W9-BLH-730

"[F]ascinating ... electric ... LaPlante brings [Hutchinson's trial] alive.... What LaPlante has reconstructed here supplies a welcome new podium for a brave Puritan theologian who wouldn't hold her tongue."
　　　—Christian Science Monitor

"The most full-scale biography of Hutchinson to date, and a readable, useful account of the challenges women faced ... in an era when women were expected to be silent. Diligently researched and well-crafted."
　　　—Minneapolis Star Tribune

"A new biography well worth reading ... Anne Hutchinson is among the most neglected, most important figures in United States history."
　　　—Nick Gillespie, *Reason* magazine

"[A] well-researched account ... LaPlante paints a fascinating portrait ... [and] deftly depicts the gritty world of colonial New England."
　　　—Booklist

"[Hutchinson's] crime and her trial are skillfully recounted ... [a] timeless story."
　　　—Providence Journal

"This book is New England history at its best. But it carries with it a message for today as well. Once again America faces the same question that the Bay Colony faced: liberty versus security. Let's hope that the lessons of Anne Hutchinson's banishment are not lost on those entrusted with ensuring that we are both strong and free."
　　　—Michael Dukakis, former governor of Massachusetts

"A discursive and charming exploration of the life and times of Anne Hutchinson—by a descendant. A personal and appreciative tribute."
　　　—Edwin Gaustad, author (with Leigh E. Schmidt) of *The Religious History of America*

"Anne Hutchinson, New England's foremother and Harvard's midwife, is here rescued from Puritan obscurity and re-introduced to twenty-first century America. Her passionate, non conformist intelligence makes her the most significant woman in pre-Revolutionary America."
—Peter J. Gomes, author of *The Good Life*

"*American Jezebel* offers a spirited biography of Anne Hutchinson, a stirring figure who pushed the limits of Puritan dissent and paid heavily for it. Hutchinson's story has often served as an emblem by which to take measure of the public voices of women in American culture, and LaPlante's rendering suggests how deeply resonant that history remains."
—Leigh E. Schmidt, Princeton University

"A vivid account, full of surprising twists and turns. In her richly documented book, Eve LaPlante tells the nearly incredible story of a woman who managed, in a male-dominated, religion-obsessed world, to shape the future of New England and New York."
—Susan Quinn, biographer of Marie Curie and Karen Horney

"What makes *American Jezebel* so extraordinary is how LaPlante enables Hutchinson to come alive through her own words . . . not as a simple saint or sinner, but as a textured human being."
—Ted Anthony, canada.com

"Fast-paced and elegant . . . LaPlante's first-rate biography offers glimpses into the life and teachings of a much-neglected figure in early American religious history."
—*Publishers Weekly* (starred review)

"A powerful and fascinating book that deserves wide reading."
—*Boston Globe*

"Remarkably successful . . . traces the vein of an ongoing ambivalence about powerful public women in America . . . particularly good on the sexual mores of the Puritans. . . ."
—Laura Miller, salon.com

"[A] powerful biography of a woman who refused to still her voice."
—*Dallas Morning News*

"Drawing on a staggering amount of historical detail, twelve-generation descendant Eve LaPlante plots her forebear's downfall with the vivid immediacy of a novel."
—*BookPage*

"[LaPlante is] the master of biography as thriller. She tells a familiar story with a novelist's panache . . . makes her kinswoman's fate into a riveting drama. . .an enthralling narrative."
—*The New York Sun*

"To all those teachers around the country who have asked me: what true heroes can I tell my students about? I would reply: tell them about Anne Hutchinson. And read Eve LaPlante's biography of her to make her and her courage come alive."
—Howard Zinn, author of *A People's History of the United States*

"*American Jezebel* is a stunning book, exquisitely written, that fills in a crucial piece of American history. A founding mother, Anne Hutchinson exemplifies the best in the American spirit. She's a woman everyone will want to—and should—know about."
—Carol Gilligan, author of *In A Different Voice* and *The Birth of Pleasure*

ALSO BY EVE LAPLANTE

Seized

AMERICAN JEZEBEL

The Uncommon Life of
✦ ANNE HUTCHINSON, ✦
the Woman Who Defied the Puritans

Eve LaPlante

HarperOne
An Imprint of HarperCollinsPublishers

HarperOne

AMERICAN JEZEBEL: *The Uncommon Life of Anne Hutchinson, the Woman Who Defied the Puritans.* Copyright © 2004 by Eve LaPlante. All rights reserved. Printed in the United States of America. No part of this book may be used or reproduced in any manner whatsoever without written permission except in the case of brief quotations embodied in critical articles and reviews. For information, address HarperCollins Publishers, 195 Broadway, New York, NY 10007.

HarperCollins books may be purchased for educational, business, or sales promotional use. For information, please e-mail the Special Markets Department at SPsales@harpercollins.com.

HarperCollins Web site: http://www.harpercollins.com
HarperCollins®, ▩®, and HarperOne™ are
trademarks of HarperCollins Publishers.

FIRST HARPERCOLLINS PAPERBACK EDITION PUBLISHED IN 2005

Designed by Joseph Rutt
Map on page 35 reproduced by permission of the
Guildhall Library Corporation, London.
All other maps by Topaz Maps Inc.

Library of Congress Cataloging-in-Publication Data
LaPlante, Eve.
American Jezebel : the uncommon life of Anne Hutchinson, the woman who defied the
Puritans / Eve LaPlante.
p. cm.
ISBN 978-0-06-075056-5
Includes bibliographical references (p.).
1. Hutchinson, Anne Marbury, 1591–1643. 2. Hutchinson, Anne Marbury,
1591–1643—Political and social views. 3. Puritans—Massachusetts—Biography.
4. Women—Massachusetts—Biography. 5. Social reformers—Massachusetts—
Biography. 6. Antinomianism—Massachusetts—History of doctrines—17th century.
7. Freedom of religion—Massachusetts—History—17th century.
8. Massachusetts—History—Colonial period, ca. 1600–1775.
9. Massachusetts—Biography. I. Title.
F67.H92L37   2003
973.2'2'092—dc22

[B]   2003056944

HB 06.21.2021

To David and
Rose, Clara, Charlotte, and Philip

CONTENTS

ILLUSTRATIONS

A NOTE ON THE TEXT

This is a work of nonfiction. All quotations are from the historical record, largely from the lengthy transcripts of the four days in 1637 and 1638 when Anne Hutchinson was brought to trial before the Great and General Court of Massachusetts and then the First Church of Boston. In citing these transcripts I have for the sake of clarity modernized spelling and added punctuation and occasionally emphasis. In quoting the Bible, I use the King James Version except when the quotation is in the words of a seventeenth-century speaker. In those cases the translation is from the Geneva Bible, which Anne Hutchinson and her Puritan contemporaries used.

All sources for the book are listed in the bibliography. All dates are from the historical record, which in the seventeenth-century English world was based on the Julian calendar, created in 45 BCE by Julius Caesar, rather than on the modern Gregorian calendar, created by Pope Gregory in the late sixteenth century. England and its colonies maintained the old calendar (and its use of March 25 rather than January 1 as the start of a new year) until 1752 as a way of avoiding the innovations of a pope. To modernize any seventeenth-century date in the book, simply add eleven days to it.

I have sought the assistance and advice of many historians, other scholars, curators, and preservationists, who are named in the acknowledgments. If despite all their help the text contains any errors of fact, the responsibility is mine.

You certainly think right when you think Boston people are mad. The frenzy was not higher when they banished my pious great grandmother, when they hanged the Quakers and . . . the poor innocent witches, than the political frenzy has been for a twelve-month past.

—THOMAS HUTCHINSON
Governor of Massachusetts
August 1770

INTRODUCTION

But history, real solemn history, I cannot be interested in.... The quarrels of popes and kings, with wars or pestilences, in every page; the men all so good for nothing, and hardly any women at all.

—JANE AUSTEN

One warm Saturday morning in March, as I let my children out of our minivan alongside a small road in rural Rhode Island, a part of America we'd never visited before, a white pickup truck rolled to a stop beside us. Leaving my baby buckled in his car seat, I turned to the truck's driver, a middle-aged man with gray hair. "This is where Rhode Island was founded, you know," he said to me. "Right here. This is where Anne Hutchinson came.

"And you know what?" the friendly stranger added, warming to his subject. "A lady came here all the way from Utah last summer, and she was a descendant of Anne Hutchinson's."

For a moment I wondered how to reply. "See those girls there?" I said, pointing at my three daughters, who watched us from a grassy spot beside the dirt road. "They're Anne Hutchinson's descendants too."

In fact, I had driven my children from Boston to Portsmouth, Rhode Island, to explore the place that their eleventh great-grand-mother, expelled from Massachusetts for heresy, had settled in 1638.

Anne Hutchinson is a local hero to the man in the pickup, but most Americans know little about her save her name and the skeleton of her story. To be sure, Hutchinson merits a mention in every textbook of American history. A major highway outside New York City, the Hutchinson River Parkway, bears her name. And a bronze statue of her stands in front of the Massachusetts State House near that of President

John F. Kennedy. Yet Hutchinson herself has never been widely understood or her achievements appreciated and recognized.

In a world without religious freedom, civil rights, or free speech—the colonial world of the 1630s that was the seed of the modern United States—Anne Hutchinson was an American visionary, pioneer, and explorer who epitomized the religious freedom and tolerance that are essential to the nation's character. From the first half of the seventeenth century, when she sailed with her husband and their eleven children to Massachusetts Bay Colony, until at least the mid-nineteenth century, when Susan B. Anthony and others campaigned for female suffrage, no woman has left as strong an impression on politics in America as Anne Hutchinson. In a time when no woman could vote, teach outside the home, or hold public office, she had the intellect, courage, and will to challenge the judges and ministers who founded and ran Massachusetts. Threatened by her radical theology and her formidable political power, these men brought her to trial for heresy, banished her from the colony, and excommunicated her from the Puritan church. Undeterred, she cofounded a new American colony (her Rhode Island and Roger Williams's Providence Plantation later joined as the Colony of Rhode Island), becoming the only woman ever to do so. Unlike many prominent women in American politics, such as Abigail Adams and Eleanor Roosevelt, Hutchinson did not acquire power because of her husband. She was strong in her own right, not the wife of someone stronger, which may have been one reason she had to be expunged.

Anne Hutchinson is a compelling biographical subject because of her personal complexity, the many tensions in her life, and the widespread uncertainty about the details of her career. But there is more to her story. Because early New England was a microcosm of the modern Western world, the issues Anne Hutchinson raised—gender equality, civil rights, the nature and evidence of salvation, freedom of conscience, and the right to free speech—remain relevant to the American people four centuries later. Hutchinson's bold engagement in religious, political, and moral conflict early in our history helped to shape how American women see ourselves today—in marriages, in communities, and in the larger society.

Besides being a feminist icon, Hutchinson embodied a peculiarly American certainty about the distinction between right and wrong, good and evil—a certainty shared by the colonial leaders who sent her away. Cast out by men who themselves had been outcasts in their native England, Hutchinson is a classic rebel's rebel, revealing how quickly outsiders can become authoritarians. The members of the Massachusetts Court removed Anne because her moral certitude was too much like their own. Her views were a mirror for their rigidity. It is ironic, the historian Oscar Handlin noted, that the Puritans "had themselves been rebels in order to put into practice their ideas of a new society. But to do so they had to restrain the rebellion of others."

Until now, views of Anne Hutchinson in American history and letters have been polarized, tending either toward disdain or exaltation. The exaltation comes from women's clubs, genealogical associations, and twentieth-century feminists who honor her as America's first feminist, career woman, and equal marital partner. Yet the public praise is often muted by a wish to domesticate Hutchinson. The bronze statue in Boston, for instance, portrays her as a pious mother—a little girl at her side and her eyes raised in supplication to heaven—rather than as a powerful figure standing in the Massachusetts General Court, alone before men and God.

Her detractors, starting with her neighbor John Winthrop, first governor of Massachusetts, derided her as the "instrument of Satan," the new Eve, and the "enemy of the chosen people." In summing her up, Winthrop called her "this *American Jezebel*"—the emphasis is his—making an epithet of the name that any Puritan would recognize as belonging to the most evil and shameful woman in the Bible. Hutchinson haunted Nathaniel Hawthorne, who used her as a model for Hester Prynne, the adulterous heroine of *The Scarlet Letter.* Early in this 1850 novel, Hutchinson appears at the door of the Boston prison.

> This rose-bush, by a strange chance, has been kept alive in history; but whether it had merely survived out of the stern old wilderness, so long after the fall of the gigantic pines and oaks that overshadowed it,—or whether, as there is fair authority for believing, it had sprung up under the footsteps of the sainted Ann [sic] Hutchinson, as she entered the prison-door,—we shall not take upon us to determine. Finding it so directly on the threshold of our narrative, which is now about to issue

from that inauspicious portal, we could hardly do otherwise
than pluck one of its flowers and present it to the reader.

Hutchinson never "entered the prison-door" in Boston, as Hawthorne
imagines, but she is rightly "a rose at the threshold" of a narrative that
is itself a sort of prison.

"Mrs. Hutchinson," Hawthorne's eponymous story in *Tales and
Sketches*, depicts her as rebellious, arrogant, fanatical, and deeply anxiety provoking. "It is a place of humble aspect where the Elders of the
people are met, sitting in judgment upon the disturber of Israel," as
Hawthorne envisions her 1637 trial. "The floor of the low and narrow
hall is laid with planks hewn by the axe,—the beams of the roof still
wear the rugged bark with which they grew up in the forest, and the
hearth is formed of one broad unhammered stone, heaped with logs
that roll their blaze and smoke up a chimney of wood and clay."

Apparently unaware that the Cambridge, Massachusetts, meetinghouse that served as Hutchinson's courtroom had no hearth, Hawthorne
continues,

> A sleety shower beats fitfully against the window, driven by the
> November blast, which comes howling onward from the north-
> ern desert, the boisterous and unwelcome herald of a New
> England winter. Rude benches are arranged across the apart-
> ment and along its sides, occupied by men whose piety and
> learning might have entitled them to seats in those high Coun-
> cils of the ancient Church, whence opinions were sent forth to
> confirm or supersede the Gospel in the belief of the whole
> world and of posterity.—Here are collected all those blessed
> Fathers of the land. . . .

"In the midst, and in the center of all eyes," Hawthorne imagines,
"we see the Woman." His Anne Hutchinson "stands loftily before her
judges, with a determined brow. . . . They question her, and her answers
are ready and acute; she reasons with them shrewdly, and brings scripture in support of every argument; the deepest controversialists of that
scholastic day find here a woman, whom all their trained and sharpened
intellects are inadequate to foil."

In *Prophetic Woman*, a trenchant analysis of Hutchinson's role in America's self-image, Amy Schrager Lang observes, "As a heretic, Hutchinson opposed orthodoxy; as a woman, she was pictured as opposing the founding fathers, who, for later generations, stood as heroes in the long foreground of the American Revolution. In the most extreme version of her story, Hutchinson would thus come to be seen as opposing the very idea of America." A woman who wielded public power in a culture suspicious of such power, she exemplifies why there are so few women, even today, in American politics, and why no woman has attained the presidency.

Unlike most previous commentators, I aim neither to disdain nor to exalt my central character. I strive instead for a balanced portrait of Anne Hutchinson's life and thought, in all their complexity, based on painstaking research into all the available documents, which are extensive considering she was a middle-class woman living in a wilderness four centuries ago. I've had the pleasure of visiting all the sites of her life—in Lincolnshire and London; in Boston, England, and Boston, Massachusetts; and in Rhode Island and New York. In rural England I climbed the steps to the pulpit where her father preached and sat on a bench in the sixteenth-century schoolroom where he taught village boys to read Latin, English, and Greek. I walked on the broad timbers of the manor house that was being built as twenty-one-year-old Anne and her new husband returned from adolescent years spent in London to the Lincolnshire town of Alford to start a family. I touched the plague stone that Alfordians covered with vinegar, their only disinfectant, during the 1630 epidemic that killed one in four of the town's residents. In the Lincolnshire Wolds I explored Rigsby Wood, where she took her children to see the bluebells bloom each May. Back in the States, I kayaked to an isolated beach on a Rhode Island cove where she lived in the colony she founded, and I rode on horseback through the North Bronx woods to the vast glacial stone marking the land on which she built her final farmstead.

I first heard of Anne Hutchinson when I was a child and my great-aunt Charlotte May Wilson of Cape Cod, an avid keeper of family trees, told me that Hutchinson was my grandmother, eleven generations back. Aunt Charlotte was a character in her own right, a crusty Victorian spinster with Unitarian and artistic leanings, a proud great-granddaughter of the Reverend Samuel Joseph May, a niece of the nineteenth-century painter Eastman Johnson, and a first cousin twice removed to Louisa May Alcott. Longtime proprietor of the Red Inn, in Provincetown, Massachusetts, Aunt Charlotte served tea and muffins every morning to her guests, including me. Evenings, after the sun set over Race Point Beach, she would nurse a gin and tonic and read aloud from her impressive collection of browning, brittle-paged volumes of poetry. When she recited Vachel Lindsay's "The Congo"—"Mumbo-jumbo will hoo-doo you. . . . Boomlay, boomlay, boomlay, boom!"—her aging eyes closed and her ample torso swayed.

Even earlier, curled into an armchair in her little red house across Commercial Street from the inn, hardly a block from the Provincetown rocks where the Pilgrims first set foot on this continent in November 1620, I listened to Aunt Charlotte's tales of the exploits of our shared, known ancestors. My aunt seemed to favor the abolitionist and minister Samuel Joseph May and Samuel Sewall (1652–1730), the judge who so repented of his role in condemning nineteen "witches" to death in Salem Village in 1692 that for the rest of his days he wore beneath his outer garments a coarse, penitential sackcloth. "For his partaking in the doleful delusion of that monstrous tribunal," James Savage observed in 1860, Judge Sewall "suffered remorse for long years with the highest Christian magnanimous supplication for mercy." To me, though, Anne Hutchinson was most compelling on account of her vehemence, her familiarity, and her violent death.

Once I was old enough to pore over the minute glosses around the edges of my great-aunt's handwritten genealogies, I read wide-eyed of the dramatic contours of Anne Hutchinson's life. At fifty-one, after her husband died, she moved with her younger children from Rhode Island to New York, to live among the Dutch. When her Dutch neighbors, who often skirmished with local Indians, advised her to remove her family during an anticipated Siwanoy raid, she stayed put. Always an iconoclast, she had long opposed English settlers' efforts to vanquish Indian tribes. Not for the first time, she risked her life for her beliefs.

As a sixteen-year-old in high school American history class, I listened, ashamed, as my teacher described the religious sect called Antinomianism and Hutchinson's two trials. The ferocity and moral fervor I associated with her were attributes I disliked in my relatives and feared in myself. Reading about her, I'd learned that one of her heresies was knowing that she was among God's elect and then presuming that she could detect who else was too. Since then, I've come to see that this view, which her opponents imputed to her, was not hers alone. An excessive concern with one's own and others' "spiritual estate" was also typical of her judges. Salvation—who had it, who didn't—was the major issue of her day, as it may be, in various forms, today.

In my high school classroom I raised my hand despite my adolescent shame. Called on by the teacher, I blushed and said that Hutchinson was my great-great-great . . . great-grandmother. The teacher's bushy white eyebrows rose in an expression that I interpreted as horror. Not long ago, though, I ran into him and recalled the scene. I was wrong about his reaction, he said. It was more like awe.

Now, as an adult studying Hutchinson's story, I understand his response. Among a raft of fascinating ancestors, Anne is most alluring and enigmatic. As a wife, mother, and journalist living in modern Boston—a palimpsest of the settlement where Anne had her rise and fall—I am intrigued by her life and thought. How, in a virtual wilderness, did she (like countless other women) raise a huge family while also (unlike the rest) confronting the privileged men who formed the first colony and educational center of the United States? According to Harvard University, it is she rather than John Harvard who "should be credited with the founding of Harvard College." In November 1637, just a week after her first trial and banishment, colonial leaders founded Harvard to indoctrinate young male citizens so as to prevent a charismatic radical like Hutchinson from ever again holding sway in Massachusetts, observes the Reverend Peter J. Gomes, the Plummer Professor of Christian Morals at Harvard University.

Were she alive today, Anne Hutchinson might be a minister, a politician, or a writer. Four hundred years ago, when the vast majority of women could not even write their names, how did she emerge boldly to question the leading men of the day as to the nature of salvation and grace? What fueled her self-confidence and her sustained anger at colonial authorities? Where did she find the strength of character to stand for hours before scores of seated men, parrying their every Gospel quotation, replying again and again with wit? This book is a response to these and other bedeviling questions. Through it, I hope, Anne Hutchinson may claim her rightful place as America's founding mother.

Early New England and New York

ENEMY OF THE STATE

"Anne Hutchinson is present," a male voice announced from somewhere in the crowded meetinghouse, momentarily quieting the din that filled its cavernous hall. The meetinghouse of Cambridge, Massachusetts, a square structure of timber and clay with a thatched roof, served as the community's city hall, church, and courthouse—the latter its role this chilly Tuesday in November 1637. Hearing the news that the defendant had arrived, scores of bearded heads in black felt hats turned to find the one woman in the crowd.

There was nothing auspicious about Anne Hutchinson's appearance as she stood in the doorway alongside several male relatives and supporters, awaiting the start of her trial. She was forty-six years old, of average height and bearing, with an unremarkable face. Her petticoat fell almost to the ground, revealing only the tips of her leather boots. Against the cold she wore a wool mantua, or cloak. A white coif covered her hair, as was the custom of the day. Besides that and her white linen smock and neckerchief, she wore all black. She was a stranger to no one present, having ministered as midwife and nurse to many of their wives and children. All knew her to be an active member of the church of Boston, the wife of the wealthy textile merchant William Hutchinson, the mother of twelve living children, and the grandmother of one, a five-day-old boy who just that Sunday had been baptized. There was, in short, no outer sign to suggest she was an enemy of the state.

Enemy she was, though, indeed the greatest threat Massachusetts had ever known. More than a few men in the room, including several of the ministers, considered her a witch. Others believed the Devil had taken over her soul. The governor, John Winthrop, who was waiting in an antechamber of the meetinghouse to begin the trial over which he would preside, suspected her of using her devilish powers to subjugate men by establishing "the community of women" to foster "their abominable wickedness."

Anne Hutchinson's greatest crime, and the source of her power, was the series of weekly public meetings she held at her house to discuss Scripture and theology. At first, in 1635, the evening meetings had been just for women, who then were generally encouraged to gather in small groups to gossip and offer mutual support. Soon scores of women, enchanted by her intelligence and magnetism, flocked to hear her analysis of the week's Scripture reading, which many of them preferred to the ministers' latest interpretation. "Being a woman very helpful in times of childbirth and other occasions of bodily infirmities, [Hutchinson] easily insinuated herself into the affections of many," an official observed. Her "pretense was to repeat [the ministers'] sermons," the governor added, "but when that was done, she would comment upon the doctrines, interpret passages at her pleasure, and expound dark places of Scripture, and make it serve her turn," going beyond "wholesome truths" to "set forth her own stuff." One minister, Thomas Weld, reported that her "custom was for her scholars to propound questions and she (gravely sitting in the chair) did make answers thereunto." This was especially grievous in a time when the single chair in every house was for the use of the man alone.

Men had begun to accompany their wives to Hutchinson's meetings in 1636, and as her audiences swelled she offered a second session of religious instruction each week, just as the colonial ministers liked to give a Thursday lecture as well as their Sunday sermon. The Reverend Weld lamented that members of her audience, "being tainted, conveyed the infection to others," including "some of the magistrates, some gentlemen, some scholars and men of learning, some burgesses of our General Court, some of our captains and soldiers, some chief men in towns, and some eminent for religion, parts, and wit." Anne Hutchinson had "stepped out of [her] place," in the succinct phrase of the Reverend Hugh Peter, of Salem—she "had rather been a husband than a wife; and a preacher than a hearer; and a magistrate than a subject."

It was painfully clear to Governor Winthrop, who had an excellent view of her comings and goings from his house directly across the road from hers in Boston, that Anne Hutchinson possessed the strongest constituency of any leader in the colony. She was, he confided in his journal, "a woman of a haughty and fierce carriage, a nimble wit and an active spirit, and a very voluble tongue." Her name was absent (on account of her sex) from every offensive political act and document, he observed, but she was behind them all. "More bold than a man," she was Virgil's *dux foemina facti,* "the woman leading all the action"—the breeder and nourisher of all the county's distempers, the sower of political and religious discord. Before Mistress Hutchinson had arrived in America, in the fall of 1634, all was sweetness and light, he recalled. Now that she was here, all was chaos.

Through a side door of the meetinghouse, the forty magistrates of the Great and General Court of Massachusetts filed into the dimly lit room. This court of no appeal, the only court available to the fledgling colony's roughly seven thousand settlers, comprised the governor, a deputy governor, seven of their assistants (chosen by the freemen to serve as the colony's board of directors), and thirty-one deputies, prominent freemen chosen by the colony's fourteen towns (forerunners to the state's legislators). The judges that day included the assistant Simon Bradstreet, of Cambridge, thirty-three, who as colonial secretary was expected to take notes; Salem's John Endicott, the righteous, forty-nine-year-old former soldier who had recently tried to pass a law forcing all women to wear veils, as in the Old Testament; and Deputy Governor Thomas Dudley, who at sixty-one was the oldest judge.

Eight ministers in black robes also joined the procession, not to judge the defendant but to give testimony, as witnesses. Colonial ministers, despite their vast public power, were not allowed to hold public office, a distinction that kept Massachusetts from being a theocracy. These divines included the Reverend Zechariah Symmes, with whom Anne had sparred over theological matters during the grueling trip across the Atlantic Ocean, and John Wilson, Boston's senior pastor, who had recently called Anne out of that meetinghouse on account of her heresies. In England these Puritans had been hounded by church authorities, silenced, and in a few cases imprisoned, but here in Massachusetts they ran the state church. Still, most had come reluctantly to this land where, an anonymous female colonist admitted, "the air is sharp, the rocks many, the trees innumerable, the grass little, the winter cold, the summer hot, the gnats in summer biting, the wolves at midnight howling." Back in 1629, while planning their first trip here, the founders had put ministers first on their long list of "supplies."

Just that morning, there had been a last-minute change in the roster of men arrayed before Anne Hutchinson. Governor Winthrop had hastily appointed two new judges to replace three who had expressed support for Mistress Hutchinson. Notwithstanding the change, this group of ministers and magistrates possessed the "highest concentration" in the colony of wealth, intelligence, and power.

To a man, they wore greatcoats, leather gloves, and hats against the cold, in addition to their standard loose white linen shirts, knickers, and thick stockings tied with cloth garters. All had leather shoes, and most of their hats were lined in the brow with leather. The meetinghouse lacked a fireplace, and the bitter chill of winter had arrived early that year. Just the week before, in an early November ice storm, a young man had frozen to death while trying to cross the nearby Charles River in a skiff.

Every judge but one took his seat on one of the wooden benches at the front of the hall that faced the crowd. The last judge to enter the hall was the governor, who approached the single desk and cushioned chair before the benches and sat down.

Governor John Winthrop, a small man of forty-nine with a tense, worried mien, was not only the architect of this trial but also its leading magistrate, serving as both chief judge and chief prosecutor. Winthrop had been born in Suffolk, England, in 1588, attended Trinity College, Cambridge, for two years, during which he considered becoming a clergyman, and was trained as a lawyer in London. He worked as a government attorney and justice of the peace, and, as squire of the manor of Groton, in Suffolk, he was admitted in 1628 to the Inner Temple, one of the Inns of Court in London that train English lawyers. Although he was considered a strong candidate for Parliament, he never had a chance to run for office in England.

In the late 1620s John Winthrop and other pious Puritans saw England as in a decline. Men were treated like cattle, he believed, and money trumped morals. He was increasingly offended by the "papist," or Catholic, leanings of the Anglican Church under King Charles I, who had ascended the throne in 1625. True religion was about to expire, Winthrop feared. William Laud, whom Charles had chosen to become Bishop of London in 1628, leaned toward Arminianism—the belief, put forward by a Dutch minister named Arminius, that people by their own free will can achieve faith and salvation—which especially offended Puritans, who so emphasized divine grace as against the ability of humans to effect their own salvation. Furious at Bishop Laud, the Puritans appealed to Parliament, which decided to suppress his "popery" in the state church. As a result of this and similar parliamentary challenges to his rule, King Charles abrogated Parliament in March 1629, a decision that cost John Winthrop his government post.

The following summer the forty-two-year-old gentleman barrister joined a company of Puritan gentry wishing to leave England and form a new colony in America, with the approbation of the king, who granted the colonial charter. The Massachusetts Bay Company, as it was called, chose Winthrop as its first governor, in recognition of his political and administrative skills, which Hawthorne noted in "Mrs. Hutchinson" (1830): "In the highest place sits Winthrop, a man by whom the innocent and the guilty might alike desire to be judged, the first confiding in his integrity and wisdom, the latter hoping in his mildness." In Winthrop's personal journal, which is now a primary source on early Massachusetts, the new governor saw himself as the Moses of a new Exodus, embarking on a second Protestant Reformation—withdrawing from the church of England as it had withdrawn a century earlier from the church of Rome. In the spring of 1630 he led a flotilla of eleven ships carrying nearly a thousand nonconformist Protestants like himself across the Atlantic Ocean. Unlike the Separatists who nine years earlier had founded Plymouth Plantation, Winthrop aimed not to separate from his country but to extend its reach while purifying its church—hence the name *New* England.

Now, in 1637, Winthrop had been elected to his fifth one-year term as colonial governor, after having lost the office for three years, most recently to the young Sir Henry Vane, a supporter of Hutchinson. Each spring, according to the royal charter, the governor was elected from among the members of the General Court by the members themselves. But in 1633 voting rights were extended to all male members of the state church who were at least sixteen years old—roughly one-quarter of the adult population. After this, Winthrop, who had been chosen governor first in 1630 and reelected three times, had been defeated—in

1634 by Thomas Dudley, in 1635 by John Haynes, and in 1636, most distressingly, by the Hutchinsonian Vane. By this time, increasing numbers of citizens were traders, merchants, sailors, and brokers, who had more commercial and mercantile concerns than the earlier émigrés, who tended to support Winthrop. Ironically, the highest-born immigrant of all—Vane, the idealistic son of a member of the king's Privy Council—was, together with the free-thinker Anne Hutchinson, the champion of Boston's burgeoning middle class.

Winthrop's concerns in court that day in November 1637 were both internal and external. King Charles, alarmed by rumors he had heard of Separatism in the American church and a dangerously independent spirit in its government, was threatening to revoke the colonial charter he had granted the settlers in 1629 and to send a royal governor to rule them. In addition, the colonists increasingly feared aggression by the French, the Spanish, and the Dutch, who were also exploring and settling the continent, and by the native tribes. Just the summer before, Massachusetts had fought and won the Pequot War, their first campaign against the natives, on the coast of what would become Connecticut. That war had ended in July with the massacre by colonial soldiers of almost every Pequot man, woman, and child—a "divine slaughter," in the words of the Cambridge pastor Thomas Shepard, who was present in the courtroom that day.

To Winthrop's dismay, Anne Hutchinson opposed war against the native tribes. Her attitude toward the natives reminded the governor of the Reverend Roger Williams's "dangerous" refusal to support the conversion (and, if necessary, killing) of Indians in the name of Christ. As Williams put it, "Jesus never called for the sword of steel to help the sword of spirit." Believing the English king had no right to give away land that was not his, the Reverend Williams, of Salem, in 1635 had written a letter to Charles I saying it was evil to take Indian lands without payment. Massachusetts Bay authorities persuaded Williams not to send the letter and continued to watch him warily. They rejected his novel concept of freedom of conscience—"Forced worship," he believed, "stinks in God's nostrils." In October 1635 they asked him to retract criticisms of their involvement in church affairs in Salem. He refused, continuing to preach his unorthodox message about religious liberty. That winter they banished him, and he later settled Providence

Plantation, forty miles to the southwest, where he was no longer such an irritant. But now Mistress Hutchinson was spreading similarly noxious views. During the summer of 1637, most of her male followers refused to enlist in the Pequot War, presenting a serious problem for the governor and for the Reverend Wilson and Captain John Endicott, the leaders of the military campaign.

"Reducing" Mistress Hutchinson—correcting or subduing her—would help Winthrop on all these counts, by showing his strength and unifying the colony to which he was devoted. Massachusetts Bay was, after all, his New Canaan, his ideal "city upon a hill" for all the world to emulate. He had uttered these now-famous words in the spring of 1630 on board the *Arbella* as he and his company sailed toward the New World (or, according to some historians, on the dock in Southampton just prior to the ship's departure): "God shall make us a praise and glory, that men shall say of succeeding plantations, the Lord make it like that of New England. . . . The eyes of all people are upon us." Having given up so much to come here, Winthrop could not abide the thought of Massachusetts threatened or split: the salvation of the colony was the central goal of his career.

John Winthrop's large white ceremonial ruff stood out against the black of his coat. He had a long, somber face, a trim gray beard, and arched eyebrows that looked as though they had been penciled on. The son of a successful lawyer who had served in Parliament and a grandson of the wealthy Adam Winthrop—who had received a large grant of monastic lands, including the manor of Groton, in Norfolk, as a result of Henry VIII's split from Rome—Winthrop had a prim, aristocratic air. Glancing toward the rear of the meetinghouse, where the rabble stood, he called out, "Mistress Hutchinson." A roar of support for her rose. Winthrop banged his gavel on his desk, silencing the crowd. "Mistress Hutchinson," he repeated.

Emerging from the crowd, Anne Hutchinson walked slowly toward his desk, looking straight ahead. At her throat a brass fastener held the corners of her cloak. She stopped at the center of the room, where she was expected to stand throughout the trial, and faced the governor.

"Mistress Hutchinson," he began, looking around to ensure that he had the attention of all, "you are called here as one of those that have troubled the peace of the commonwealth and the churches here."

Massachusetts was now split between his supporters and hers. Most of her support came from Boston, where both Hutchinson and Winthrop lived. His support came from the freemen of certain outlying towns, such as Cambridge, and most of the clergy. Only two ministers backed her, and one of them—her brother-in-law John Wheelwright—had already been censured and now, only four days before, banished. She also had the support of most colonial merchants and businessmen, who resented the alien exclusion law that Winthrop had imposed earlier that year to prevent more Hutchinsonians from immigrating ("such persons as might be dangerous to the commonwealth" could not stay longer than three weeks without the court's permission), and the wage and price controls recently imposed by the court and ministers. Not surprisingly, these early settlers were as likely to rebel against the authoritarianism of state and church here in New England as they had been in Old.

"You are known to be a woman that hath had a great share in the promoting and divulging of those opinions that are the cause of this trouble," the governor said to Anne Hutchinson, "and to be nearly joined not only in affinity and affection with some of those the court had ... passed censure upon." He meant her many allies—such respected men of the colony as the town assessor, William Colburn; William Aspinwall, who was a notary, court recorder, and surveyor; William Coddington, the richest man in Boston; the prominent silk merchant John Coggeshall; the innkeeper William Baulston; William Dyer, the milliner; and the Pequot War hero Captain John Underhill—all of whom faced disfranchisement on account of their recent petition in support of her brother-in-law John Wheelwright.

The Reverend Wheelwright, the forty-five-year-old husband of Anne's husband Will's youngest sister, Mary, had arrived in Massachusetts with Mary, her mother, and their five children seventeen months earlier, in May 1636, the month that many considered the start of the current crisis. Around this time other ministers had begun warning Winthrop that they feared Hutchinson's activities and views, and they wondered if her minister, John Cotton, one of the two preachers at the First Church of Boston, might also be tainted. That summer, in 1636, Winthrop had lost the governorship to Vane, a twenty-three-year-old aristocrat who lodged in Boston with the Reverend Cotton and attended Anne Hutchinson's meetings. The most highly placed immigrant to Massachusetts, Vane at first, in 1635, had been warmly received by colonial leaders because, as Winthrop noted, he was the "son and heir to Sir Henry Vane," comptroller of the king's household, a privy councilor, and a chief adviser to King Charles. Royal authorities had allowed the younger Vane to venture to Massachusetts for three years in hopes that the hardships of the New World would drive some sense into the charming but irresponsible youth who had been alienated from them by his conversion to Puritanism. Largely on account of Vane's social status and his eagerness, he had quickly assumed a role in Massachusetts as an adviser and mediator between magistrates more than twice his age.

In the fall of 1636, with Vane in power, the congregation of the Boston church had invited Wheelwright to serve there alongside their pastor, John Wilson, a Winthrop ally whose theology they disliked, and their beloved first teacher, John Cotton. Winthrop was deeply offended by this move by his own congregation. Using a little-known rule that required all actions of the church to be unanimous, Winthrop thwarted the move and assigned Wheelwright to a church ten miles to the south, in Mount Wollaston. Allowing Hutchinson's brother-in-law to preach in Boston, noted Winthrop in his journal, would "raise doubtful disputations." It would also strengthen Mistress Hutchinson.

But removing Wheelwright did not solve Winthrop's problem. The majority of the congregation continued to oppose Wilson, even more openly than before. On at least one occasion Anne Hutchinson stood up and walked out during his sermon, which she felt interpreted Scripture wrongly. Other women followed her out of the meetinghouse, wishing also to show their displeasure. The court could not ban such leave-takings, though, which could always be attributed to feminine distress or "infirmities." Meanwhile, male Hutchinsonians began to query Wilson provocatively during the question period after his sermons. Wilson's colleague the Reverend Thomas Weld, listing the congregation's derisive terms for its senior pastor, reported, "Now the faithful ministers of Christ must have dung cast on their faces, and be no better than Legal Preachers, Baal's Priests, Popish Factors, Scribes, Pharisees, and Opposers of Christ Himself."

In this conflict, as in most if not all battles in early Massachusetts, each side identified with the ancient Jews, God's chosen people, and

identified the other side with the pagan worshipers of Baal. These settlers, all of them Puritans, were conscious of themselves as the succes-
sors of ancient Israel, the people with whom God made a covenant. The
Antichrist—the Catholic Church, which they also called the Great
Whore of Babylon—had triumphed in Europe and was trying to con-
quer England under Charles and Laud by moving its church back toward Rome. While these Puritans had felt united in England, where
they shared the common enemy of the "papist" hierarchies of church
and state, in New England they were reduced to fighting among themselves.

The crisis had reached its peak in early December 1636, eleven
months before Anne Hutchinson's trial. The ministers held a conference with Cotton, Hutchinson, and several members of the Boston
church who supported her. To his colleagues' dismay, Cotton did not
completely agree with the others on doctrine, and Hutchinson "did
conceive that we were not able ministers of the gospel," the Salem minister Hugh Peter lamented. In sum, "she was a woman not only difficult
in her opinions, but also of an intemperate spirit."

A few days later, at the General Court meeting, it was suggested
that Vane was to blame for this conflict as well as for the colonists'
growing fears over external threats such as the Indians and the French.
A distraught Vane, still only twenty-three years old, burst into tears
and resigned, saying he had been called back to England on business.
Winthrop and his allies would have accepted his resignation happily
had not a group of Hutchinsonians succeeded in convincing Vane to
stay through the end of his term the following May. He consented, but
his power was sorely compromised.

At the same time, on December 7, 1636, the General Court dismissed from its members the person in the colony most closely linked
to Anne Hutchinson. "Upon the churches' request," the court record
states, "Mr. William Hutchinson was discharged from assisting at the
particular courts."

In hopes of reconciliation and unity in the colony, the court pro-
claimed a Fast Day to be held on January 19, 1637. Fast Days—the reverse of Thanksgiving Days, when people feasted—were a central civic
ritual in the colonial world, imported from Europe. The entire community ceased its daily work and went to church to repent and pray collec-

tively for peace and order, civic health, and an end to sin and dissension. Believing that God protects those who obey his rules, they fasted as a way of avoiding God's terrible judgment on those who do evil.

Even on the Fast Day, Wheelwright continued to oppose other ministers openly. Asked by Cotton to prophesy in public, Wheelwright accused Wilson and most of his brethren of failing to maintain Christ properly in doctrine and worship. The orthodox ministers, Wheelwright said, were leading their flocks to damnation. Those among us who wish to return Christ to our presence, he said, "must prepare for a spiritual combat," "put on the armor of God," and "show themselves valiant. They should have their swords ready," and "fight with spiritual weapons." Further fueling the fires of dissent, Wheelwright addressed his congregation as "brothers and sisters" rather than just "brethren" and used as examples of valor not only David and Barak but also the women Deborah and Jael. To the court and the other ministers, it was unthinkable to credit a woman with public power.

The General Court ordered Wheelwright to appear before it in March, as it had called up Roger Williams for reproach a year and a half before. Wheelwright, a tall man with large features, curly hair, a mustache, and a goatee, told the court he would answer no questions because the hearing was unfair. Promptly found guilty of sedition and "contempt of the civil authority," he was silenced, for the second time in his career, for in 1632 the Church of England had censured him, prompting his eventual exile to Massachusetts. The court delayed Wheelwright's sentencing until May, when a new governor would be elected to replace Vane.

In a chaotic annual election that May, which was held in Cambridge because Hutchinson enjoyed little support there, Winthrop was returned to the governor's chair. In the meantime, fifty-eight freemen who supported Hutchinson—respected citizens of Boston, Charlestown, Ipswich, Salem, and Newbury—signed a petition remonstrating against her brother-in-law Wheelwright's conviction. Over that summer, for the first time ever, church membership in Boston began to decline. Winthrop saw the country he had built tipping toward disaster.

Late that summer Winthrop set out to rectify the situation. The General Court banished Wheelwright and gave him two weeks to leave. Roger Williams offered him a place in Providence Plantation, but

Wheelwright decided to flee north, where he camped beside a waterfall on the Squamscott River and eventually founded Exeter, New Hampshire. The court called up all the men who had signed the petition, accused them of sedition, and warned them that if they did not desist they would lose the right to vote. In early November the General Court under Winthrop's leadership banished several prominent Hutchinsonians. The men who had signed the petition were disfranchised and disarmed. Now, with the trial of Mistress Hutchinson, Winthrop hoped to settle the problem once and for all. The men they had removed were "but young branches" of the problem, in Winthrop's view. Anne Hutchinson was its roots and trunk.

"You have spoken diverse things, as we have been informed, very prejudicial [damaging] to the honor of the churches and ministers thereof," Governor Winthrop continued, according to transcripts that were made that day of the trial. "And you have maintained a meeting and an assembly in your house that hath been condemned by the general assembly as a thing not tolerable nor comely in the sight of God nor fitting for your sex." One of her greatest crimes, in his view, was her criticism of the ministers with whom she disagreed. At her meetings, he had been told, she said only two ministers in the colony preached the truth. One was her brother-in-law Wheelwright. The other was John Cotton, formerly England's most influential Puritan preacher, whom Winthrop and other leaders had wooed to Massachusetts. Wooing him, they had inadvertently wooed Anne too. In the summer of 1634, a year after Cotton departed England to avoid imprisonment for his nonconformity, the Hutchinsons had followed him. Their journey was one of many that had led to the current face-off in the Cambridge meetinghouse.

Anne Hutchinson stood silently before the governor, listening closely but mindful of God. She did not yet know the nature of the charge against her. Indeed, even Winthrop himself was not yet sure what charge to use against the first female defendant in the New World. He couldn't accuse her of contempt against the state or of sedition because as a woman she had no public role. She could not be silenced or punished with disfranchisement because as a woman she had no voice or vote.

Winthrop concluded his opening remarks with two threats. "If you be in an erroneous way we may reduce you," and "If you be obstinate in your course then the court may take such course that you may trouble us no further."

Still omitting any specific charge against the defendant, he prompted her to speak by asking, "Do you not assent and hold in practice to those opinions and factions that have been handled in court already, that is to say, do you not justify Mr. Wheelwright's sermon and the petition?"

Anne replied, "I am called here to answer before you, but I hear no things laid to my charge." These words, transcribed by two observers in the courtroom, are her first-ever recorded words. They show her as she was, clever and undeterred. She was calling the governor's bluff, exploiting his failure to charge her with any crime.

"I have told you some already," Winthrop sputtered, "and more I can tell you."

"Name one, sir," she replied. Anne, with no lawyer or adviser, would have to speak for herself throughout the trial. By colonial decree—in contrast to English common law—she had no right to counsel, and even her husband could not testify on her behalf. Ministers and deputies of the Massachusetts court were present as witnesses and to advise the prosecution, but the defendant was allowed no legal assistance or advice.

"Have I not named some already?" the governor said to her.

"What have I said or done?" she repeated. As they both knew, she had done nothing criminal. As a woman, she had no publicly sanctioned role. Her actions were invisible.

She shifted her weight from foot to foot, trying to find a comfortable position. Cold and tired, she longed to sit down. She was still nursing her youngest child, nineteen-month-old Zuriel, and she believed she was now pregnant for the sixteenth time.

She had risen that day with the sun, which rose each morning over the ocean beside her house on the Shawmut peninsula—then the center of the colony and now a slender strip of downtown Boston. After her usual morning prayer, Scripture reading, and breakfast of corn mush (cornmeal with milk or molasses), baked apples or stewed pumpkin, and cider, Anne had set out with William for the Charlestown ferry, almost a mile from their house. Ordinarily they made a

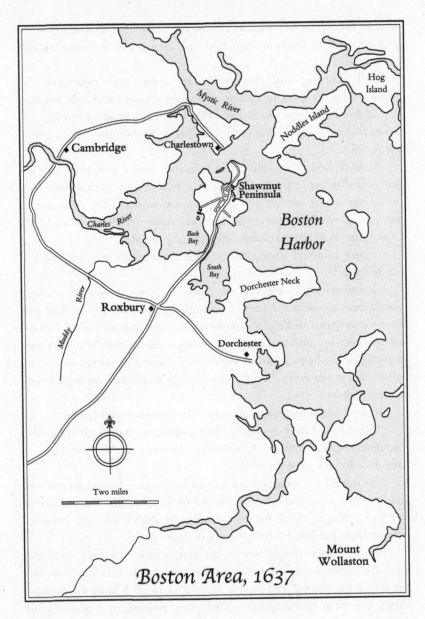

Boston Area, 1637

trip of this length, roughly five miles to Cambridge, on horseback or by coach, but they had traveled on foot because of the ice, which could break a horse's leg.

At the ferry landing they had met William's younger brother Edward, a thirty-year-old whom the court had also called that day because of his signature on the petition supporting Wheelwright. Edward and his wife, who had two young sons, had come to Boston in 1633 on the same ship as John Cotton. As the ferry crossed the mouth of the Charles River that morning, the ferryman had told the Hutchinsons of the man dying on the river the week before. During their four-mile walk inland from Charlestown to Cambridge, they had passed Indian encampments, a few colonial houses and farms, the expansive marshland that bordered the northern bank of the river, and deep forest, extending for miles north and west, beyond what was known. The same trip today, by subway or car, takes twenty minutes, but on foot it took the Hutchinsons more than two hours that morning in 1637.

Unexpectedly, the walk had exhausted Anne. This pregnancy seemed different from all the rest, although each one was distinct in her mind. The first, twenty-four years before, was Edward, born in her hometown of Alford, Lincolnshire, just ten months after her wedding day; Edward was now father to her new little grandson, Elishua. The rest had followed at intervals of roughly a year and a half. Her second child and first daughter, Susan, had died at sixteen when the bubonic plague ravaged Alford. Anne's third child, Richard, was now twenty-one. Faith, twenty, was her oldest living daughter. Then came eighteen-year-old Bridget. Francis, just seventeen, could already vote alongside his father and older brothers. Elizabeth, her next child, had died at eight, three weeks after Susan, also of the plague. Then came sweet William, who survived toddlerhood but died before he turned six. Samuel, now almost thirteen, was a year shy of the age at which he would be allowed to stand beside his brothers and father as freemen; since the voting age had been lowered to sixteen, boys of fourteen and fifteen were also permitted to vote. Eleven-year-old Anne. Mary, age nine. Seven-year-old Katherine. William, who arrived after the first William died, was already six years old. Little Susan, the last born in England, was nearly four. And then came Zuriel, the only baby born in the New Jerusalem, who was baptized in the Boston meetinghouse on

March 13, 1636, and given the Old Testament name, which means in Hebrew "my rock is God," belonging to the Levite chief prominent during the Exodus. Not one of those fifteen pregnancies had produced the faintness and fatigue she felt now.

The governor was talking again, describing her guilt by association. "Why for your doings, you did harbor and countenance those that are parties in this faction that you have heard of. If you do countenance those that are transgressors of the law, you are guilty too."

"That's a matter of conscience, sir." With this remark, a woman with no formal schooling had fought the Cambridge-educated lawyer and governor to a draw. She was saying that her beliefs were her own business, not in the public realm, and therefore not actionable in court.

Having advanced nothing, Winthrop turned to a new line of questioning in the hope of humbling her. He introduced the fifth commandment, "Honor thy father and thy mother," which he and other colonial leaders interpreted to mean, "Honor the fathers of the commonwealth."

Her clever, hypothetical riposte was "But put the case, sir, that I do fear the Lord *and* my parents; may not I entertain them that fear the Lord because *my parents* will not give me leave?" That is, should human authority take precedence over the divine?

This was a reasonable question in a time and place with little separation of church and state. The very concept of such a separation would not be introduced in Massachusetts society until more than a half century later, following the debacle of the witch trials in Salem Village. The settlers had come with the express purpose of creating a community in which to worship God rightly. Their charter "of the Governor and Company of the Massachusetts Bay in New England" mandated that the "people, inhabitants there, may be so religiously, peaceably, and civilly governed, as their good life and orderly conversation may win and incite the natives of the country *to the knowledge and obedience of the only true God and Savior of mankind, and the Christian faith, which,* in our royal intention and the adventurers' free intention, *is the principal end of this plantation.*" Although some of the founders of Massachusetts, including most notably John Winthrop, had been trained in English common law, their new code of laws arose largely from the Bible, which they saw as containing all history—past, present, and future. Public funds paid all church expenses. Only men who were admitted to church membership had the right to vote. Becoming a church member involved a lengthy interview in which one had to show "evidence" of being elect, and thus saved, by God. In this way, political power was limited to those who were, in the eyes of the church, saints.

Moreover, the few men of the General Court jointly held multiple powers that would later be divided among the judicial, executive, and legislative branches of government. A court system—in the modern sense of the word *court*—did not exist, according to Elizabeth Bouvier, a court archivist in modern Boston. "The judicial, administrative, legislative, and executive functions were then all intertwined in the General Court, as well as the religious authority—all of it!" This court's vast power over the populace limited people's freedom to a degree that is unimaginable today. People were banned, for instance, from wearing any fur, lace, or colorful cloth, and all citizens, whether or not they were church members, were required to attend Sunday services.

Despite their vast powers, the magistrates were mindful of the even greater power, across the ocean, of the English monarchy. All of the General Court's authority came from the royal charter, granted to Winthrop and his company in 1629, which the Catholic-leaning King Charles I could revoke at any time. By bringing the physical document of the charter to America in 1630, Winthrop had put six thousand miles between it and any English effort to retrieve it. Four years later the ship that carried the Hutchinsons to Boston had also carried King Charles's written demand that the charter be returned, which the colonists so far had ignored. Partly because of their concerns about the charter, the judges of Massachusetts needed to maintain the peace in the colony and some semblance of honor and fairness—along the lines of English common law and Puritan political theory—in their dealings with Anne Hutchinson. They could not simply banish her without reason.

"Your course is not to be suffered for," or tolerated, Winthrop reminded her. "[It is] greatly prejudicial to the state. It is to seduce many honest persons that are called to those meetings, and your opinions—being known to be different from the word of God—may seduce many simple souls that resort unto you." Despite the governor's aloof and chilly mien, his temper could rise. "And now these opinions have flown off from magistrates and ministers since they have come to you. And, besides that, it will *not well stand* with the commonwealth that families should be neglected for so many neighbors and dames and so much time spent. We see *no* rule of God for this. We see *not* that any should have authority to set up any other exercises besides what authority hath already set up. And so what hurt comes of this, *you* will be guilty of, and *we* for suffering you."

"Sir," she said calmly, "I do not believe that to be so."

"Well, *we* see how it is. We must therefore put it away from you or restrain you from maintaining this course. We are *your* judges, and not you ours, and we *must* compel you to it."

"If you have a rule for it from God's word you may." Boldly, she held him to his own standard, that all authority must come from the Bible. "If it please you by authority to put [my teaching] down, I will freely let you, for I am subject to your authority. I desire that you would then set me down a rule by which I may put them away that come unto me and so have peace in so doing."

Rather than answering her, the governor deflected her question. "Yes, you are the woman of most note, and of best abilities, and if some others take upon them the like, it is by your teaching and example, but you show not in all this by what authority *you* take upon *you* to be such a public instructor."

Anne had a good answer for him, from the book of Titus, but she could not give it. Suddenly, without warning, she fell to the floor. She had fainted before the court.

2

THIS IMPUDENT
PURITAN

Although entirely without formal schooling, like virtually every woman of her day, Anne Hutchinson had been well educated at her father's knee. Francis Marbury, a Cambridge-educated clergyman, schoolmaster, and Puritan reformer, was her father. In the late 1570s, more than a decade before her birth, his repeated challenges to Anglican authorities led to his censure, his imprisonment for several years, and his own public trial—on a charge of heresy, the same charge that would be brought against his daughter, of refuting church dogma or religious truth. Marbury's trial was held in November 1578 at Saint Paul's Cathedral in London, fifty-nine years and an ocean distant from her far better known trial.

His trial left an abiding mark on her, though, and its themes foreshadow those of hers. During a lengthy period of church-imposed house arrest that coincided with Anne's first three years of life, her father composed from memory a biting transcription of his trial, which he called "The conference between me and the Bishop of London" with "many people standing by." This dramatic dialogue, published in the early 1590s as a pamphlet, was one of the central texts he used to educate and amuse his children. "Thou art a very ass, an idiot, and a fool," his buffoonish bishop chides Marbury the hero, in a dramatic style not unlike that of his contemporary William Shakespeare, who was then a decidedly non-Puritanical playwright and actor living in London. The other texts Marbury used to teach his daughters and sons—the Bible, first available in a printed English translation around 1540, and Foxe's *Book of Martyrs: A History of the Lives, Sufferings and Triumphant Deaths of the Early Christian and the Protestant Martyrs*, a 1583 compendium of martyrs emphasizing those of post-Reformation England, particularly during the reign of the Catholic queen "Bloody" Mary—were available to most children in sixteenth-century English Puritan gentry homes. What was unusual in Anne's house was the third text, authored by her father, as well as the simple presence of her father, who was forced by church authorities to remain, unemployed, at home.

The Reverend Francis Marbury was born in the fall of 1555 in London, where he was baptized on October 27 in the Church of Saint Pancras, Soper Lane. His parents, William Marbury and Agnes Lenton, had come from Lincoln and Northampton, both Midland shires more than a hundred miles north of London. Francis and his six siblings were raised in Grisby, Lincoln, their father's ancestral home. The family was lesser gentry, although a great-great-grandfather in the fifteenth century, Sir Thomas Blount of Grisby, was a knight.

Francis left home at age seventeen to attend Christ's College, Cambridge. At the time, Cambridge drew all the gifted Puritan school-boys of sufficient status, who considered Oxford too Catholic. Francis spent four years studying at Cambridge, received a master's degree, and was soon ordained a minister of the Church of England.

Anglicanism had replaced Roman Catholicism as England's state church in 1534, when King Henry VIII broke from Rome, declaring himself the "Protector and Only Supreme Head of the Church and Clergy of England." With this move, King Henry and thus England joined the waves of change that are now dubbed the Reformation, when religious reform inspired by the likes of Martin Luther, John Calvin, and Huldrych Zwingli drew large swaths of Europe away from the Church of Rome.

English Puritanism, which began in the late 1550s, was a Reformed sect aimed at further ridding the English church of Catholic tendencies and practices. The name *Puritan* came from the sect's stated aim of pu-rifying the church—creating a "true" church, like the early church in the years following the resurrection and ascension of Jesus Christ. Pu-ritans themselves rejected the "vile" term Puritan, seeing themselves as "nonconformists" or "true" Anglicans, while the Anglicans they op-posed were seen as papists.

The areas of dispute between Puritans—for the slur stuck—and Anglicans included the training of clergy, the order of the service, cler-ical vestments, and church ornamentation. Puritans considered many

English clergy poorly educated (lacking a university degree and knowledge of Greek and Hebrew) and thus ill equipped for preaching, which
they saw as a high skill, meriting elaborate preparation. This conflict
over the quality of preaching arose in part, according to a history of
seventeenth-century Lincolnshire, because of "the growing formalism of
the Church." Many people viewed the service of the Anglican Mass "as a
kind of charm" to ensure their salvation "if they could afford sufficient
celebrations after their death," and preaching "was little practiced."

Besides stressing the importance of sermons, Puritans wished to
simplify the service and the church. Kneeling for the sacrament of communion, using a ring in marriage, and even having a cross in the church
were "romish" or "popish" habits, they felt, "awful vestiges" of Catholicism, which smacked of Antichrist, a term they used for anything
friendly to Satan or hostile to God. The Puritans shrank the number of
sacraments from seven to two or three, leaving only baptism, communion, and sometimes marriage. They renounced as superstitions the
calendar of saints' and holy days.

Inspired at first by King Henry VIII's 1548 order to remove images from churches as "corrupt, vain, and superstitious," English
Protestants of the late sixteenth and seventeenth centuries destroyed
much of the legacy of medieval England, including stained glass windows, fabrics, icons, and rood screens and lofts. Protestants preferred
less-adorned churches than did Catholics, and Puritans far surpassed
Anglicans in this regard. To avoid any pagan idolatry, such as the second commandment forbade ("Thou shalt not make for thyself a carved
image"), Puritan ministers forsook the surplice—the loose-fitting white
ceremonial vestment worn by Catholic and Anglican clergy—for a
black preaching gown and skullcap. (White symbolized the sacrificial
Mass and the priestly role that they rejected.) Shocking many, Puritans
wore hats in church (following Jewish practice), refused to bow or kneel
during worship (which they saw as a violation of the third commandment), and allowed pigs and chickens in the church, and some of them
didn't even know the Lord's Prayer. During this period of upheaval, as
the English church adapted to the Reformation, behaviors such as these
divided towns, congregations, and even families.

Francis Marbury's first assignment was as a deacon, or assistant
minister, at a church in Northampton, in central England, the main

town of the shire in which his mother had been born. Without apparent concern for his future career, Deacon Marbury preached to his Anglican congregation that the Anglican bishops were but politicians. They lacked true understanding of the Bible, he said, and they chose ministers without concern for their training or their zeal. In a period when relatively few English ministers had a university degree—fewer than 30 percent of those in neighboring Lincolnshire at the start of the seventeenth century, for instance, a percentage that would rise to almost 90 by the end of the century—Puritans advocated an educated ministry.

The Reverend Marbury's sharp, public attacks prompted his bishop to withdraw the young man from his post and send him to jail. Francis was freed several months later but censured as a preacher and ordered never to return to Northampton. Within weeks, the brash twenty-two-year-old was back, preaching in Northampton as before. Church authorities arrested him again, detained him, and sent him to London to stand trial in November 1578 before the ecclesiastical Court of High Commission.

This court, charged with enforcing conformity in the church, inquired into and punished crimes ranging from heresy, violations of canon law, and libels against the monarch to incest, adultery, and gambling. It answered only to God and the monarch—not to Parliament or English common law—and was active under Queen Elizabeth in harassing Puritans. After secretly gathering evidence and charges, the court called up the defendant, stating neither the accusations against him nor the names of his accusers. If he refused to vow to make "full, true, and perfect answers" to the court, he would be fined for contempt. The judges, all bishops or ministers, acted also as prosecutors.

Francis Marbury, like his daughter a half century later, stood before his seated judges, who gathered in the consistory hall in the southwest corner of Saint Paul's Cathedral, a vast thirteenth- and fourteenth-century Norman and Gothic structure that also served, after the Reformation, as London's center of trade. Almost thirty years earlier, in 1549, Protestant preachers had incited a mob to sack Saint Paul's, destroying its altar, wall hangings, and many stone tombs. A dozen years after that, in a lightning fire on June 4, 1561, the church lost its nearly five-hundred-foot steeple, at the time the tallest in Europe, which was never rebuilt. The interior of the church—which would burn to the ground in the

Great Fire of London in 1666—was derelict by Marbury's time. Pamphleteers and merchants hawked their wares in stalls planted along the stone floor of the nave, which a late-sixteenth-century observer called "a brothel for the ears." Merchants stored barrels of ale and books, wood, and coal in the church's vaults. Despite the disrepair inside, large crowds often gathered outside the church's south wall, at an open-air pulpit called Paul's Cross, to hear Puritans like Marbury preach.

The Court of High Commission met in the consistory, a large fenced-in room adjacent to the cathedral's main door. Two long benches of dark oak lined the room's longer, north and south, walls. Bishop John Aylmer, the portly presiding judge, who was then in his late fifties, occupied a wooden throne set alone on the west wall. Francis Marbury faced Bishop Aylmer from the middle of the room, where he was flanked by two rows of the dutiful Anglican officials who were members of the court.

Bishop Aylmer did most of the questioning of the defendant, just as Governor John Winthrop would in Massachusetts in 1637. As at Anne's trial, supporters of the defendant clustered to the rear and sides of the hall.

"What have you to say to us?" Bishop Aylmer demanded of Marbury, beginning the trial.

"Nothing but God save you both," replied the defiant deacon, demonstrating a wit and confidence his daughter would inherit. Pressed further, according to his transcript, Marbury outlined his main charge, that the bishops were "killing" souls by ordaining uneducated ministers. "I say the bishops of London and Peterborough and all the bishops of England are guilty of the death of as many souls as have perished by the ignorance of the ministers of their making whom they knew to be unable." This was mild language from a Puritan, compared to petitions to Parliament from the same period, which described Anglican ministers as "dumb dogs, unskillful sacrificing priests, destroying drones, or rather caterpillars of the Word."

"Thou speakest of making ministers," Bishop Aylmer replied. "The bishop of Peterborough"—Lord Edmund Scambler, then present in the hall, who had ordained Marbury the previous year—"was never more overseen in his life than when he admitted *thee* to be a preacher in Northampton."

"Like enough so (in some sense) I pray God those scales may fall from his eyes," Marbury retorted.

"Thou art a very ass, thou art mad, thou art courageous, nay thou art impudent," the bishop said, adding to his brethren, "By my troth I think he be mad"—a notion that would also cross the minds of some of Anne Hutchinson's judges at her trial.

"Sir, I take exception against swearing judges," Marbury said. "I praise God I am not mad, but sorry to see *you* so out of temper."

"Did you ever hear one more impudent?" the bishop asked the room.

"I humbly beseech you, sir, have patience," the twenty-three-year-old defendant pleaded, half in jest. "Give this people better example. I am that I am through the Lord." Then, making the same sort of shift that his daughter would make on the stand, he turned from the present human realm to the spiritual: "Though I fear not you, yet I fear the Lord."

To prove his claims against the church, Marbury quoted Scripture, which was seen by all as the final authority in all matters, religious and otherwise. Regarding the bishops' killing of souls, he said, "If they order unable or unmeet ministers, they give imposition of hands over hastily to those men, which to do, the Apostle saith"—in 1 Timothy 5:22—"is to be 'partaker of other men's sins.'" He also quoted the prophet Hosea 4:6, "My people are destroyed for lack of knowledge," and asked, "But who should teach them knowledge?"

A church commissioner named Lewys broke in to demand of Marbury, "What trial would you have more than this? [Bishop Aylmer] is an honest man, and like to prove learned in time."

"But in the meantime the people perish," the defendant replied. "You will not commit your sucking child to a dry milk nurse, be she never so honest."

Choosing a different metaphor, the Reverend Lewys said, "A good life is a good sermon, and such slay no souls though they be not so exquisite."

Jousting with his opponent's figure of speech, the Reverend Marbury said, "To teach by example *only* is good in a matron whom silence beseems." He brought up Paul's letter to Titus, which reads, "Thou shouldest set in order the things that are wanting, and ordain elders [ministers] in every city. . . . For a bishop must be blameless, as the steward of God... Holding fast the faithful word as he hath been taught, that he may be able by sound doctrine both to exhort and to convince the gainsayers" (1:5–9). Marbury told the bishops, "The Apostle tells Titus they must be able to convince the gainsayers. These [comments of yours] are but evasions."

Impatient, Lewys remarked, "This fellow would have a preacher in every parish church," referring to the Puritans' drive to ordain not only better-educated but also more ministers.

"So would Saint Paul," Marbury said, referring again to Titus.

"Where wouldst thou have them?" Lewys demanded.

"In Cambridge, in Oxford, in the Inns of Court," Marbury replied, "yea and some," he added, in a nod to his jail time and that of many nonconformists who had troubled the state church, "in prison. We doing our part, the Lord would do his part."

The role of the clergyman was much debated during this period, in large part because the Protestant Reformation's emphasis on grace over faith had changed the clerical role. When Luther and Zwingli, both Catholic clergymen, discarded their collars and took wives, they ended the special status of the Catholic priest as a vessel through which God gives humanity divine grace. In Reformed theology, grace is free to all who are chosen by God, even without priestly intervention. Each believer receives the body of Christ "only by his own personal faith," Luther wrote. This new doctrine would lead to quarrels among Protestants and, in America, among Puritans over the proper role of the "faithful shepherd." For early Puritans like Marbury, ministers were needed not to channel grace but to spread God's word through prophecy, evangelism, and preaching.

Bishop Aylmer cut in to ask Marbury where the church would find money to train more priests: "Where is the living for them?"

"A man might cut a good large thong out of *your* hide, and the rest would not be missed," Marbury retorted. "If a living be the default, they are to blame which have too much," he added, implicating his judges. Over and over, Marburg told the consistory, he would give up everything to gain something for God. Underlying his defiance was a deep faith, which he would pass to Anne.

Archdeacon Mullins said the church could not ordain more priests until "nobler" men sought clerical work.

Marbury observed, "It is better to have nothing than that which God would not have."

Bishop Aylmer asked, "How provest thou that God would not have them, when we can get no better?"

Marbury replied, "Doth he not say," in Hosea 4:6, "'Because thou hast rejected knowledge, I will also reject thee, that thou shalt be no priest to me'?"

"Thou art an overthwart proud Puritan knave!" the bishop cried. "Thou wilt go to Northampton, and thou wilt have thine own saying to die, but thou shalt repent it."

"I am no Puritan," Marbury said, for he considered himself a member in good standing of the Church of England, subscriber to all its doctrines. "I beseech you to be good to me. I have been twice in prison, but I know not why."

Bishop Aylmer ordered the bailiff to "have him to Marshalsea," a London prison that was notorious for the maltreatment of inmates. At Marshalsea, Queen Elizabeth's henchmen took pleasure in throwing together the two diametrically opposed camps, Puritans and Catholics. "There," the bishop gloated, "he shall cope with the papists."

Marbury's final words to the court, which his daughter Anne would hear and read innumerable times, were, "I am to go whither it pleases God, but remember God's judgments. You do me open wrong. I pray God forgive you."

The church court convicted Francis Marbury of the crime of heresy—corrupting the dogmas of Christ—for questioning the judgment of his superiors. Heresy was a shifting category, its meaning changing with the political tide. During the reign of Queen Mary, who was Catholic, the Puritan minister Hugh Huddleston said, "It is heretical or heresy for a woman to govern the state, for that were to make the woman above the man." A few years later, when the Protestant Queen Elizabeth ascended the throne, Huddleston's nonconformist colleagues would have liked to strike that definition.

The punishment for Marbury's crime was two years in jail. He spent them in Marshalsea prison, on the seamy south side of the Thames—the opposite bank from the city of London and Saint Paul's—where prisons and other distasteful establishments such as brothels, taverns, theaters, and bear- and bull-baiting arenas were relegated.

In 1580, when he was twenty-five, the Reverend Francis Marbury was released from prison for the third time. He moved to the remote market town of Alford, Lincolnshire, where he was considered sufficiently reformed to be allowed to preach and teach. In this town his daughter Anne would be born and spend more than half her life.

Alford (pronounced "Olford") lies 140 miles north of London and six miles from England's central eastern coast. It is set, according to local historian Reginald Dudding, in "a wide-stretching valley, bounded on the west by the gentle slope of the Wolds," hills that rise from the flatlands of eastern Lincolnshire. At that time inhabited by fewer than five hundred people, Alford consisted of a central market square, one state-run Anglican church, several dozen small, thatched-roof houses, and extensive surrounding arable fields. The sixteenth-century historian Leland described Alford as "all fact and reeded"—reed thatched—"and a brook runneth by." The brook, which remains today, is a remnant of the ford that gave the town its name and its market status. A ford—part of a river so shallow that one can wade across—was in medieval times a gathering place, which led to barter, the mother of markets. In Marbury's day the town's population doubled every Tuesday and Friday as vendors gathered with their fish, flowers, produce, and baked goods, as they still do today.

Ascending the Wolds to the west of Alford, residents could see many windmills on the horizon and on a clear day, to the east, the North Sea dotted with passing ships, beyond which lay Holland, another hotbed of Puritanism. Residents of this English coastal region imagined—there appears to be no historical basis for it—that flotsam washing ashore here came from the 1588 destruction of the Spanish Armada, the mighty fleet of warships appareled with banners of the Virgin Mary that King Philip of Spain had sent into English waters. After a nine-day naval battle, the Spanish ships that had escaped English guns ran into a storm—the "Protestant wind"—which caused the most losses. Already in late-sixteenth-century Lincolnshire, there was a sense of a vast world beyond, and a world-encompassing battle between evil and good.

The Reverend Marbury was clearly capable, personable, and outwardly conforming, for he was soon appointed curate, or deputy vicar, of the local church. The vicar, or senior priest, of Alford then was the

North
Sea

Scrooby

Lincolnshire

Alford

Lincoln

Trent

Boston

The Wash

East Anglia

Great Ouse

Northampton

Cambridge

Canons
Ashby

ENGLAND

Oxford

LONDON

River

Thames

Canterbury

Southampton

Portsmouth

Strait of Dover

Isle of
Wight

FRANCE

Southeastern England

Reverend Joseph Overton, of whom little is known. Preachers in Lincolnshire at the time were known for their verbal stamina, with sermons lasting two hours or longer. These clerics "exalted preaching above the sacraments," according to the Lincolnshire historian Dudding, and their views were "chiefly Puritan and Calvinistic."

The church of Saint Wilfrid's, in which Francis Marbury preached, still stands on a slight rise beside the main road through Alford. Named for a seventh-century English bishop who preached to the Saxons and the Celts, the church was erected in the 1350s on the site of an earlier church. A handsome, airy building of naturally green sandstone, it has Gothic arches atop its windows and doors and a square tower containing large bells whose tolling announces services, as they did in Marbury's day.

One enters the church through thick, oak-paneled Gothic doors studded with nail heads and decorated with a clover trefoil design, which open at the turn of the original round brass handle. Inside, 650-year-old octagonal columns line the aisles, and at the rear an ancient staircase leads to the bell tower. Despite oak pews and carvings, the church is pleasantly light. Its walls, originally covered with religious paintings, are whitewashed with lime, and the medieval stained glass was long ago broken, leaving most windowpanes clear amid delicate tracery. The fourteenth-century rood screen, the barrier between the nave and altar of a medieval church, survives, remarkably, despite the post-Reformation purification of English churches and minimal Victorian renovations (such as the addition of roof pinnacles) to this church. Carvings depicting the passion of Christ—a cock, a crown of thorns, nails, a cup, a tunic, a ladder, and tools—float above the altar, beside which a local knight and his wife lie in marble effigy.

During his first decade in Alford, Francis Marbury preached from the rood loft, an enclosure above the screen from which medieval priests preached. But King James I ordered in 1603 that every English church should have a pulpit, to bring the priest closer to the people. The rood loft in Saint Wilfrid's was removed, although the start of the spiral staircase leading to it can still be seen behind the newer Jacobean pulpit. Made of dark oak, the pulpit is carved with arabesque figures of Adam and Eve, a medieval man and woman, flowers, rams, and horns. The Reverend Marbury had to ascend several steps to the pulpit, raise its metal latch, and pass through its oaken half door in order to preach.

This pulpit is still used every Sunday morning, when the current vicar of Alford offers one of two weekly services at the church. The church was far busier in Elizabethan times: there were daily morning prayers and evensong, two sermons on Sundays, and one sermon each on Wednesdays, Fridays, and feast days. Holy Communion was given thirteen times a year, monthly and on Christmas Day. At the Lord's Supper, Marbury offered his congregation wine along with the bread, one of the innovations of post-Reformation Anglicanism. The silver chalice that he sipped from, which was made in 1537 from melted-down medieval chalices, is now in a bank vault in Louth, thirteen miles to the north.

Along with his ministry, in 1585 the Reverend Marbury became schoolmaster at the Alford Free Grammar School, one of England's earliest free schools. These were public schools, free to the poor, begun by Queen Elizabeth. The Alford free school began in 1570 with a fifty-pound grant from a local merchant. Marbury was its third master. During its early years the school was located above the church's charming front porch. This schoolroom remains, atop a stone staircase leading up from a miniature version of the church's main door, located just west of the larger door. Six days a week, from early morning until late afternoon, Marbury's students, all boys, sat on wooden benches in the unheated schoolroom, scribbling on slates with chalk dug from nearby fields. The curriculum included reading, writing, arithmetic, and biblical exegesis in the original languages of Scripture, Hebrew and Greek, as well as English. The Latin Vulgate Bible had gone out with the Reformation, but most English boys studied Latin too, reading from Horace, Cicero, and Pliny. One of Marbury's students, a John Smith of nearby Willoughby, born in 1579, would become Captain John Smith and found the colony of Jamestown, Virginia, and chart the coastline of New England.

Around the time Francis Marbury returned to work, he married Elizabeth Moore, a young woman of whom practically nothing is known. The couple lived up the road from the church in a small timber-frame house with whitewashed mud walls, a thatched roof, and one or two bays. Near the house was a barn "all of timber building and mud walls" and enough arable land to cultivate crops, graze sheep and cows, and provide pasturage for the horse he needed for transport. The Reverend Marbury grew wheat, beans, root vegetables, and hay, and the family produced its own cheese, butter, and wool. His wife gave birth to three daughters—Elizabeth, in 1581; Mary, born in 1583 and deceased two years later; and Susan, in 1585—and then she died.

Within a year of his first wife's death, Francis married Bridget Dryden, a midwife about ten years his junior from a prominent Northampton family of religious dissenters. Twenty-five-year-old Bridget, who joined Francis, his two daughters, and one or two servants in their cottage, had been born and raised in the manor of Canons Ashby, Northampton, where she likely heard her future husband preach. Bridget's ancestors were said to include the eighth-century monarch Charlemagne, although such claims cannot be proven. It was a point of pride in the Dryden family that an uncle, Sir Anthony Cope, who opposed Queen Elizabeth's efforts to steer a middle course between the Catholics and the Puritans, was imprisoned in the Tower of London in 1587 for trying to revise along Puritan lines the state-approved Book of Common Prayer. Bridget's grandfather John Dryden was a close friend of the humanist and theologian Erasmus of Rotterdam (1467–1536), who had lectured at Cambridge and encouraged reading the Bible in the vernacular. Sir Erasmus Dryden, Bridget's older brother, was grandfather to the seventeenth-century poet and playwright John Dryden, who was thus a first cousin once removed to Anne.

The first child of the marriage that would produce Anne Marbury Hutchinson was a girl named Mary, born in 1588. Two years later Francis and Bridget had a son, John, who died in infancy. In the midsummer heat of July 17, 1591, their third child, Anne, arrived.

At the time of Anne's birth, all the Marbury children were girls—ten-year-old Elizabeth and six-year-old Susan, Anne's two half sisters, and three-year-old Mary. The lack of sons may help explain why Anne's schoolteacher father accorded her so much attention in a time when only boys were sent to school and taught to read and write. Another factor may have been the growing suspicion among the ruling class in Elizabethan England that girls and women could be schooled. The powerful female monarch, who at the time of Anne Marbury's birth had spent more than half of her fifty-seven years on the throne, knew French, Italian, Spanish, Welsh, Latin, and some Greek besides her native tongue and wrote eloquently in music and words. As the prominent London headmaster Richard Mulcaster put it, "That young maidens can learn, nature doth give them, and that they have learned our experience doth teach us. What foreign example can more assure the world than our diamond," Queen Elizabeth, "at home?"

After Anne, the next Marbury baby was another girl, Bridget, born in 1593. Francis's first surviving son, also named Francis, did not arrive until Anne was three years old. Ten more children followed—Emma, Erasmus, Anthony (who died at two), Bridget (born after the death of her older sister Bridget at age five), Jeremuth, Daniel and Elizabeth (who both died at nine), Thomas, Anthony, and Katherine, the last, born in 1610. In all, Bridget Marbury bore fifteen live children (just as her daughter Anne would), twelve of whom survived early childhood.

At the time of Anne's birth, the Reformation had spread across Europe. The continent that a century earlier had been almost entirely Roman Catholic was now split between Rome and various Protestant sects. The Renaissance was in full swing. In 1591, when Anne arrived, Cervantes was forty-four; Francis Bacon was thirty; Shakespeare, Christopher Marlowe, and Galileo Galilei were twenty-seven; and Ben Jonson and John Donne were nineteen years old. In the coming two decades René Descartes, Caravaggio, Rembrandt, and John Milton would be born.

In tiny Alford in Lincolnshire, the period just preceding Anne's birth was pivotal for her father. In the summer of 1590, after a decade of relative quiet, according to ecclesiastical court records, Francis Marbury was again in trouble with authorities. In his midthirties, apparently happily married and employed, he felt emboldened to challenge his superiors again. Some suspected him of authoring the Marprelate Tracts, satiric diatribes against Catholic tendencies in the Church of England that were published in London in 1588 and 1589 under the pseudonym "Martin Marprelate." There is no evidence linking Marbury to these tracts, for which the printer, the only known culprit, was executed in 1593. Nevertheless, in lectures at Saint Wilfrid's, the Reverend Marbury freely denounced the Church of England

and its head, the queen, for selecting ill-educated bishops, who in turn chose poorly trained ministers. The bishops were "self-seeking soul murderers," he charged, using the terminology of his trial. Outraged at his renewed defiance, the Bishop of Lincoln forbade this "impudent Puritan" from preaching, stripped him of his living as a teacher, and placed him under house arrest. This punishment was imposed the year Anne was born.

Imprisoned with his family in his modest house in Alford, Francis tended his gardens, revised and published his magnum opus, and tutored his children. He read aloud to the girls from his dialogue, which posed him as the brave hero opposing the bishop, who was clearly a buffoon. To teach the children to read, Francis assigned them portions of his transcript, of Scripture, and of John Foxe's *Book of Martyrs*. Foxe's work was a lively account of the "atrocities" and "instruments of torture [such as] the rack, the gridiron, [and] the boiling oil" inflicted on Protestant martyrs, from the scourging and crucifixion of the evangelist Philip in 54 CE to the burning at the stake of a Puritan named Anne Askew in 1546. During Anne Hutchinson's childhood, Queen Elizabeth ordered that for her people's edification a copy of Foxe's *Martyrs* should be chained to a lectern in every parish in England. This book provided compelling reading to Anne and her siblings, much as the tales of Andersen and Grimm would do for children of later centuries.

Stripped of his students and of his pulpit, Francis Marbury was in an almost unbearable situation. To survive, he turned his prodigious and focused attention on his own little girls, particularly the brilliant, inquisitive Anne, who as the youngest at the time of this incarceration was least burdened by household chores.

Meanwhile, Francis continued to fight for his freedom. He begged each year to be returned to his posts, pleading to church authorities that he was not a Puritan. "I subscribe to the Elizabethan Book of Common Prayer, and none other," he wrote to the Bishop of London, John Aylmer, who was now in his seventies. Marbury said he was expelled "for cause to me utterly unknown." He asked other ministers of the church to vouch for his good character, which they did in letters to the bishop. Finally, after three years of house arrest, in 1594—just months after Bishop Aylmer's death—Francis recovered his license to teach and to preach.

Now a middle-aged patriarch, the Reverend Marbury decided to make a change. Never again would he openly question the Church of England or its head, the monarch. For the rest of his life he would curb his tongue.

This new, conformist attitude would lead, eleven years later, to a pastoral assignment at a London parish just north of the Thames. The summer Anne turned fourteen, Francis was offered the post of vicar of the Church of Saint Martin's in the Vintry, in London. Francis was delighted: his move toward the establishment was complete. That fall the Marburys packed all their belongings on wagons and traveled 140 miles south to London, where on October 28 they moved into the vestry attached to the church.

This was a promotion for the Reverend Marbury. The size of a parish was an index of its pastor's success, and the parish of Saint Martin in the Vintry was relatively large. In 1638, the nearest year in which parish size was recorded, most of London's ninety-six other parishes had only a few hundred communicants while Saint Martin in the Vintry had 1100, more than the entire population of Alford. Although the Vintry was slightly poorer than most parishes, based on its rents and tithes, its residents included wealthy wine merchants descended from the early-fourteenth-century immigrants from Bordeaux who gave the neighborhood its name.

The timing of the move—not long after the purging of the Puritan preachers by King James I, who succeeded his childless cousin Queen Elizabeth upon her death in March 1603—also indicates that Francis was back within the Anglican fold, at least by outward appearances. Early in his reign King James tried to appease the Puritans but then swung the other way. Now, faced with a shortage of ministers in London, he called on men like Marbury whose troublesomeness seemed but a memory.

Saint Martin in the Vintry was in central London, almost at the midpoint between Saint Paul's Cathedral, where Francis had been tried, and the prison in which he had spent two uncomfortable years. To Anne and her siblings, who had grown up in a rural outpost, this neighborhood must have seemed unimaginably vibrant and cosmopolitan. The church and vestry were less than a hundred yards from the great river that was the main highway of the largest city in the world.

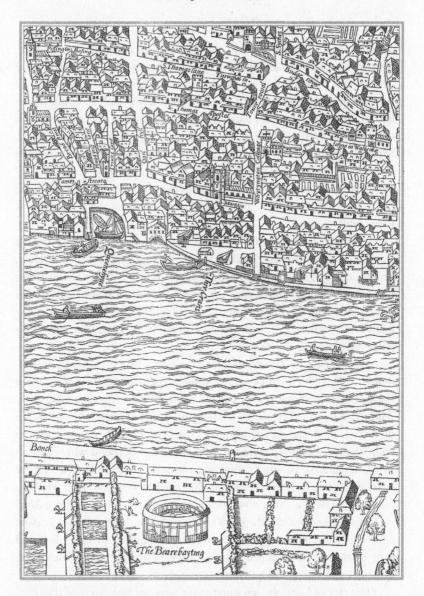

The church of Saint Martin in the Vintry appears, with a Y on its steeple, in the upper center of this portion of the 1562 "Agas" map of London. The Great Fire of London destroyed this neighborhood north of the Thames in 1666.

Wider and shallower than it is now, Spenser's "silver-streaming" Thames was the scene of royal pageants and civic ceremonies. In winter, on the rare occasion when it froze, carnivals were set upon its icy surface and fires lit, and vendors sold their wares upon it. The rest of the year it was crowded with small boats and the sails of ships, which had to unload at London Bridge. Barges for the king, the archbishop of Canterbury, and the lord mayor of London plied its muddy waters. Manors along the Thames had private boats and landing places. To cross the river, one could walk across the bridge or cry "eastward ho!" or "westward ho!" to hail a ferry, at the cost of a penny. The east side of the bridge was London's main port, which throughout this period was the world's largest.

A quarter mile east of the Vintry along the river was the Tower of London, that symbol of English power serving alternately as fortress, prison, and palace, which had been built in 1078 under William the Conqueror. In the mid-sixteenth century, Queen Elizabeth had been imprisoned here during the reign of her half sister, Mary, and then she had been crowned here. James I had ordered in 1603 that the royal jewels be displayed in the Tower.

Adjacent to the Tower was the river's only bridge, now called London Bridge, a thirteenth-century stone structure cluttered with more than a hundred shops, one of which had been the medieval chapel of St. Thomas à Becket. The severed limbs and heads of criminals were often displayed on spikes on the bridge's Great Stone Gate, on its southern end, which led to the forbidden Bankside neighborhood where prostitutes, drunkards, rowdy hordes, and playwrights such as Christopher Marlowe roamed. In the very year that the Marburys arrived, William Shakespeare was a short distance away, across the river, creating *Measure for Measure*. Besides the plays of Shakespeare, Marlowe, Ben Jonson, and their contemporaries, the pleasures of Bankside included bull and bear baiting in ring-shaped theaters, cock fighting, taverns, alehouses, brothels, gambling, and bowling.

The city of London, one square mile situated just north of the river, from the Tower to Saint Paul's, was an overcrowded clutter of three- and four-story buildings on cobbled, refuse-littered medieval streets, its skyline dominated by the steeples of hundreds of churches, which served as the community and religious centers of most Londoners' lives. The bubonic plague occasionally swept through the city, shrinking its population, although the Marburys avoided it. At the turn of the seventeenth century the city had roughly 200,000 residents, twice as many as just fifty years before. In 1603, according to the historian John Stowe, London "consisteth of diverse streets, ways, and winding lanes, all full of buildings, on the bank of the River Thames. . . . There is now a continued building of tenements, about half a mile in length of the bridge." Vast, open fields surrounded the urban chaos. The late Queen Elizabeth and her successor, King James, hunted in the remote woods that are now Hyde Park.

On November 5, 1605, just a week after the Marburys arrived, London buzzed with the news of a secret plot to reintroduce Catholicism as the state religion. A group of Catholic men intended to blow up the Houses of Parliament in which the members of parliament and the king were gathered for a session. The plot was foiled when authorities discovered thirty-six barrels of gunpowder in a cellar beneath the Palace of Westminster. They caught and tortured the leaders of this "gunpowder plot," Robert Catesby and Guy Fawkes, whose capture is still commemorated in parts of England as Guy Fawkes Day.

Francis Marbury was at the opposite end of the religious spectrum from these rebels, for he considered the Church of England too Catholic rather than not enough. Despite the outward conformity that he adopted in order to support his family, Francis was still a dissenter at heart. Yet he followed the rules well enough to be able to supplement his income by taking on other parishes. From 1608 he served also in the parish of Saint Pancras, Middlesex, several miles northwest of the city, where he traveled on horseback once or twice a week to preach. Early in 1610 Marbury replaced that secondary assignment with the less strenuous one as rector of Saint Margaret's, New Fish Street, a short walk east of Saint Martin in the Vintry.

Outwardly at least, fifty-five-year-old Francis Marbury had made peace with Anglican authorities. But the strain of this charade—concealing his convictions about worship and faith—may have contributed to his sudden death, in London, in February 1611. Nevertheless, the seeds he had planted in his nineteen-year-old daughter, Anne—a willingness to question and even to show contempt for authority, a confidence in the rightness of one's own views, a deep faith in God, and a desire to share that faith through teaching—would bear fruit in Massachusetts long after his death.

3

A MASTERPIECE
OF WOMAN'S WIT

On that bitterly cold Tuesday in November 1637, the session of the General Court of Massachusetts halted the moment the defendant, Anne Marbury Hutchinson, dropped to the floor. Her husband and his brother Edward ran from the back of the hall to help her to her feet. Governor Winthrop did not rise, but "gave her leave to sit down, for her countenance discovered some bodily infirmity," as he explained that evening to his wife, Margaret, who was in bed following a miscarriage, after which the defendant had ministered to her.

In the courtroom Anne Hutchinson accepted the bench offered her and agreed to continue with the trial. A manservant refreshed the heated coals in the brass foot warmers that lay beneath the boots of her forty judges.

Addressing the question asked just before her collapse, she told the court that she found her authority to run public meetings in Paul's letter to Titus, which describes older women as "teachers of honest things." She said, "I conceive there lies a clear rule in Titus, that the elder women should instruct the younger, and then I must have a time wherein I must do it."

Winthrop corrected her, noting that Titus 2:3–5 states, "Elder women must instruct the younger about their business, and to *love* their husbands and *not* to make them clash." The entire passage reads, "The elder women likewise, that they be in such behavior as becomes holiness, not false accusers, not subject to much wine, but teachers of honest things, That they may instruct the young women to be sober minded, that they love their husbands, that they love their children, That they be temperate, chaste, keeping at home, good and subject unto their husbands, that the word of God be not evil spoken of."

Ignoring aspects of this passage—as she had to ignore other statements of the apostle Paul requiring silence and obedience of women—
Hutchinson cited another Scripture. In the Acts of the Apostles 18:26, a
married couple, Aquila and Priscilla, "took upon them to instruct [the
man] Apollos, more perfectly, yet he was a man of good parts, but they,
better instructed, might teach him." A marginal note in the Geneva
Bible, which she used, justified the revolutionary idea that a woman
could teach religion, even to a man: "Apollos, a godly and learned man,
did not refuse to profit in the school of a . . . woman: and so became an
excellent minister of the Church."

Winthrop mocked her. "See how your argument stands? Priscilla,
with her husband, took Apollos home to instruct him privately, therefore
Mistress Hutchinson without her husband may teach sixty or eighty?"

"I call them not. But if they come to me, I may instruct them."

"Yet you show us not a rule."

"I have given you two places of Scripture," she answered, growing
impatient.

"But neither of them will suit your practice."

Her calm dissolving into sarcasm, she said, "Must I show *my name*
written therein?"—meaning in Scripture.

This retort seems especially ironic in light of how rarely women's
names appear in the records of colonial America. But Winthrop could
not appreciate Hutchinson's wit. Her speech and actions were most un-
seemly in a woman, he and his peers believed. Although he had not noticed it when she first arrived in Boston, he was sure now that her
behavior was out of place, which suggested the presence of evil, or the
Antichrist.

In the courtroom he defended his position by citing two other passages. In 1 Corinthians 14:34–35, the apostle Paul admonishes all
women to be silent in church and all wives to seek spiritual guidance
from their husbands. And 1 Timothy 2:12 states, "I permit not a woman
to teach, neither to usurp authority over the man, but to be in silence."
This general wish for silence from women extended also into the
courtroom, as Winthrop had earlier explained to Hutchinson: "We do
not mean to discourse with those of your sex."

Winthrop was arguing for nothing more than the role expected of
any seventeenth-century Englishwoman. The model woman then—

modest, meek, submissive, virtuous, obedient, and kind—was solely occupied with supervising and maintaining the home, cooking, sometimes brewing and dairying, and bearing and rearing children. She was expected to suffer all these in silence, as in the oft-quoted passage from Genesis 3:16: "Unto the woman he said, I will greatly multiply thy sorrow and thy conception; in sorrow thou shalt bring forth children." The other role a woman could assume was that of nurse or midwife, which Anne and her mother did. Complex discourse, deep thought, and books of all kinds were believed to tax a woman's weak mind and keep her from pleasing her husband, who was her superior intellectually. A woman who aimed for more was asking for trouble, Winthrop was sure. After Anne Hopkins, a well-read Connecticut woman who was married to the governor of Hartford, suffered a breakdown in 1645, Winthrop confided in his journal that her error was "giving herself wholly to reading and writing. . . . If she had attended her household affairs, and such things as *belong to women,* and not gone out of her way and calling to meddle in such things as are *proper for men,* whose minds are stronger, she had kept her wits, and might have improved them usefully and honorably *in the place God had set her."*

Luckily for the governor, all of his female intimates conformed to this model of femininity. Margaret (his third wife, for the first two had died, as was common, in childbirth) signed letters to him, "your faithful and obedient wife," and said she felt she had "nothing within or without" worthy of him. His sister signed letters to him as "Your sister to command." The wife of his son John described herself to John as "thy ever loving and kind wife to command in whatsoever thou pleasest so long as the Lord shall be pleased to give me life and strength." All these women cheerfully obliged the governor. Why couldn't Mistress Hutchinson?

This bout of biblical squabbling between Hutchinson and Winthrop over social identity and status ended in another standoff. Neither side was willing to accept the validity of the other's view. This impasse was a microcosm of the state of the state, and in Winthrop's mind was unacceptable. Impasses such as these could not be let stand. Something or someone had to be removed so that the colony could be at peace.

As for Hutchinson, the basis for her determined interpretation of Scripture was her exhaustive study over many decades of her 1595 edition of the Geneva Bible. This Bible, whose copious marginal notes greatly influenced Puritan thinking, was the one used in most Reformed homes. It was named for the Swiss city where most of the translation had been done. It first came to America in 1620 aboard the *Mayflower*. Published from 1560 until 1644, the Geneva was for nearly a century the most popular English Bible. The King James Version, completed in 1611, would not gain wide acceptance until the 1640s.

The Geneva, one of the first English translations of the Bible, was also the first to contain both New and Old Testaments with chapter and verse divisions. A 1408 English church decree forbade as heresy any translation of the Bible into the "vulgar English tongue," but with the split from Rome in 1534 and the spread of Reformation theology, Henry VIII had a new need. The first great English translator, the Oxford-educated priest William Tyndale, read Martin Luther in the 1520s and then finished his translation while in exile in Germany, where he was martyred in 1538. A Reformer, Tyndale believed that all Christians should independently study the New Testament and count it as the final authority in all matters of doctrine and life.

This was the case in Cambridge, Massachusetts, in 1637. For both Hutchinson and her judges, there was no more important text than the Bible. Scripture gave them their law, much of their culture, and most of their understanding of human emotions and relationships. They inhabited the New Israel, which was chosen by God, and saw themselves as "the people of God," like the biblical Jews. In the words of John Cotton, "The same covenant which God made with the national church of Israel and their seed ... is the very same (for substance) and none other which the Lord maketh with any Congregational Church and our seed."

On a more practical level, the Holy Bible was one of the few texts available to the colonists of New England, who prior to 1660 had no active printing presses and imported little reading matter from London or Holland. A few of the best-educated men here, including the ministers, had libraries of biblical commentaries and works of Latin, Greek, and Hebrew, and some even wrote poetry, but dramatists and composers did not exist on this continent. The novel, of course, had yet to be invented. Most homes contained fewer than four books, at least one of which was the Bible. According to early Massachusetts probate records, the Bible was present in more than half of the households, and some houses had two or three. In addition, there was often a book of psalms, a primer, an almanac, a catechism, or a chapbook—a small book of stories, songs, or rhymes.

It is not possible to exaggerate the importance of Scripture to this community. Children learned to read, if they did at all, from the Bible. Families studied it together daily, reading it aloud over several months—from Genesis through to Revelation—and then starting again. Many settlers knew much of it by heart and readily applied it to such events as thunderstorms, sudden inexplicable deaths, or the passing of a comet overhead. For most if not all of those present at Anne's trial, the Good Book occupied hours of thought every day. "The life of the Puritan was in one sense a continuous act of worship," the historian Patrick Collinson observed, "pursued under an unremitting and lively sense of God's providential purposes and constantly refreshed by religious activity, personal, domestic and public. [The Puritan was] much in prayer; with it he began and closed the day." Knowing God through the Bible and serving God through action were the most important human activities.

Anne, her judges, and many of their contemporaries read the Bible with an intensity that many of us now associate only with studying a poem, when we carefully plumb the meaning of each word. Scripture was the source not only of meaning but also of truth. Studying the Bible enabled one to live in God's way, according to his dictates. Nowadays, the Bible may seem like an antique, a relic from which we learned stories in childhood, or it may seem nonessential, the gratuity in the drawer beside the bed in every roadside motel. But to the Puritans, the Bible, recently translated, was new, relevant, and powerfully true. For them, the Word was the world.

As one's sole and constant reading matter, the Bible is not a bad choice, for it abounds in drama, poetry, and mystery. The Puritans had little else in the way of entertainment, in part because they spurned most forms of amusement except alcohol in moderation, tasty food, and matrimonial sex. In the Bible they found countless intriguing questions that served to occupy their minds as they performed the menial tasks necessary to settle a wilderness. What do these words of Christ's mean? they asked themselves. More compellingly, they worried, Have I Christ in my heart or not? Have I true grace? How does one prepare for saving grace? How do I know I am saved? What is the right evidence of this? How shall I go into heaven? These sorts of questions kept Puritans awake at night imagining the very flames of hell and roused them hours before dawn, their hearts in a panic.

The events foretold in the book of Revelation—pouring of vials, unfolding of seals—were as real to them as the dirt beneath their feet. They were actively awaiting Judgment Day, when the Holy Spirit would descend from heaven to condemn some and redeem others. In which group will I be? Do I deserve to partake of the Lord's Supper after services? How do I know I have a sign or seal of God's grace? How can I, such a great sinner, sit down to the Lord's Table?

These were among the questions asked by Anne's peers in casual conversation, during childbirth, or around a sickbed, which she felt competent to address. A ministerial word from the midwife Hutchinson, as she wiped a laboring woman's brow or soothed a teenager mourning her dead mother, was eagerly received. As naturally as the women of Boston sought protection from the cold of winter, they came to Anne to quiet their anxieties about salvation (being saved by God), assurance (knowing with certainty that one is saved), and God's great and mysterious gift of his grace. Many of them were illiterate, all had the constant burden of keeping house for their families, and most had little opportunity for mental stimulation. In these lives of physical labor, Anne's brilliant explorations of subtle points in Scripture and sermon provided them with inspiration and even entertainment.

In running women's meetings, in fact, Anne was following local custom, as she explained to the court. Upon her arrival in Boston in 1634, she had noted that local women met regularly in their homes to discuss the weekly Bible reading and the ministers' sermons—occupying their minds with theology while keeping their hands busy with quilting and embroidery. These religious discussions, sometimes called "gossipings," grew out of the ban on women participating in any activities at church. Women were barred not only from the ministry but also from voting on church membership, participating in services, and talking in the church. Within the meetinghouse they were segregated from men, entering by a different door and sitting in a separate side of the building. This custom, which has no precedent in the churches of England or Rome, was an innovation of the colonists and a few Reformed sects in Europe, with Old Testament origins. In

Orthodox Judaism men and women worship separately, and women do not participate in services.

Despite women's exclusion from many aspects of worship in New England, they felt as much anxiety as did the men about their spiritual well-being. The women too had risked their lives by crossing the ocean to worship God freely. Concern about their soul's salvation was rarely far from their minds, particularly in light of the Puritan belief that salvation is not possible unless one was chosen by God before birth—predestined, or "elect." Unlike the men, women had few ways of salving their religious fears. One Boston woman suffered such "utter desperation" over "her spiritual estate"—whether before birth she was damned or saved—that "one day she took her little infant and threw it into a well, and then came into the house and said, now she was sure she should be damned, for she had drowned her child." This extraordinary act shows the depth of the spiritual fear and how great the need for certainty.

Meetings like Anne's had been held by Puritans in England also, and while they were not encouraged by church authorities, they were allowed. Known as "conventicles," these meetings were hard to distinguish from those regularly held by Puritan families and small communities for praying, repeating sermons, reading the catechism, and singing of psalms. While women were not directed to run conventicles, and were officially banned from doing so, the division between mother and preacher blurred in a culture that encouraged daily reading and discussion of Scripture and sermons, both inside and outside the family. In this way, women in England assumed leading public roles at the local level, especially over female servants and children. Beyond that, of course, and officially at all levels, they were barred from public power in the church.

In Boston, Anne at first offered theological counseling and advice to other women only in the privacy of their homes and avoided the regularly scheduled gossipings, for which she felt no need on account of her own strong sense of communion with God. Unlike many of her peers, she was not deeply troubled about her spiritual estate. Day after day, year after year, she prayed, studied Scripture, and felt reasonably confident that her estate was secure. Of course, as she well knew, a Puritan can never completely abandon doubt, for that alone is a sign that one is not saved. But as much as one could feel confident about her relationship with her Savior, Anne Hutchinson did.

Her initial avoidance of the women's meetings in Boston prompted public suspicion, a friend had warned her in 1635. "Because I did not go to such meetings," she told the court, "they said I was proud, and I to prevent such aspersions took it up. But it was in practice before I came," she added defensively. "Therefore I was not the first" to instruct other women at home, implying that she should not be found guilty of doing what many respectable women did.

While she was not the first woman to share with others her thoughts on Scripture and faith, she was likely the best trained, the brightest, and the most influential to do so. Her magnetism had several sources. It came from her extremely high social status, which her judges acknowledged each time they addressed her as "Mistress," a term reserved for only the wealthiest and most prominent women. Lower-status women were "Goodwife" or, in many cases, given no such appellation.

Social status was critical in a culture in which even seating in church was determined by wealth: those with more money sat up front. Anne's husband, William, had brought to New England a purse containing a thousand gold guineas. This vast sum, equal to many millions of dollars today, enabled him to purchase an acre in the best part of Boston—right across the road from the governor's carefully chosen plot—and to build on it a handsome timber house with a stone foundation and several gables on the second floor. Will Hutchinson was admired by all, including his wife's many opponents. John Winthrop, for instance, called him "a peaceable man of good estate." Within six weeks of the Hutchinsons' arrival, in November 1634, Will was elected a magistrate of the Massachusetts General Court, the highest authority in the colony.

Anne's power also came from her role as a trusted midwife and nurse, on whom settlers depended at crucial moments of life and death. Many women died in childbirth, and nearly half of their children were dead before their fifth birthday. Even in England, the chance of surviving to age forty was only one in ten. A nurse-midwife with a good record for saving lives was held in high esteem by women and men alike. Anne's happy and fruitful marriage, as well as her evident success as the mother of a large family, also contributed to her social standing.

Her religious meetings had begun informally, in 1635, with five or six other women present. To her, they seemed a natural outgrowth of the spiritual teaching that she slipped into her visits to women's bedsides. Week after week, at an appointed hour on an appointed evening, more women came to hear Anne talk about Scripture and salvation. In time, some of these women brought their husbands and sometimes other freemen, such as Sir Henry Vane, the newcomer who became governor in 1636. But Anne never solicited anyone to listen to her, she reminded the court. Her crowd grew of its own accord.

Demand was so great that by 1636 she ran two evening meetings a week in the large parlor of her comfortable house overlooking the sea. She sat behind a table that held her Bible, opened to whatever passage she was discussing. As she talked she skipped from passage to passage; she knew large sections of Scripture from memory. She analyzed the mysteries of God's grace and salvation, the recent sermons of the ministers (those she admired and those she did not), and her experiences of "revelation," times when biblical passages directly informed her life, even suggesting future events. Her audiences for these sessions often numbered eighty men and women—estimated as nearly one in five of the adults in Boston—who stood or sat on benches or on the floor. Anne Hutchinson always had a chair, which set her apart. When Governor Vane attended, an extra chair was found, and he sat at her right hand.

Most of the colony's leaders were unaware of her "preaching" to women until after she began to influence men. But by the spring of 1636 the news was out. A woodworker named Edward Johnson reported with alarm to authorities that upon arriving in Boston he was told by a local man, "I'll bring you to a woman that preaches better Gospel than any of your blackcoats that have been at the Ninniversity" (perhaps a compound of *ninny* and *university*). Hutchinson was, Johnson said, "a woman of another kind of spirit, who has had many revelations of things to come," a "masterpiece of woman's wit" who "drew many disciples after her, and to that end boldly insinuated herself into the favor of none of the meanest," suggesting she touched society's highest tiers. Commenting also on Hutchinson, the Reverend Thomas Weld observed that in New England "the weaker sex prevailed so far, that they set up a Priest of their profession and sex." In Weld's view, women are "the weaker to resist; the more flexible, tender, and ready to yield," and able "as by an Eve, to catch their husbands also," so that Hutchinson gained advocates "almost in every family."

She was actively proselytizing, and many of her followers were too, visiting other parishes and encouraging their members to evaluate whether their preachers had the seal of the spirit. At her meetings she remarked that some ministers did not appear to her to have this seal. The biblical seal, described in Paul's letter to the Ephesians 1:13, is a mark placed on a person's forehead to show he belongs to God. She claimed, it was said, to know whether people were saved, or sealed by God, which understandably angered the orthodox ministers. Her criticisms of them were not unlike her father's charges, in his London trial, that too many divines were ill educated and uninspired. A few months before the trial, the Massachusetts court had ordered her to stop her meetings. Like her father, who returned to preach in Northampton despite the bishop's ban, she had ignored the court's order.

In the courtroom she asked the governor, "If any come to my house to be instructed in the ways of God, what rule have I to put them away? Do you think it not lawful for me to teach women, and"—she couldn't resist adding—"why do you call *me* to teach the court?"

"We do *not* call you to teach the court," Winthrop replied angrily, "but to lay open yourself." Pausing to collect himself, he said women's meetings were acceptable only if they did not intrude on women's duties and subservience to men. "I grant you a time for" religious instruction, "but what is the purpose" of bringing women "together from their callings" at home "to be taught of you?" Quoting Corinthians on the need for women to honor and obey their husbands, he added, "You must take [Titus] in this sense, that elder women must instruct the younger about their [domestic] business and to love their husbands and *not* to make them to clash." This was consistent with Winthrop's lifelong philosophy that it was always best to reduce conflict. Throughout this troubled period, Winthrop maintained the view that the only colony that would survive was a united colony. People holding dangerously unorthodox views had to be brought into the fold or, if necessary, removed.

A new voice was heard for the first time in the trial. "I am not against all women's meetings, but do think them to be lawful," observed

Simon Bradstreet, a thirty-three-year-old assistant who also served as the colony's secretary. Bradstreet, who sat with the six other assistants on the first bench behind the governor's desk, had come to Massachusetts in 1630 as part of Winthrop's group. Before making the transatlantic trip he had married Anne Dudley, who would later gain renown as the Puritan poet Anne Bradstreet. His wife's strivings to excel in a profession reserved for men may have prompted in him compassion for Anne Hutchinson. While Anne Bradstreet never commented on Anne Hutchinson in her published work, she no doubt was aware of the trial because her husband and father were members of the General Court. At the time, Anne Bradstreet was a twenty-five-year-old mother too busy with three small children to attend the celebrated event just a block from her house.

Simon Bradstreet seemed to offer Anne Hutchinson her first line of support. Yet he urged her to consider abandoning her course "because," he explained, "it gives offense." While not unlawful, in his view, her meetings were dividing the colony and thus should cease. He, like Winthrop, saw conciliation as the best path to stability.

In response to Bradstreet's display of pragmatism, Hutchinson said, "Sir, in regard of *myself* I could [stop my meetings]. But for *others* I do not yet see light, [although I] shall further consider of it."

Anne would not be moved until she saw light to do so. At forty-six, she was already a decade older than her father was when he reformed his practices to suit the authorities. Unlike him, though, she would persist in preaching and teaching what she believed, even at the risk of her family's security. All around her, men like John Wheelwright and Roger Williams were banished for their beliefs, and still they carried on. If worst came to worst, she was confident, she and hers could survive outside Massachusetts.

No one else in the meetinghouse responded to Simon Bradstreet's remarks, in part because they did not advance the governor's cause. At the same time, Bradstreet's opening emboldened other judges to come forward to challenge the defendant.

STRANGE OPINIONS

"I would go a little higher with Mistress Hutchinson," the deputy governor began, urging a more forceful approach. Thomas Dudley, a stout, energetic man of sixty-one with a gray beard and thick, white hair, had been a soldier in Queen Elizabeth's army and then steward of the Earl of Lincoln's estate. In 1630 he had come with Winthrop to Massachusetts as its first deputy governor, accompanied by his wife, Dorothy, several of their children, and their son-in-law, Simon Bradstreet. The Dudleys and Bradstreets had known the Hutchinsons in England, for the families all worshiped in the church at Boston, Lincolnshire, where John Cotton preached. Dudley had been elected governor of the colony for the 1634–35 term and was now serving as deputy governor for the sixth time. He generally disagreed with Winthrop on matters of public policy, and the two men often sparred. But the governor and deputy governor were in complete agreement on the subject of Mistress Hutchinson. Failing to find a way to remove her would risk the health of the colony to which they both had devoted their lives.

"About three years ago we were all in peace," Dudley said, referring to the length of the Hutchinsons' stay. Then "Mistress Hutchinson, from that time she came, hath made a disturbance." She had "vented diverse of her *strange* opinions and had made parties in the country [and] Mistress Hutchinson hath so forestalled the minds of many by their resort to her meetings that now she hath a potent party in the country." Strange opinions alone were not a crime; many citizens had odd beliefs. What made her dangerous to the government was her "potent party," or many powerful supporters, throughout the colony. Dudley's choice of the word *potent* underscores his point, for in the lexicon of a seventeenth-century Englishman this masculine term could not properly be applied to any woman.

"Now," he continued, "if all these things have endangered us as from that foundation, and if *she* in particular"—he pointed a finger at Hutchinson—"hath disparaged all our ministers in the land that they have preached a covenant of *works*, and only Mr. Cotton a covenant of *grace*, why this is *not* to be suffered."

A *covenant of works* as against a *covenant of grace*. This simple formulation, opaque to many modern readers, was the crux of the issue between Anne Hutchinson and the orthodox ministers, which had rent the colony. And despite all their efforts to resolve it in 1637, this issue would vex the ministers and the people of New England for well over two centuries.

The argument was over salvation, or redemption by Christ, the subject of greatest concern to the colony's seven or eight thousand souls. Salvation, which they called "justification," was the goal of the covenant, or contract, between God and humanity. In the first covenant, outlined in the Old Testament, God gave humanity the gift of perfect and eternal life in exchange for good behavior. Adam broke this covenant with his disobedience, leaving his descendants deprived. In Genesis 17:7 God said to Abraham, "I will establish my covenant between me and thee and thy seed after thee in their generations for an everlasting covenant, to be a God unto thee and to thy seed after thee." God then made a new covenant through Jesus Christ, offering fallen humanity yet another chance at justification. The Puritans believed, with Calvin, that God had to elect a person's soul before birth in order for that person to be eligible for salvation. Human beings were granted this gift of saving grace, but they had to prove their worthiness by displaying faith and performing works, such as good deeds and socially appropriate behavior. In this view, held by Winthrop and the orthodox ministers, people's works demonstrate that they are saved.

This Puritan concept of works is a far cry from what they would have considered the Catholic notion that one can attain salvation simply by going through the motions of the sacraments—one of the issues that propelled the Protestant Reformation. To these Puritans, works entailed not mindless repetition of prayers or taking of sacraments, but rather a constant striving to cleanse one's soul and lead a righteous life, visible and apparent to others. They called this striving "sanctification"—literally, being a saint, which was the standard term of self-description by members of the early American church. "Sanctification is *evidence of* justification," the orthodox ministers told their congregations. In other words, if you follow the rules and laws of church and state, then you can have assurance that you are elect and thus saved. This causal link between sanctification (doing good works) and justification (being saved) was not consistent with the writings of Luther and Calvin—they would have considered it heretical in light of their doctrine that people can do nothing to earn or effect their own salvation—but it was for the leaders of Massachusetts an appealing theological conceit. To create their new society, the founders were naturally drawn to a theology that enforces obedience.

Anne Hutchinson openly rejected this view of salvation, deriding it as a covenant of works. In her view, only God's grace can bring justification; hence her covenant of grace. She saw external works (sanctification) as not irrelevant to salvation but not necessary for it and possibly deceptive in suggesting that someone has been saved. In her view, a hypocrite can go through the motions of good works while lacking true grace, which comes freely—without human effort or intervention—as a gift of the Holy Spirit. She believed the covenant of works dangerously emphasizes a soul's outward appearance of sanctification, while her covenant of grace depended only on God's grace, which may be unseen. There is voluminous scriptural support for her view, particularly in the Epistles of Paul, which had deeply influenced Calvin and other Reformation theologians. The apostle Paul repeatedly emphasized this point, as in Ephesians 2:8–9, "For *by grace are ye saved*, through faith," and "*not [by] works*, lest any man should boast."

On the theological battlefield, Hutchinson and Wheelwright attacked as "legalists" the clerics who linked works and redemption. They in turn called her and her supporters "opinionists." As everyone in the courtroom knew, any male freeman who dared to challenge a preacher would soon find himself in court, charged with disrespect and possibly disfranchised or banished. What would happen to a woman who did so was anyone's guess.

A few months before the trial, Winthrop had written in his journal, "Every occasion [in Massachusetts] increased the contention and caused great alienation of minds, and the [church] members of Boston (frequenting the lectures of other ministers) did make much disturbance by public questions, and objections to their doctrines, which did in any way disagree from their opinion; and it began to be as common here to distinguish between men, by being under a Covenant of Grace, or a Covenant of Works, as in other countries between Protestants and Papists."

Anne Hutchinson's theology arose from her strong sense of communion with the Holy Spirit, which arose early in life. This feeling enabled her to free herself from the orthodox notion that ministers are needed as an intervening means of grace between humans—including women—and God. It also kept her from the worries over assurance—"How do I *know* if I am saved?"—that plagued many of her peers. She believed, according to those who spoke with her, that she had received the Holy Spirit. To her, any striving after signs of grace was a sure sign that grace was not present. This theology, with its immediate, felt sense of God's presence, offered assurance to others whose experiences at the meetinghouse had left them anxious about their estate. "Seek for better establishment in Christ," she advised, "not comfort in duties," or "works," which are only "sandy foundations" compared to Christ, who is rocklike and secure. When faced with reports of the controversy of grace against works, according to John Winthrop, she replied, "Here is a great stir about graces and looking to hearts, but give me Christ. I seek not for graces, but for Christ. I seek not for promises, but for Christ. I seek not for sanctification, but for Christ. Tell not me of meditation and duties, but tell me of Christ."

Winthrop and most of the ministers chose to see this Christ-centered view of the world as dangerously nihilistic—as an encouragement to people to "do nothing" and still expect salvation. This doctrine appealed to "many profane persons," he felt, because "it was a very easy, and acceptable way to heaven—to see nothing, to have nothing, but wait for Christ to do all." Hutchinson's teachings, he added, "quench all endeavor." If people could be convinced that works had no relationship to salvation—if attending church, studying the Bible, and otherwise following the rules had nothing to do with the grace they coveted—then even "many good souls, that had been of long approved godliness, were brought to renounce all the work of grace in them, *and to wait for this immediate revelation.*" His use of the word *revelation* was a direct reference to Hutchinson, who had described receiving signs from God, sometimes after opening the Bible at random and reading a passage. To the orthodox leaders, revelations came only to ministers, who mediated between God and humans. Cotton, however, encouraged revelations: "Do not be afraid of the word revelation," he lectured in 1636: "you will feel his grace in your souls." But Winthrop and the other ministers thought it risky to allow ordinary people to read divine meaning into current events, as if they had the status of clergymen.

Anne Hutchinson's challenge to the power of Massachusetts's civil and religious elite was effective in part because her theology arose from a basic tenet of Calvinism, the basis for Puritan belief. Puritanism rejected the Laudian Anglican emphasis on rituals and works, just as the Protestant Reformation was founded on the rejection of Catholicism's focus on sacraments and works. Calvin's central message was that salvation is God's free gift, which humans, in their utter unworthiness and depravity (as encapsulated in the Reverend Thomas Shepard's last words, "Lord, I am vile, but thou art righteous"), cannot attain by any earthly striving. This is consistent with Hutchinson's teaching. Calvin and Luther had rejected as heresy any link between sanctification (doing good works) and justification (being saved), and in the late twentieth century it was rejected as well by the Roman Catholic Church.

By remaining true to a fundamental doctrine of the Reformation, Anne Hutchinson's theology took Puritanism to its farthest reaches. If Puritanism was a seeking after more intimacy with and knowledge of God than Catholicism offered—through reading the Bible in the vernacular, considering Scripture alone and with others, and in some cases even experiencing the revelation of God's word—then Hutchinson's theology approached God even closer, to receive his word direct, an idea that the colonial leaders could not abide.

In addition to revelations, her doctrine involved prophecy, the power to know the future, usually as a result of Scripture study. "Wonder stories" similar to Hutchinson's were common, according to noted colonial historian David Hall. Many people believed in astrology, portents, and prophecy. Queen Elizabeth herself had employed a court astrologer, whom she consulted regularly. Even the theologian John Foxe stated that John Hus in 1416 had prophesied the Protestant Reformation. And in the mid-seventeenth century, on the eve of the English civil war, both sides—the Parliament and the court—hired astrologers to glean sympathetic readings of the planets and stars.

In early Boston Anne had a reputation as a prophetess. John Winthrop reported in his journal that "her godliness and spiritual gifts" led people to "look at her as a prophetess, raised up of God for some great work now at hand, so she had more resort to her for counsel about matters of conscience and clearing up men's spiritual estates than any minister (I might say all the elders) in the country." Even more troubling to him, she took "upon her infallibly to know the election of others, so as she would say that if she had but one half hour's talk with a man, she would tell whether he were elect or not." Winthrop could have assurance that he knew God's will, but she could not. Similarly, her judges believed that the gift of prophecy fell only on ministers, thus only on men.

Hutchinson's reputation for prophecy arose, apparently, from two predictions she made aboard the *Griffin*, the ship that brought her to America. God had revealed to her the date the ship would arrive in America, and—according to her daughter Faith—Anne had prophesied that "a young man on the ship should be saved, but he must walk in the ways" of God. At the time, many people saw God's hand in such events as the passing of a comet or even the Sunday drowning of boys playing on the frozen river in winter—God punishes Sabbath breakers. An earthquake that shook England just before Christmas in 1601 was soon the occasion of a London pamphlet, *The Wonders of the World, the Trembling of the Earth, and the Warnings of the World before the Judgment Day*. For colonists, as for Europeans then, supernatural and natural forces operated in the world, and God was the most powerful force of all. His "providence," David Hall noted, "accounted for everything that happened in everyday life" and was open to interpretation as a sign of God's judgment or his mercy. There was little, if any, distinction between the moral (sin) and the physical (sickness).

While most ministers preferred the idea that revelation ended with the apostles of Christ, several ministers of Massachusetts claimed visions and prophesied. John Wilson often used prayer to heal the sick and to affect future events. During the Pequot War, for instance, when he was chaplain of the expedition to subdue the natives, he said he had deflected an arrow from a man's chest through prayer. He reported that his dreams while sleeping worked as prophecy. John Cotton encouraged his congregations in England and America to open themselves to God and to experience "revelations." In John Wheelwright's Fast Day speech, he claimed actually to see the approach of the "terrible day" when all the enemies of Christ "shall be consumed" by fire.

Hutchinson's collective doctrines are now termed Antinomianism, a label Winthrop first attached to her that her nineteenth-century critics adopted and that historians today use without a sense of condemnation. Literally "against or opposed to law," Antinomianism means in theology that "the moral law is not binding upon Christians, who are under the law of grace," in the words of David Hall. Had Anne heard this term applied to her, she would have rejected it because of its association with licentious behavior and religious heterodoxy, both of which she opposed.

At the time of her trial, her brother-in-law Wheelwright was banished for promulgating this doctrine, and most of its other prominent adherents were disfranchised and censured, and still Anne Hutchinson was not the only influential settler proclaiming its truth. John Cotton, a minister at the colony's largest and most influential church, often reminded his congregation that good behavior alone is but a work that any hypocrite can perform. He warned against undue confidence in works, stating that a "true saint"—every Puritan's personal goal—was overcome with a sense of his own helplessness. Rather than counting on duties for assurance, Cotton lectured, the sinner must look to God. The person who waited for Christ, whose heart was "emptied of every thing besides," could be judged elect and hence eligible to join the church. No sanctification, Cotton emphasized, can help "evidence to us" our justification. This was in clear conflict with the orthodox view of salvation, and it is where Anne Hutchinson found much of her support.

Fifty-two-year-old John Cotton was seated in the courtroom, listening silently, as Thomas Dudley rebuked the defendant with whom the minister had a long and close connection. Cotton had spent years nourishing Anne's spiritual development in Lincolnshire, he had invited her to follow him to New England, and he had supported—perhaps passively—her insurrection against his brethren. At repeated meetings with Winthrop and other ministers, Cotton had vouched for Hutchinson's character and beliefs. In his view, "Mistress Hutchinson was well beloved, and all the faithful embraced her conference, and blessed God for her fruitful discourses," both at her meetings and in her work as a midwife and nurse. The previous August, at the Religious Synod intended to address the conflict over salvation, he had carefully chosen his words. "The Spirit doth evidence our justification in *both* ways," he said, conceding the validity of the other side without compromising his own. A pious and magnetic man who seemed to enjoy the admiration of all, Cotton was skilled at balancing opposing views. He had avoided any notice by the court. While someone else in his position might have been in a quandary, John Cotton enjoyed a preternatural calm.

In the courtroom Thomas Dudley, who towered over his fellow magistrates, lumbered toward his conclusion. "And therefore," he cried, "being driven to the foundation [of our troubles], and it being found that Mistress Hutchinson is she that hath *depraved* all the ministers and hath been the cause of what is fallen out, why we must *take away the foundation* and the building will fall."

Summoning her intellectual and physical resources, the wan defendant rose again to defend herself.

"I pray, sir, prove it," Hutchinson said. If the magistrates could prove she had slandered the ministers of the colony, they could justify banishing her. The charge would be fomenting sedition—threatening the state's stability, or breaching the peace—the same crime they had pinned on Wheelwright. To avoid the charge of sedition, Anne had decided to try a new approach. Rather than arguing with the magistrates over biblical interpretation, as she had done before, she would contest their charges. She would deny the allegations, as her father had done in his heresy trial, and if that were not possible because the charges were true, she would challenge her judges to provide evidence.

She also employed linguistic subterfuge. "Prove it that I said they preached nothing but a covenant of works," she told Dudley, adding the *nothing* to make the charge more comprehensive, thus easier to deny.

Dudley caught this, showing more wile than the governor had. "*Nothing* but a covenant of works!" he retorted. Of course she had said other things, including some with which he might agree. "Why a *Jesuit* may preach truth sometimes!"

"Did I ever say they preached a covenant of works, then?" she relented.

"If they do not preach a covenant of grace clearly, then they preach a covenant of works," Dudley replied, quoting what he had been told she said.

"No, sir," she corrected him. "One may preach a covenant of grace *more clearly* than another, so I said."

"When they do preach a covenant of works, do they preach truth?" he persisted, trying to corner her into admitting she had traduced, or maligned, the ministers.

"Yes, sir," she said, evading his trap. "But when they preach a covenant of works *for salvation*, that is not truth." Works have value, she suggested, but they alone cannot bring salvation. Only God can do that.

Frustrated, Dudley continued, "I do but ask you this: when the ministers do preach a covenant of works, do they preach a *way* of salvation?"

Unable to agree, she refused to answer: "I did not come hither to answer questions of that sort."

"Because you will deny the thing," he persisted.

"But that is to be *proved* first," she said, fending off Dudley as well as she had Winthrop.

"I will make it plain that you *did* say that the ministers did preach a covenant of works—"

"I deny that."

"—and that you said they were not able ministers of the New Testament, but Mr. Cotton only."

"If ever I spake that, I *proved* it by God's word," she retorted, implying that the court proved nothing.

Taking her remark as an admission of guilt, a chorus of judges murmured, "Very well, very well."

She raised her head and declared, "If one shall come unto me in *private*, and desire me seriously to tell them what I thought of such a one, I must either speak false or true in my answer."

Colonial society distinguished between private and public acts and considered only the latter actionable in court. Choosing her words carefully, Hutchinson hoped to avoid prosecution by showing that her statements were outside the public domain. Most, if not all, of her comments about ministers had been made in private conversation or in meetings with officials that she considered private. Had ministers been able to use private statements made by members of their flock against them in court, people could never speak in confidence with their ministers, something every Puritan expected to do.

Her gender could also work as a shield. If her activities were not public, none of them could be punished publicly. In addition to protecting her, her gender suggested certain courtroom tactics. If her sarcasm did not work, she affected modesty to try to convince the men. When the court charged her with prophesying, she said, "The women of Berea are commended for examining Paul's doctrine; we [women at meetings] do not [do more than] read the notes of our teacher's sermons, and then reason of them by searching the Scriptures." If a woman has no public power, she suggested, then she cannot be condemned for private opinions and acts. It was a good argument. No one knew if it would succeed.

Ignoring her distinction between her private acts and public, actionable, acts, Dudley continued hotly in the same vein. "Likewise, I will prove this, that you said the gospel in the letter and words holds forth *nothing* but a covenant of works"—implying that she had done the unimaginable act of denying the Holy Bible itself—"and that *all* that do not hold as you do are in a covenant of works."

"I deny this, for if I should so say, I should speak against my own judgment," she replied, sounding like her father. Her actual statement, misconstrued in the retelling, had been that the *spirit* of the gospel, rather than the letter and words therein, holds forth the covenant of grace. For her, the spirit was more important than the letter of the Bible, just as the heart was more important than the external appearance.

Like her teacher Cotton, Anne Hutchinson believed herself to be an instrument of the Holy Spirit. For both of them, as for many Puritans, conversion was not intellectual but deeply emotional. Humans are utterly unable to effect their own salvation, Cotton preached. To argue otherwise, he felt, was to open the way for a Roman Catholic covenant of works, that is, to see human beings as actors who can affect God's disposition toward them. For Cotton, salvation is a completely inner experience, dependent not on anything you or even your minister does but solely on your relationship with the Holy Spirit. It does not depend on law in any way, even the Law of the New Testament. As Cotton stated, "Even the New Testament is dead to one who has not the Spirit." He added, in *A Treatise of the Covenant of Grace,* "If there were no revelation but the word, there would be no spiritual grace revealed to the soul. . . . There is need of greater light than the word of itself is able to give; for it is not all the promises in Scripture that have . . . wrought any gracious changes in any soul. Without the work of the Spirit, there is no faith. . . ." In an early sermon, in England, he had said that Christians "must never rest in any Scripture they read, or ministers they hear, before they have examined things by the testimony of the Spirit," that is, in their own hearts. Anne Hutchinson took him at his word.

If we trace the lineage of this doctrine even further, we find Cotton's mentor at Cambridge, the great Puritan divine William Perkins, preaching that humanity can do nothing to bring about its own conversion and salvation. All is in God's hands. While "the doctrine of the Papists now is that the [human] will, so it be stirred up by God, can do it"—achieve salvation—"the certain truth is that the will cannot." Humanity can claim only a "new and fleshy heart," which is the "gift of God." Without God's intervention, we can do "nothing but sin." These were the words of the Cambridge preacher who, according to Anne's teacher John Cotton, "laid siege to and beleaguered [my] heart."

In the courtroom, Hutchinson found support for her argument in 2 Corinthians 3:6: "Who also hath made us able ministers of the new testament; not of the letter, but of the spirit: for the letter killeth, but the spirit giveth life."

Dudley and Winthrop were getting nowhere with her, they both knew. Between her clever parries and her just claim that as a woman she had no public role and thus no boundaries to exceed, they could make no charge stick. Yet the fact remained, she did not act as a woman must. What was not obvious was how to charge and punish her.

Governor Winthrop determined that, in order to bolster the case that she traduced, or maligned, the ministers, the ministers themselves should testify. If they could catch her in a major theological error, then there would be reason to humiliate her publicly. At Winthrop's request, the ministers looked around the hall, each hoping another would speak first. None wanted to testify. They did not recall well the details of their meeting with her eleven months before. And, as all were aware, if as a group they gave divergent testimony, that would serve her.

Breaking the silence, the Reverend Hugh Peter, of Salem, said, "Our brethren are very unwilling to answer, unless the court command us to speak." A short, stocky man with beady eyes and a flushed face, Peter was said to be "demagogic," "bullying," and "peculiarly forcible in language and speech." Born in Cornwall in 1599, he had graduated from Cambridge and preached in London, where Archbishop Laud had briefly imprisoned him for nonconformity. The Reverend Peter's hatred of the formalism of the English church had driven him to Rotterdam and then, in 1635, from Plymouth, England, to Massachusetts, on the same ship as Sir Henry Vane.

In response to the Reverend Peter, whom the governor considered "a man of a very public spirit and singular activity," Winthrop commanded the ministers to speak. "This speech [between Hutchinson and you] was not spoken in a corner but in a public assembly, and though *things were spoken in private*, we are to deal with them in public."

Six ministers who had been at the December 1636 meeting acquiesced. Hugh Peter, Thomas Shepard (of Cambridge), Thomas Weld and John Eliot (both of Roxbury), George Phillips (Watertown), and Zechariah Symmes (Charlestown) all testified that she had indeed spoken critically of them. "Briefly," the Reverend Peter said crossly, "she told me there was a wide and a broad difference between our brother Mr. Cotton and ourselves. I desired to know the difference. She answered that he preaches the covenant of grace and you the covenant of works, and that you are not able ministers of the New Testament, and know no more than the apostles did before the resurrection of Christ. [I] then put it to her, 'What do you conceive of such a brother [who preaches the covenant of works]?' She answered he had not the seal of the spirit," meaning he was not saved.

Hutchinson replied, "If our pastor would show his writings" about the December meeting, "you should see what I said, and that many things are not so as is reported."

The Reverend John Wilson, the senior pastor of the Boston church, had taken notes of the December meeting between him, his supportive brethren Weld and Peter, Hutchinson, and the Reverends Cotton and Wheelwright. "Sister Hutchinson," Wilson said, "for the writings you speak of, I have them not. And, I must say, I did not write down *all* that was said. Yet I say that what is written [here in previous testimony] I will avouch." Governor Winthrop asked Hutchinson for her copy of Wilson's notes, which she had left at home. Neither she nor Wilson produced in court a copy of his notes from the meeting, which both of them considered favorable to their side.

The Reverend Wilson and Mistress Hutchinson knew each other well, rather too well, they would have agreed. A tall, angular man of forty-eight, Wilson had been pastor of her church as long as she had been in Boston. For most of the first year after her September 1634 arrival, though, Wilson had been away in England, leaving her favorite, his associate John Cotton, in charge. Wilson's absence arose from his long struggle to convince his wife, Elizabeth, to cross the ocean. He had come in 1630, but she did not arrive, with their children, until 1635, on the same ship as Anne's nemesis Hugh Peter and her ally Henry Vane.

The Reverend John Wilson, thought by many to be her "chief persecutor," had a stern face and a nasal voice that irritated some of his parishioners. His devotion was so rigorous, it was said, that he allowed no talking at supper on Sundays except words about God. A minister's son born in Windsor, England, in December 1588, Wilson had attended Eton and then Christ's College, Cambridge. In 1609 he took a master's degree from King's College, Cambridge, where he excelled in Latin poetry. His heart was "opened to Christ" by noted Cambridge divines Dr. Lawrence Chaderton, Richard Rogers, and William Ames. Wilson's nonconformist refusal to bow or kneel in chapel cost him his fellowship at King's College, whose grand sixteenth-century chapel to him reflected pagan idolatry. He served as a minister in Sudbury, Suffolk, during the 1620s but rarely preached. Hutchinson and others saw evidence of this lack of experience whenever Wilson lectured in Boston. In her, in turn, the zealous minister saw the force behind the opinionists, the group determined to oust him. It was she who inspired women to walk out during his sermons, and she who aroused men to fire provocative theological questions at him afterward.

Three weeks before the trial, on a Sunday in October, the Reverend Wilson had stopped in the middle of a sermon to chastise Anne

Hutchinson, who sat silently before him on the women's side of the Boston meetinghouse, for her "monstrous errors." He referred to theological errors that he and his brethren had decried at their Religious Synod in Cambridge in August.

"Depart this assembly!" he had commanded her.

Anne Hutchinson had stood up, swung around, and, in the company of her friend Mary Dyer, departed the meetinghouse. She was afraid of no man, only God.

The previous summer, she had inadvertently interfered with his feeling of authority in the Pequot War, where he had served as chaplain. Puritan ministers were given prominent roles in military campaigns and sometimes even asked to relieve officers. At the May meeting of the General Court, Winthrop and Dudley had been elected again partly through Wilson's strenuous efforts, and in return the minister had been appointed to accompany the troops. A few months later, during the Pequot campaign, Captain John Mason, of Connecticut, had left his command post to Wilson one evening so that the chaplain could "seek divine direction in prayer." During that long summer night, the Reverend Wilson discovered just how little clout he had among the 150-man Massachusetts contingent, who had been told by the twenty-six Bostonians how much antipathy toward him his congregation felt. The fact that so few men of Boston enlisted was also Hutchinson's fault, he felt, because she vocally opposed the war against the natives.

The next courtroom witness against Hutchinson was yet another minister with whom she had sparred. Zechariah Symmes was a strait-laced Oxford graduate in his late thirties who had met Hutchinson in July 1634 in a town on the English coast a few days before they both departed for America on the same boat. *Corrupt* and *narrow* were the words that first struck him to describe her. In casual conversation about their destination, he noted, "she did slight the ministers of the word of God." As the daughter of a minister who considered most ministers poorly trained to preach, she felt little compunction about challenging the erudition of any divine.

The *Griffin* had set sail that July three years earlier with the Reverend Symmes, twelve Hutchinsons, and about 150 other passengers and crew members aboard. This voyage, like the hundred-odd other voyages of "God's people" to their New Canaan in the 1630s, was tedious and unpleasant. For passengers in the ship's cramped, dank hold, the hours ran on endlessly, as they would for more than two months. The ocean swelled, the vessel pitched and yawed, the children whined, and the farm animals crushed in the belly of the boat cried out in confusion. Besides the 100 cows that John Winthrop had ordered from England, the 300-ton ship carried scores of pigs, chickens, and geese; mattresses and furniture; and barrels of bread, cheese, butter, dried beef, peas, oatmeal, beer (45 tons), Spanish wine ("10 gallons a person"), and water (6 tons). It was armed with guns to protect against pirates, who approached once, only to be scared away by gunfire. Despite the crew's daily washings down of the decks with beer vinegar, the boat stank of excrement, both human and animal.

Each day, as was the custom on ships to the New World, the minister or ministers aboard led services of worship, prayer, and singing. Some, like Symmes, preached on deck for four hours or more. This would have been acceptable to Anne if she had agreed with him. But his preaching was erroneous, she determined after listening closely for several days: he was preaching a covenant of works.

One burning hot afternoon in late August on that ship, as Symmes lectured on love of neighbor "as a means of evidencing a good spiritual estate," he said, "In our love we will 'grow in grace,' for we must strive always to lay up a 'stock of grace.'" This suggestion that a soul could effect its salvation through its own effort infuriated Anne. She held her tongue until the question period after the sermon. Defying the rule against women speaking during religious services, she said, "Your words bear a legal savor, and they do not correspond with my understanding of the doctrine."

Symmes, not understanding her point about salvation, replied, "Were not the words of the Apostle John precise and clear on this point: 'We know that we have passed from death into life, because we love the brethren. He that loveth not his brother abideth in death.' What could possibly be more explicit?" He reminded her that as a woman she had no right to question him. "For the man is not of the woman, but the woman of the man," he said, quoting 1 Corinthians 11:8.

Indignant, she threatened to expose him once they reached America. He in turn promised to report her to the authorities. Undeterred, she challenged him to predict what day the ship would arrive in Boston, a date she knew because it had been revealed to her during her Scripture study. "What would you say if we should be at New England within these three weeks?" she dared him, suggesting a date of arrival much earlier than anticipated.

He denied the veracity of her revelation, and they argued so loudly that many passengers could hear. For the rest of the trip—which apparently ended on the day she had predicted—she ignored the Reverend Symmes. She held women's meetings, at which she offered up her own interpretation of Scripture, and she urged other women to ignore him too.

Landing in Boston on September 18, 1634, Symmes promptly reported Hutchinson's offensive behavior and words. Deputy Governor Dudley responded by asking the Reverend Cotton "to enquire of her," which he did. Cotton subsequently assured Dudley that she was "not of that mind" Symmes had described. "And then," Dudley recorded, "I was satisfied that she held nothing different from us."

On Sunday, November 2, Anne was admitted to full membership in the Boston church—a privilege that was granted to fewer than half of the colony's inhabitants. Because of Symmes's complaint, she had to wait a week longer than her husband, who had expressed no objectionable views, to join the church.

In court now, the Reverend Thomas Shepard, of Cambridge, concurred with his colleagues as to Hutchinson's stated views: "Also to same." A thirty-three-year-old graduate of Emmanuel College, Cambridge, Shepard had arrived in Massachusetts in October 1635. Like many colonial ministers, Shepard had been silenced in England by Archbishop Laud. "You prating coxcomb!" the archbishop had denounced Shepard: "I charge you that you neither preach, read, marry, bury, or exercise any ministerial function in any part of my diocese, for if you do . . . I will be upon your back and . . . everlastingly disable you." Now a subscriber to orthodoxy, Shepard had spent much of the summer of 1637 in this very building sermonizing about the dangers of Hutchinson's theology. He had also enjoyed a warm correspondence with his colleague Cotton in which he tried to point out the various ways in which works can evidence grace. Although they were on opposite sides of this doctrinal issue, Cotton had signed off as "your affectionate though weak brother," and Shepard had called Cotton his "dear friend." In a pamphlet Shepard had just composed to refute Antinomianism, *The Parable of the Ten Virgins,* he outlined how God makes room for human striving. God and humans work together, as in Colossians 1:29: "Whereunto I also labor, striving according to his working, which worketh in me mightily." Overly emphasizing grace, as he felt Hutchinson and Cotton did, was a way for "slothful" sinners to escape the demands of the law. The answer to spiritual anxiety, he felt, lies in constant striving. He had no patience with the argument that people are helpless to achieve grace, a stance that set Shepard apart from Calvin, Luther, and most other Reformed theologians of the day.

Summarizing the six ministers' testimony, Thomas Dudley said to Hutchinson, "I called these witnesses, and you deny them. You *see* they have proved this, and you *deny* this, but it is *clear.* You [did] say they preached a covenant of works and that they were not able ministers of the New Testament. Now there are two other things that you did affirm, which were that the scriptures in the letter of them held forth nothing but a covenant of works, and likewise that those that were under a covenant of works cannot be saved."

"Prove that I said so," she repeated, as defiant in court as her father. One reason for her unwillingness to answer was, of course, that she was not a minister. All her comments about others' spiritual estates—made in private, under duress—were not acceptable from anyone but a clergyman.

"*Did* you say so?" Governor Winthrop demanded.

"No, sir, it is your conclusion."

"What do I do charging of you," Dudley wondered, "if you deny what is so fully proved?"

Winthrop too was astonished by her effrontery. "Here are six *undeniable* ministers who say it is true," he said, "and yet you deny that you did say that they preach a covenant of works and that they were not able ministers of the gospel. It appears plainly that you have spoken it, and whereas you say that it was drawn from you in a way of friendship, you did profess then that it was out of conscience that you spoke."

"They *thought* that I did conceive there was a difference between them and Mr. Cotton," she replied. In fact, she had been reluctant to speak openly, knowing her answers would offend. But when the Reverend Hugh Peter pressed her to "answer the question directly as fully and as plainly as you desire we should tell you *our* minds," she opened up. As a later witness, Thomas Leverett, attested the next day, the Reverend Peter "did with *much* vehemency and entreaty urge her to tell what difference there was between Mr. Cotton and them." Further urged to elaborate, she had again answered indirectly, saying, "The fear of man is a snare, but they that trust upon the Lord shall be safe." But still the ministers had pursued the point. "And being asked wherein the difference was, she answered that they did not preach a covenant of grace *so clearly as* Mr. Cotton did. And she gave this reason of it: because that as the apostles were for a time without the spirit so until they had received the witness of the spirit they could not preach a covenant of grace so clearly."

Pressed by the ministers in private, she had admitted what she believed: that a minister who, in her view, was not sealed with the spirit could not preach a covenant of grace "so clearly as Cotton." The logic was obvious: How could someone who is not sealed with the spirit— who is not even within the covenant of grace—preach clearly of that covenant?

In court, the two sides had reached yet another stalemate. Outside, dusk was descending over the wooden houses of Cambridge, the farms, the hills, the forest, and the great marsh that extended south to the coiled river named for Charles their king. Even in the windowless meetinghouse, those present could feel the cold of night encroach.

"Mistress Hutchinson," Governor Winthrop said with perhaps some frustration in his voice. "The court, you see, has labored to bring you to acknowledge the error of your way so you might be reduced [corrected or subdued]. The time now grows late. We shall therefore give you a little more time to consider of it, and therefore desire that you attend the court again in the morning."

Anne rose to start the long walk home. Joining her husband and his younger brother Edward at the back of the meetinghouse, she talked briefly with supporters. Someone gave her a handwritten transcript of the day's proceedings and a copy of the Reverend Wilson's record of their meeting the previous December. It is likely—based on the hour, the season, the distance to her house, and her obvious physical weakness—that she was encouraged to stay the night in Cambridge. Rather than making the dangerous ten-mile round trip to Boston and back, she might rest before her appearance in court the next morning. Her five youngest children—Zuriel, Susan, William, Katherine, and Mary, ages nineteen months to nine years—were at home in the care of her older daughters, her husband's two unmarried cousins who lived with them, and her servants. Certainly her neighbor John Winthrop, who had chosen Cambridge for this trial because it was out of her reach and filled with his sympathizers, had no trouble finding a spare mattress on which to rest. His twenty-five-year-old daughter, Mary, and her husband, Thomas Dudley's son Samuel, lived next door to the Cambridge meetinghouse.

The crowd dispersed quickly, eager to escape the silence and dark of night. As a rule, the settlers went to bed early, often by eight, and rose by daybreak.

That evening, warmed by the fire in the parlor of her temporary lodgings, Anne studied by candlelight the papers she had been given. It appears, based on her testimony the next morning, that someone knowledgeable in the law gave her legal advice. Before allowing herself to rest, she reread the day's transcript in search of points to strengthen her defense.

All in all, she had acquitted herself well before the court. John Winthrop appeared to have no specific charge with which to snare her. Her teacher John Cotton had not yet spoken, and if he would she was sure of his support.

Her success before the court may have astonished her judges, but it was no surprise to her. She was confident of herself and her intellectual tools, largely because of the intimacy she felt with God, her faith in his love and protection. Over and over, in Bible verse after Bible verse, God had shown her she had nothing to fear.

Some years before, in Alford, England, she had had a vision of the events that were occurring now. In a dream vision, she had seen herself travel to a distant land where she would find adversity and be persecuted. Like her father, she would be put to trial. With Christ's help, she would endure.

In her vision she had assumed the role of the biblical prophet Daniel, a Jew who faithfully served the royal family of Babylon. The Babylonian king loved Daniel. Envying him for this, princes in the palace told the king that Daniel prayed to the one Jewish God rather than to the Babylonian king or his many gods. Horrified, the king ordered that Daniel be thrown into the lions' den, a standard form of execution. Daniel spent six days there, during which the lions' mouths remained shut. Emerging without injury, he told the king, "The lions have not hurt me because I was innocent in the sight of God and of my king." The king, amazed, converted to Judaism and threw the princes who accused Daniel to the lions, who devoured them.

"It was revealed to me," Anne recalled, "that [some] should plot against me, and I should meet with affliction. But the Lord bid me not to fear." Like Daniel, she prayed rightly, she was despised for it, and she would triumph. God assured her, "I am the same God that delivered Daniel out of the lions' den. I will also deliver thee."

In another of the prophetic visions that came to her while studying Scripture, the Lord "did reveal himself to me, sitting upon a throne of justice, and all the world appearing before him." He said to her that "though I must come to New England, yet I must not fear nor be dismayed. The Lord spake this to me with a strong hand, and instructed me that I should not walk in the way of this people here."

These revelations, which she experienced as divine gifts, must have given her strength as she approached sleep on that harrowing Tuesday night in November 1637. "No man has any power over my body, neither can he do me any harm, for I am in the hands of the eternal Jehovah, my savior," she believed, according to her remarks in court the next day. "I am at his appointment. The bounds of my habitation are cast in heaven. No further do I esteem of any mortal man than creatures in his hand. I fear none but the great Jehovah, which hath foretold me of these things, and I do verily believe that he will deliver me."

THE END OF
ALL CONTROVERSY

The next morning the sun rose over Massachusetts Bay Colony at about twenty to seven. It came, like the ships that bore the settlers from England, from over the ocean. Winter stars lingered in the night sky even as the sun approached. Migrating geese lined the ice on the river named for the Catholic-leaning monarch from whom the Puritans had run. Deer and coyote roamed the forest, which spread north, west, and south. Wolves slept in caves in the snow. With the sun's arrival on Wednesday, November 8, 1637, the sky over the house where Anne slept—if indeed she did sleep—went from black of night to indigo blue to pale gray and then to the almost white light of a late fall New England day.

Stepping out the door of a house in Cambridge that morning, Anne would have been reminded at once that she was not at home. The streets of Cambridge, unlike the crooked roads of Boston, were neat and perpendicular. There were no seagulls cawing, as there were on the Shawmut Peninsula. From here she could not see the ocean to which she now awoke every dawn, the three hills of Boston, and her warm house with her beloved children in it. They were several miles to the east, where the still-dark sky glowed yellow.

At the time, coastal Massachusetts was a wilderness of forest, meadow, and swamp. Much of the swamp has been filled in to expand the land, and in our day the forests are different from the ones Anne saw. Then they were virgin forests of first-growth hardwoods, so lacking in undergrowth that a horse and rider could gallop through. The arable land near the ocean was inhabited by small groups of Algonquian-speaking natives—of the Wampanoag, Massachuset, Pawtucket, Neponset, and Nauset tribes—whose encampments tended to move with the seasons, in contrast to the fixed settlements of Europeans. Many of the native Indians, who had cleared much land for planting, had died in recent years of smallpox, which English fishermen had imported to America earlier in the century. Some later English émigrés saw this double "clearing" of the land as a benefice. In the words of the Reverend Cotton Mather of Boston, "The woods were almost cleared of these pernicious creatures to make room for a better growth."

On June 22, 1630, the eleven English ships of the Massachusetts Bay Company had landed in Salem (Nahumkeck) harbor, eager to impose on this wilderness a familiar sense of order and civilization. The ships carried 1000 men, women, and children; 240 head of cattle; 60 horses; and the supplies and materials needed to clear and plant land and build houses. That included 10,000 bricks, a ton of iron nails, a musket and bandolier for each man, hundreds of swords and pikes, one seine net per vessel for fishing, 400 pairs of shoes, dozens of pewter pots, and hundreds of sheets and bolsters of linen cloth.

As John Winthrop's ship, the *Arbella*, approached land, he observed that "there came a smell off the shore like the smell of a garden." A wild pigeon landed on the boat's deck just before the passengers rowed ashore, as if the Holy Spirit were blessing the fleet and its mission. Winthrop and Dudley led the settlers south from Salem along the coast to the mouth of the Charles and Mystic Rivers, where on July 1 they declared Charlestown their first town.

Charlestown seemed at first the perfect setting for the "city on a hill" that Winthrop had described before they arrived. This town—Mishawum to the natives—is on the northern bank of the Charles River where the river meets the ocean. It was the principal settlement of the Pawtucket, or Mystic, tribe, whose territory encompassed the Charles and Mystic Rivers, their estuaries, and several harbor islands. Nevertheless, King Charles had chartered to "the Colony of the Massachusetts Bay in New England" the land from just above the Merrimac River, some thirty miles to the north, to just below the Charles River, "from sea to sea." (No one suspected the next sea was three thousand miles away.) "Together, also, with all the firm lands," the company owned the "soils, grounds, havens, ports, rivers, waters, fishing, mines, and minerals, as well as royal mines of gold and silver." Delighted with these newfound holdings, the settlers, many of whom were now landed gentry in a way they could never have imagined in England, built temporary wigwams of bent saplings and bark panels. Their "meeting-place," Governor Winthrop noted, was "abroad under a tree." They laid the stone foundation for several houses, including one for him. By the end of August, Charlestown was the site of the First Church of Christ in Massachusetts.

Unfortunately, Charlestown offered little fresh spring water, which was a necessity, so the settlers considered other locales. Looking south, they saw a large swamp dotted with islands. One island was known as Shawmut, a corruption of the Algonquian word *nashauwamuk*, or "he goes by boat." Winthrop called the island Trimountaine because of its three prominent hills, which would soon be known as Pemberton Hill, Mount Vernon, and Beacon Hill. (The last and tallest, at an elevation of two hundred feet, was soon to be the site of a warning beacon sixty-five feet high.) Exploring the marshy area around Shawmut by boat, the men discovered that it was not an island but a peninsula, connected to the mainland by a slender strip of land. Thinking this peninsula a more auspicious location because of the fine spring flowing from its hills, Winthrop sought and was granted permission from the peninsula's sole English inhabitant, an eremitic clergyman named William Blackstone who lived on Beacon Hill, to move there.

On September 17 the company moved a half mile south to Shawmut, which they henceforth called Boston in honor of the Lincolnshire cathedral town. This name is said to have been chosen to entice the Puritan celebrity John Cotton, who preached at Lincolnshire's Boston, to join them there. While scattered groups of settlers put down roots in surrounding regions to which they gave English place-names such as Watertown, Medford, Roxbury, Lynn, and Dorchester, it was the Shawmut Peninsula that would be the Massachusetts Bay Company's home.

Within days, though, Dudley doubted this decision. He feared the peninsula was too exposed to attack from the sea by the French or, as was always possible, their own king. Thinking of making yet another move, he and Winthrop and their assistants rowed up the Charles River on September 30 in search of what Winthrop termed "a fit place for a fortified town." The first high ground near the river channel was at a bend roughly two miles in, near today's Larz Anderson Bridge. Landing on the northern bank, the men ascended a broad, flat hill. At a spot

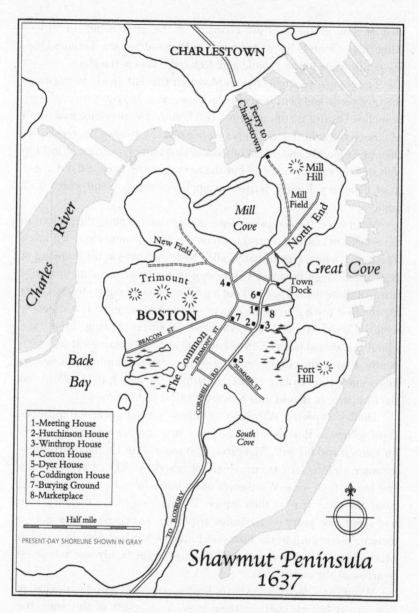

CHARLESTOWN

Ferry to Charlestown

Charles River

Mill Hill

Mill Field

Mill Cove

North End

New Field

Great Cove

Trimount

BOSTON

4

6

Town Dock

8

1

BEACON ST

7 2

TREMONT ST

3

CORNHILL RD

The Common

Back Bay

5

SUMMER ST

Fort Hill

South Cove

1-Meeting House
2-Hutchinson House
3-Winthrop House
4-Cotton House
5-Dyer House
6-Coddington House
7-Burying Ground
8-Marketplace

Half mile

PRESENT-DAY SHORELINE SHOWN IN GRAY

TO ROXBURY

Shawmut Peninsula
1637

that is now at the southwest corner of the intersection of Mount Auburn and John F. Kennedy Streets in Harvard Square, Thomas Dudley put his cane in the ground and declared, "This is the place."

The company camped out on Shawmut that fall, living in wigwams made of reeds and bent branches, in caves, or in burrows covered with branches. During that first winter, two hundred settlers died as a result of illness, the cold (temperatures were generally twenty degrees lower than in England), and a lack of food. A desperate Governor Winthrop sent to England for supplies, but the next ship, the *Lyon*, did not arrive until February. Eighty settlers promptly boarded it and sailed back home.

Meanwhile, the company's leaders negotiated among themselves an agreement to create a central town on the high ground along the river. This town, which they initially called Newtown, was at the founding of Harvard College renamed Cambridge in honor of the alma mater of many of these men. They laid out a gridiron plan of eight streets, creating the first town plan in the American English colonies. The streets—named Creek, Wood, Water, Crooked, Braintree, Spring, Long, and Marsh—radiated from a fenced common area for grazing cattle, which is now Cambridge Common. The settlers began building houses the following spring. In July 1631 eight families, including the Dudleys and the Bradstreets, moved into Newtown's first eight houses.

Dudley expected Winthrop to follow, but the governor chose instead to stay in Boston, where he had a large timber-frame house built for himself and his wife, Margaret, who was still in England with their younger children. In twenty years of marriage, Margaret Winthrop had borne four sons. Winthrop's older boys, John Jr. and Henry, had come the same year as their father. Twenty-two-year-old Henry, who had spent two years on Barbados acquiring "expensive habits and no fortune," according to the historian Edmund Morgan, had drowned in Massachusetts that first summer. The rest of the family was scheduled to arrive at the end of 1631.

Winthrop's decision to stay in Boston triggered a feud with Dudley that would last throughout their lives. As a result of this split, the Great and General Court of Massachusetts met alternately in Boston and Newtown during the 1630s, when it convened four times a year. Despite this rift, Winthrop chose in 1637 to wait to try Hutchinson until the court met in Newtown because he enjoyed far more support there than in Boston. Winthrop's support came largely from those who had been among the landed gentry or the aristocracy in England, who tended to be the first to arrive in Massachusetts, to be conservative, and to have fewer mercantile concerns than the newer émigrés.

By the time of Hutchinson's trial, Cambridge—still called Newtown for one more week—consisted of a market square, a mud-and-thatch meetinghouse, and slightly more than a hundred houses of wood, with clay mortar and thatched roofs. The meetinghouse, built in 1633, was the town's largest building, measuring roughly forty feet square. Cow fields and oyster beds lay outside the town center. There was not yet any college operating here or, for that matter, elsewhere on the continent.

An hour or so after daybreak, Anne and Will Hutchinson trod the icy roads back to the windowless meetinghouse, where the judges were gathering. As before, Anne waited in the back of the hall until the governor called her forward.

Governor Winthrop began by summarizing the previous day's events. "There were diverse things laid to [Mistress Hutchinson's] charge," he said: "her ordinary meetings about religious exercises; her speeches in derogation of the ministers among us; and the weakening of the hands and hearts of the people towards them. Here was *sufficient proof made* of that which she was accused of, in that point concerning the ministers and their ministry, as that they did preach a covenant of works when others did preach a covenant of grace, and that they were not able ministers of the New Testament, and that they had not the seal of the spirit. And this was spoken not, as was *pretended*, out of private conference, but out of conscience. And warrant from Scripture alleged the fear of man is a snare, and seeing God had given her a calling to it, she would freely speak."

Following this opening statement, he offered the defendant a chance to respond. Without hesitation, she took the legal advice of the night before and asked that the witnesses all be recalled and asked to swear an oath that their testimony was true. "The Lord hath said that an oath is the end of all controversy," she explained.

If the ministers were lying, as she suspected, it would likely appear in the form of inconsistencies or contradictions between their testimony yesterday and today. And if they were shown to be lying under oath, then they would be guilty not only of perjury but also of blasphemy—taking the Lord's name in vain, a crime against God.

Assistant Bradstreet pointed this out to her. If the ministers "should mistake you in your speeches, you would make them to *sin* if you urge them to swear."

"That is not the thing," she said. "If they accuse me, I desire it may be upon oath." She added that the ministers were not reliable because "they are witnesses of their own cause."

"It is not their cause, but the cause of the *whole country,*" Winthrop observed ominously.

The ministers knew as well as anyone the risk they took in testifying again, under oath, and were not eager to do so. They could damn themselves if they obliged Hutchinson. This, they believed, was a trap. They could not remember perfectly what she or they had said at their meeting eleven months before. They took seriously the third commandment—"Thou shalt not take the name of the Lord, thy God, in vain"—and considered an oath a solemn avowal of absolute truth.

Winthrop said supportively, "I see no necessity of an oath in this thing, seeing it is true." The ministers are "men of long approved godliness and sincerity in their course." Aiming for balance, he added, "Yet that all may be satisfied, if the elders will take an oath they shall have it given them."

"After they have taken an oath," Hutchinson insisted, "I will make good what I say."

Winthrop said, "Let those who are not satisfied in the court speak."

"We are not satisfied!" the crowd called out, delighted to have a chance to proclaim their support for Mistress Hutchinson and their distress over the court's mistreatment of her.

Winthrop quietly considered his options. "Let us state the case, and then we may know what to do. That which is laid to Mistress Hutchinson's charge is that she hath traduced the magistrates and ministers of this jurisdiction, that she hath said the ministers preached a covenant of works and Mr. Cotton a covenant of grace, and that they were not able ministers of the gospel. And she excuses it that she made it a private conference and with a promise of secrecy. Now, this is charged upon her, and they therefore sent for her seeing she made it her table talk," or casual conversation. "And then she said, 'The fear of man was a snare,' and therefore she would not be afraid of them."

The Reverend Shepard interjected, "I know *no* reason of the oath but the importunity of this gentlewoman."

John Endicott addressed the defendant directly, suggesting she was guilty of deceit: "You lifted up your eyes as if you took God to witness that you came to entrap *none*, and yet you will have them swear?" Fifty-nine-year-old Endicott wore a Vandyke beard, a square collar, and—though not a minister—a skullcap. He was also the only man present who carried a sword. Endicott appears in Nathaniel Hawthorne's story "Mrs. Hutchinson" as a choleric mix of bullishness and idealism, "ready to propagate the religion of peace by violence." Hawthorne writes, "Next came Endicott, who would stand with his drawn sword at the gate of heaven, and resist to the death all pilgrims thither, except they traveled his own path."

A former soldier, Endicott refused to be separated from the thirty-inch steel blade whose decorated handle protruded from its hilt, at his waist. He had used this sword in May 1628 to hack down a "pagan" maypole and frighten away drunken revelers. Six years later he had used it to slice from every colonial flag and regimental banner that he could find the red cross of Saint George the dragon slayer, a symbol of the English monarchy. His zeal in removing any superstitious and popish "relic of Antichrist" would be celebrated by Hawthorne in his stories "The Maypole of Merry Mount" (1836) and "Endicott and the Red Cross" (1838).

A leader of the troops against the Pequots on Block Island in 1636 and in the more recent Connecticut campaign, Endicott, according to William Bradford, the governor of Plymouth Plantation, had provoked the war with the Pequots, a tribe whose name is "destroyers" in Algonquian. This war had its origins in the Pequot killings of two questionable English traders—a Captain John Stone, of Virginia, along with his seven-man crew, in 1634, and John Oldham, a planter of Watertown, in 1636—off the Connecticut coast. After Oldham's murder, the Massachusetts General Court, under Vane, had sent a volunteer army of ninety men in four ships under Endicott and three other leaders to Block Island to avenge Oldham's death by killing the native men and capturing their island. On August 1, 1636, Endicott's ship reached

Block Island in heavy surf and a hard wind. Forty Pequots shot arrows at them and disappeared. Captain Endicott and his troops went ashore and, after searching fruitlessly for the men, plundered their villages. With sixty men Endicott sailed back across the sound to the high rocky shore near the mouth of the Connecticut River, where hundreds of Pequots lived in walled villages. The English were met by three hundred Pequot warriors, who offered to lay down their arms if the English troops would do the same. Endicott ordered his men to charge. The English, whose suits of armor protected them from the natives' arrows, burned Pequot wigwams, destroyed their canoes, and sailed home. That fall Massachusetts made a treaty with the Narragansett Indians against the Pequots, who attacked English settlements in Connecticut in reprisal. The following summer, just a few months before this trial, the combined armies of Massachusetts and Connecticut had wiped out the Pequot tribe.

In the courtroom Anne Hutchinson replied to Endicott's suggestion that she was disingenuous in asking the ministers to swear. "They say I said, 'The fear of man is a snare, why should I be afraid?' When I came unto them [at the December meeting], they urging many things unto me, and I being backward"—cautious—"to answer at first, at length this Scripture came into my mind, 29th Proverbs 25: 'The fear of man brings a snare, but who puts his trust in the Lord shall be safe.'"

In her telling, she had been doing nothing more than quoting Scripture to the ministers. They had misunderstood her and seen her words as an attack. But she meant only that if people trusted God, then they would no longer fear men.

Dudley changed the subject. "Mark what a flourish Mistress Hutchinson puts upon the business that she had *witnesses* to disprove what was said, and here is no man to bear witness."

She retorted, "If you will not call them in, that is nothing to me."

"We desire to know of her and her witnesses what they deny, and then we shall speak upon oath," the Reverend Eliot offered. "I know nothing we have spoken of but we may swear to." Several other ministers nodded.

John Coggeshall, a wealthy silk merchant in his forties who was one of the Boston deputies whom the court had just dismissed for supporting Wheelwright and Hutchinson, called out from the back of the hall. "I desire to speak a word. It is desired that the elders would confer with Mr. Cotton before they swear."

Flushed with indignation, Endicott said to Coggeshall, "I think this carriage of yours tends to further casting dirt upon the face of the judges!"

"*Her* carriage does the same," added a Winthrop supporter, twenty-six-year-old Roger Harlackenden of Cambridge, a patron of the Reverend Shepard.

William Colburn, Boston's town assessor, who, like Coggeshall, had signed the petition, said, "We desire that our teacher may be called."

Winthrop indicated his assent, so the Reverend John Cotton rose from his seat behind the judges and walked toward the defendant. Without a word or any change in expression, Cotton stood beside Hutchinson before the court.

The Reverends Eliot and Shepard repeated, "There is no reason for an oath."

"Because it is the end of all strife," Israel Stoughton, a Dorchester deputy, explained, "I think you should swear and put an end to the matter."

"Our oath is not to satisfy Mistress Hutchinson but the court," the Reverend Peter said.

Endicott drew his sword and waved it at the crowd. "The assembly will be satisfied by it!"

"If the country will be satisfied, you must swear," Deputy Governor Dudley told the ministers.

"I conceive the country doth not require it," the Reverend Shepard offered.

"Then let her witnesses be called," Dudley suggested.

"Who be they?" Winthrop asked, relieved for any diversion from the conflict over the oath.

Anne Hutchinson named three witnesses: John Coggeshall, who had just spoken briefly; Thomas Leverett, a lawyer and alderman originally from Boston in Lincolnshire; and "our teacher," the Reverend John Cotton.

Winthrop said to her, "Mr. Coggeshall was not present" at the meetings with the ministers.

"Yes, but I was," Coggeshall countered. He stepped forward and explained, "Only I desired to be silent [on the matter] till I should be called."

Staring at him, the governor said, "Will you, Mr. Coggeshall, say that she did *not* say so?"

"Yes, I dare say that she did not say all that which they lay against her," Coggeshall ventured.

Aghast that a Christian man would publicly question a minister, the Reverend Peter rebuked Coggeshall. "How *dare* you look into the court to say such a word?"

Demurring, the wealthy silk merchant said, "Mr. Peter takes upon him to forbid me. I shall be silent." And he was.

Governor Winthrop moved swiftly to Anne's second witness. "Well, Mr. Leverett, what were the words [she used]? I pray, speak."

"To my best remembrance," Leverett replied cautiously, "when the elders did send for her, Mr. Peter did with much vehemency and entreaty urge her to tell what difference there was between Mr. Cotton and them. And upon his urging of her she said, 'The fear of man is a snare, but they that trust upon the Lord shall be safe.' And being asked wherein the difference was, she answered that they did not preach a covenant of grace so clearly as Mr. Cotton did, and she gave this reason of it: because that as the apostles were for a time without the spirit so until they had received the witness of the spirit they could not preach a covenant of grace so clearly." Leverett, a close friend of Cotton's from Boston in Lincolnshire, had arrived here with Cotton in 1633 and then been named a ruling elder of the Boston, Massachusetts, church—a sign of widespread respect.

"Don't you remember," Winthrop inquired of him, "that she said they were not able ministers of the New Testament?"

Before Leverett could answer, Hutchinson said, "Mr. Weld and I had an hour's discourse at the window and then I spake that, *if* I spake it."

The Reverend Weld wondered aloud why she admitted this now, having demanded proof earlier when he had charged her with it: "Was not my answer to you, leave it there, and if I cannot prove it you shall be blameless?"

"This I remember I spoke," she said to Weld. "Do not you remember that I came afterwards to the window when you were writing?"

"No, truly," Weld said.

"But I do, very well," she said.

Frustrated by so many contradictions, denials, and evasions, Governor Winthrop turned to her final witness, the only one with sufficient power to sit among the magistrates. "Mister Cotton," Winthrop said wearily, "the court desires that you declare what you do remember of the conference."

All eyes in the hall settled on the solemn visage of Anne's closest ally. The Reverend John Cotton had deep-set, heavily lidded eyes and a mustache that he combed into two slender, waxed points. Beneath his black skullcap, his curly hair was going gray. In a few weeks he would turn fifty-three. He wore the standard Puritan clerical garb, a black robe with a white bib and collar.

Cotton had a pivotal role in the courtroom that day. Besides being Hutchinson's confidant, he was the most admired minister in the colony, one of two preachers at its largest and most influential church. He was a studious sort who avoided controversy, observed others without apparent judgment, and let few know what he believed. Now, though, he would be compelled to speak. No one present could say how he would testify, but all sensed that the outcome of the trial depended on his words.

AS THE LILY
AMONG THORNS

Six and a half years before Anne Hutchinson's birth, a struggling Derbyshire lawyer, Rowland Cotton, and his wife had their second child, a boy named John, in December 1584. Three and a half years later, when John Cotton was a child, England defeated the Spanish Armada. In Derby, as in most parts of the country, this victory over Catholic Spain prompted a monthlong harrying, or violent persecution, of English Catholics, an occurrence whose "justice" all of the boy's subsequent education would confirm. For John Cotton, as for most Puritans, the Roman Catholic Church was the reincarnation of the biblical Whore of Babylon. Ironically, years later in Massachusetts it was said that Cotton was "the unmitred pope of a pope-hating commonwealth."

Just before turning thirteen, John Cotton matriculated as a secondary-level student at Cambridge, the university where he spent the next fifteen years. The Reformation had discounted Thomas Aquinas and the other medieval Catholic scholars so that Cambridge was now a solidly Calvinist "nursery for the Puritan ministry." Cotton received his bachelor of arts degree following four years of rhetoric, logic, philosophy, and Latin disputation. Five more years of these subjects plus mastery of Greek, astronomy, and perspective led to the master's degree. During this period, Cotton entered Emmanuel College, Cambridge, where he received a series of honors, being named fellow, dean, lecturer, and, finally, head catechist. The culminating bachelor of divinity degree, which required five years of Hebrew, theology, disputation, and preaching, was granted to him in 1613, when he was twenty-eight.

A few years earlier, in his midtwenties, Cotton was converted to Puritanism and "born again." As he later recalled this intensely emotional experience, it was a sermon on grace given at Emmanuel College by the Reverend Richard Sibbes that "opened his heart" to God for the first time. Not long after, when it was his turn to preach at the university, he offered, instead of his usual arch lecture in Ciceronian Latin, a plain, literal sermon on repentance. Most of his peers were horrified, but one, the brilliant John Preston, who himself became a famous Puritan preacher, was "pierced at the heart" and converted to Puritanism. Cotton's words inflicted a wound that "no cunning in Philosophy, or skill in Physick would suffice to heal," recalled Preston, who in 1622 succeeded John Donne as the preacher at Lincoln's Inn, the law school, in London.

The summer before Cotton received his divinity degree, he left the relative security of Cambridge to begin his career. His first job was in Boston, one of Lincolnshire's largest towns, located near the mouth of the Witham River where it meets the Wash, on the North Sea. Boston is set amid the vast, level, isolated land of the Fens, a marshy area extending over thirteen hundred square miles of the shires of East Anglia, Cambridge, Peterborough, and Lincoln, in eastern England. The parish of Boston was England's largest, making it a plum assignment for a newly minted vicar. The town's name is a shortened version of "Botolph's Stone," the medieval name for its earliest church, founded by Saint Botolph, an Anglo-Saxon monk, in the seventh century.

The magnificent, fourteenth-century parish church of Saint Botolph's, also known as the "Boston Stump," appears from a distance to rise, stumplike and solitary, from the flat land all around. (The nickname may also derive from its truncated perpendicular tower, which seems to lack a steeple, or from the suspicion with which the rugged Fenlanders, who fished and fowled for survival, viewed the townspeople.) The structure of the church, which one enters from the town's marketplace through the seven-hundred-year-old Gothic-style south door, is today much as it was in the seventeenth century.

In the Middle Ages Boston had been a bustling, international seaport, famous for its fairs, its friars, and its guilds. But by 1612, when John Cotton arrived, the town had endured a half century of economic depression. Though it was now relatively quiet, it had become a center of ecclesiastical nonconformity. One of Cotton's Puritan predecessors in 1583 pleaded with church authorities to be freed from wearing the surplice, the white vestment that he considered a remnant of Catholicism, and from using rings in marriage ceremonies. In 1590 a Puritan vicar of Boston ordered the destruction of the rood screen in the church. And in 1604 the Bishop of Lincoln discharged Boston's vicar, Thomas Wooll, for not using the sign of the cross in baptisms and not wearing the surplice but using it instead as a "cushion to sit on." Wooll left an assistant in charge in Boston and went to preach in nearby Skirbeck. But it was Wooll who headed the delegation that traveled to Cambridge in 1612 to select a new permanent vicar for Saint Botolph's. Hearing that Cotton was the best young preacher there, Wooll offered him the job.

As a gift to Cotton, in acknowledgment of the importance of preaching, the church and town presented him on his arrival with a new pulpit, a lovely hexagonal wood box gilded and raised seven steps above the floor and his congregation of about a thousand souls. This carved tribute to his skill eased his adjustment to the demands of parish life. Within a year of arriving he acquired (in the parlance of the day) a wife—Elizabeth Horrocks, of a nonconformist family—something every Puritan preacher was expected to do, in part to distinguish himself from a Catholic priest. John and Elizabeth Cotton lived in the brick vicarage with gardens that adjoined the church and marketplace. Over the years they hosted many Cambridge divinity students, who were especially welcome in the vicarage, as the couple was childless.

Cotton attained a seventeenth-century form of celebrity, gaining renown during his two decades in Boston as England's preeminent Puritan preacher and intellectual. His calm manner and evident piety appealed universally, even to those who did not share his Reformed theology. In 1614 the bishop's registrar described him as "a man of great parts for his learning, eloquent and well-spoken," which explains Cotton's respectable salary the following year of a hundred pounds. He spent hours every day preparing to preach. "True happiness," he believed, "was reserved for the man who contemplated the eternal words of God rather than the man who allowed the natural world to impress its fluctuating character on him." According to the *History of Alford and Rigsby*, "The Reverend John Cotton of Boston is reported on one occasion to have preached three sermons of two hours each in two days, and his usual Sunday afternoon services lasted four hours." Some parishioners complained of wanting to "wink or nod" during the vicar's "incessant" sermons, which were usually followed by a required hour of catechism instruction. But most parishioners listened, spellbound, and some traveled long distances to hear his extravagant preaching. In response to public demand, "the saintly Cotton" added a Thursday lecture to his weekly obligation, an innovation that would become a central feature of life in New England.

The summer that John Cotton arrived in Boston, Anne Marbury and William Hutchinson were married, in London, at Saint Mary Woolnoth Church. Following their August 9 wedding, the twenty-one-year-old bride and her twenty-six-year-old husband removed to their hometown of Alford, twenty-four miles north of Boston, to furnish a house and start a family. They did not know Cotton but often went on a Sunday pilgrimage to a neighboring parish to "seek after the Lord of Hosts" by hearing a different minister preach. Among nonconformists, who valued skill in preaching over all, this was a common practice, although it defied the 1559 Act of Uniformity, which required all English people to frequent their local parish church.

The region around Alford offered many medieval parish churches within ten miles for the Hutchinsons to visit—Well, Rigsby, Bilsby, Saleby, Cumberworth, and Mumby, to cite just a few. The large market town of Boston was not so near, but someone told the Hutchinsons of Cotton's gift. One fine Sunday Anne and Will traveled to Boston to stand among the hundreds of worshipers crowding the massive nave of the Church of Saint Botolph's as John Cotton lectured for hours. From that day on, Anne and Will made the Sunday trip to Boston as often as the weather, her frequent pregnancies, and their many duties allowed.

The twenty-four-mile trip took roughly six hours. Well before dawn, Will mounted one of his horses and helped Anne onto the pillion behind him. The small children stayed home in the care of servants, although as the family grew they would hitch horses to a wagon for the long trip. But in those early days, Anne and Will rode a single horse west from Alford, across their own fields, up into the Wolds. Passing two intersections, Miles Cross and Ulceby Cross, they turned southwest on the Roman road to Boston, which was muddy in spring and fall and impassable during winter. They passed through the villages of Dalby, Partney, Spilsby, and East Keal, a region that is desolate and sparsely populated even today. Hedgerows divide vast fields of arable land that are punctuated only by occasional groves of trees. "Lincolnshire is not one of the favoured counties of England," a history of the region observes.

Ten miles south of Alford, just after East Keal, they descended from the Wolds into the Fens, where the land is as flat as Holland. On a clear day they could see the gray Boston Stump rising from the Fens, which were green or brown depending on the season. Portions of the Fens flooded in winter, but in early summer pastures appeared on which to graze cattle and make hay. So vast were these wetlands that, as Isaac Casaubon noted in 1661, the "solitary bittern," a heron, "and the imitative dotterel," a kind of plover, gave their booming calls and "sharp, plaintive cries" undisturbed.

The Hutchinsons passed the Fen towns of Keal Cote, Stickney, and Sibsey, each with its own church and lecturers, but it was Boston where Anne—and thus Will—wished to be. She was drawn to Cotton's "peculiar" theology, which combined two seemingly opposite doctrines—*absolute grace* and *conditional reprobation.* "Absolute grace" means God's grace is given absolutely to the elect so that neither good works nor faith can bring salvation. "Conditional reprobation" means that human depravity (being damned before birth) is conditional on one's misbehavior during life, which God decreed in his foreknowledge of human behavior. These two ideas—grace is absolute and controlled by God; damnation is conditional on a person's behavior—seem contradictory, but they had tremendous appeal to Anne Hutchinson.

To a brilliant, seventeenth-century Puritan woman, Cotton's theology of unmerited saving grace opened a life of studying and interpreting God's word that was otherwise denied her. Taking his doctrine of the Holy Ghost dwelling within a justified person even further than he did, she saw herself as a mystic participant in the transcendent power of the Almighty, beyond mere magistrates and ministers, who were not divine but only temporal and human. Thus his doctrine, which extended the female experience of humility to men, created in a woman like her a new feeling of pride.

It is a paradox that Cotton's theology, which minimized the importance of individual action, also enabled individuals without public power to rebel against the culture. It was the perfect theology to empower women in a society where women received status, power, and influence only through their husbands and fathers. "Women were denied training for the ministry, and indeed had no assigned roles at all in the religious life of the churches," the historians Jack Adamson and Harold Folland noted in their biography of Henry Vane. Cotton's theology enabled "a woman of strong religious sensibility to let the tongue speak something of what the heart felt." Cotton's emphasis on the individual's inability to achieve salvation echoed the pervasive inability of women to achieve public recognition. In this theology, women and men held the same troubled status as inferiors in the hands of a higher being. All power came from God, without respect to gender, rather than from male authority figures interpreting God's word. While John Cotton's doctrine excluded some, it gave Anne Hutchinson a voice.

Inspired by him, and by reports of other women who ran conventicles, Anne Hutchinson began holding meetings in her house in Alford, spreading Cotton's word among women by repeating and explicating his sermons. He was delighted to find her preparing souls for conversion by him. "She did much good in childbirth-travails, and readily fell into good discourse with the women about their spiritual estates," he remarked. She warned them not to build "their good estate upon their own duties and performances or upon any righteousness of the law." Their "conscience of sabbaths, reverence of ministers, frequenting of sermons, and diligence in calling" were "legal duties" unrelated to "saving union with Christ." Many women "were much shaken and humbled thereby, and brought to enquire more seriously after the Lord Jesus Christ." Hutchinson served to awaken people to "their sandy foundations, and to seek for better establishment in Christ." She was so skillful, Cotton added, that "she had more resort to her for counsel about matter of conscience and clearing up men's spiritual estates, than any minister" he knew.

Despite their evangelical collaboration, Hutchinson and Cotton seemed, on the surface, a study in contrasts. Where she was assertive and bold, he was conservative and conciliatory. Where she was zealous and clear, he was cautious and circumspect. Where she was witty, even sarcastic, he was literal and plainspoken. Where she reveled in the excitement and openness of dialogue, he was solitary. Where she could thrive amid the shrieks and fluids of childbirth, he preferred the intensity of texts in ancient tongues. Yet they developed over twenty years a trusting friendship, which continued in the new Boston.

Only three weeks before her trial, on a balmy October night in 1637, Hutchinson had sought and received private advice from Cotton about a matter that, had the other ministers and magistrates learned of it, would have caused an outcry. The matter was the birth of a deformed stillborn to a Boston couple, an event that most of their neighbors would have seen as evidence of God's displeasure with the baby's parents.

On October 17, Mary Dyer, the twenty-six-year-old wife of the milliner, William Dyer, went into labor two months before her due date and lost consciousness. The midwife Jane Hawkins, who was attending her at home, sent a man on horseback to summon Mistress Anne Hutchinson to assist at the birth. Later that evening, with both midwives present, Mary Dyer delivered a stillborn female with extensive deformities of the head, spinal column, and extremities.

To protect Mary and her husband from public shame, Hutchinson and Hawkins swaddled the tiny corpse, concealing its deformities. When Mary Dyer regained consciousness, the midwives told her only that her baby had died. But what to do with the body? Anne Hutchinson proposed that they bury it and not speak of it again. The risk of this, as both she and Jane Hawkins knew, was that if townspeople heard what had happened, they would suspect evil intent, which would only intensify the Dyers' shame. English common law allowed a midwife to bury a dead baby in private, as long as "neither hog nor dog nor any other beast come into it," but the Massachusetts court had forbidden this practice as a way of preventing attempts at abortion. Anne Hutchinson thought to ask the Reverend Cotton for his advice.

Well past midnight, she walked from the Dyers' house, at the corner of what is now Summer Street, to the Cottons' gabled mansion, which was surrounded by a large garden, on the lower slopes of Pemberton Hill. Despite the glow of moonlight on the peninsula, Anne could not see the reds and yellows of the scattered trees in the town. She had one purpose.

As she approached the Cotton house, with its unique double-sash windows containing diamond-shaped panes, she saw a single light burning. Her teacher was awake, working. A "universal scholar," in the words of his grandson Cotton Mather, John Cotton usually studied "twelve hours in a day . . . resolving to wear out with using than with rusting." Anne tapped on the parlor window, and the minister let her in. In the candlelight, she described Mary Dyer's birthing and requested his counsel.

Yes, conceal it, Cotton agreed, aware of the English custom and law. She thanked him and went back out into the night. Before dawn, she and Jane Hawkins buried the baby. According to one account, Cotton accompanied the midwives and dug the grave. A few other women who had been present at the difficult birth knew of the baby's state. But no man in the colony save John Cotton, William Dyer, and probably Will Hutchinson knew that the midwives and the minister had conspired to save the Dyers additional pain.

In the long view of history, Cotton is an enigmatic character who embraced unorthodoxy yet despised controversy. In his writings he was cautious, according to Moses Coit Tyler, who observed that Cotton's "vast tracts of Puritanic discourse" contain not "a single passage of eminent force or beauty." Cotton saw his own Reformed Christianity as the sole true religion, and he rejected toleration of other religions because they "tell lies in the name of the Lord." He repudiated the nascent concept of democracy, asking, "If the people be governors, who shall be governed?" Although Copernicus's and Galileo's ideas about the universe were current among Puritans, Cotton was convinced that the earth does not move. If it did, he argued, then "when a man throws a stone, the same way the earth moves, he might easily overtake" it and "be under the stone when it should fall."

Despite his deeply conservative tendencies, Cotton's theological inclinations drew him to preach dangerous things, fomenting dissent. In England his unorthodoxy prompted church authorities to investigate him repeatedly. Eventually they called him to the Court of High Commission in London for questioning by the archbishop, as Anne's father had been summoned a generation earlier. Unlike Francis Marbury, however, Cotton avoided imprisonment. He went into hiding and fled to America, where the ripples of the stones he dropped in his sermons had now brought Massachusetts to the brink of civil war.

Cotton mediated skillfully between his contradictory tendencies, impressing all who met him with his brilliance at conciliation. He learned from his mentor, the Reverend William Perkins, a fellow of Christ's College, Cambridge, to "temper his show of doctrine with expedience." In 1587, when Perkins was reprimanded by church authorities for lecturing too vehemently against kneeling at the sacrament and facing east, he chose neither to give in nor to continue with defiance. Instead, he maintained his principles but worded them more carefully, preserving his reputation as the greatest living Cambridge preacher. Perkins showed Cotton "how to practice what one believed and yet retain favor," according to his biographer. As Cotton later explained, "Zeal must be according to knowledge, knowledge is no knowledge without zeal, and zeal is but a wildfire without knowledge."

Like Anne Hutchinson, John Cotton felt an unusually strong sense of having been called by God. Based on his writings, he suffered none of the spiritual struggles that afflicted his contemporaries. This resulted partly from his nature. In addition, he was convinced that the world he lived in was about to end in an apocalyptic conflagration, to be replaced by a world like that in the days after the resurrected Christ was revealed to his apostles. At any moment God would usher in this purified, covenanted, Christian world. This great hope, which he shared with all, enabled him to avoid discouragement. The Roman Catholic Church would dissolve, and a true church would be established in England. He considered himself a member in good standing of the Church of England, which he believed contained many godly men. At the same time, he believed the Anglican bishops were in a succession that led ultimately to Rome and thus to the Antichrist.

This vision created problems for Cotton in Boston, Lincolnshire, where some of his parishioners were orthodox, preferring the rituals and views of the Anglican hierarchy. Among this minority, the most troublesome parishioners subscribed to Arminianism, the doctrine that people need not wait passively for God's grace but can work their own salvation. Rejecting the Calvinist notion that predestination and election are unconditional, the Arminians gave free will a role. To disarm them, Cotton minimized God's apparent arbitrariness in damning human beings. Predestination is so absolute, he preached, that to earn reprobation one must also behave badly. The Arminian party shrank.

A larger problem remained—how to reconcile his nonconformity with the distasteful structure and demands of the church hierarchy. In Anglicanism, as in Catholicism, every parish resident was automatically a member of the church. Everyone but the most notorious sinner was compelled, or at least expected, to attend and participate at church. All were entitled to the sacraments of the Church of England. In this open sort of congregation, there were surely some, if not many, souls that were reprobate, or foreordained to damnation. How could the Reverend Cotton preach to people whom God had not elected before birth as eligible to receive his saving grace?

John Cotton found his answer to this dilemma in chapter 2 of the Song of Solomon. "As the lily among thorns, so is my love among the daughters" was the passage. The lily, he believed, was the community of the elect, while the thorns were those with whom the elect hold fellowship, who could be reprobate. True believers need not separate from the church, he decided, but they must display within the larger congregation their special status. As he later explained, "The church may be Christ's love, yea, and a fragrant and pure flower in his sight and nostrils, and yet live amongst briars and thorns."

Having solved his dilemma, he set out cautiously to distinguish "the lily" from "the thorns." Once this process of identification was complete, he withdrew into a tighter group with the "lilies," worshiping specially with them. With them he entered into a covenant with the Lord, promising "to follow after the Lord in the purity of his worship" and hoping for the intimacy with God that the ancient Jews enjoyed. Only the lilies were qualified to receive the Lord's Supper, which, he wrote, should be given only to those who "experienced a work of regeneration in their souls." They were also allowed to absent themselves from obligations that he considered idolatrous, such as kneeling at the Lord's Supper and at prayers.

In creating this congregation within a congregation, Cotton started the first Congregational church, although he did not coin that term until 1642. In later Congregationalism as it developed in New England in the 1630s, membership was restricted to "saints," people who could convincingly describe in public an experience of saving grace. In this "pure" church, members clearly professed their faith, showed knowledge of doctrine, and walked with God. Its high standards for membership would lead to decades of conflict among the ministers of Massachusetts as to the proper method of testing candidates for actual signs of grace.

This idea of a congregation within a congregation may sound exclusive, and indeed it was, but to a seventeenth-century woman of exegetical bent it opened doors that were otherwise shut. Covenanted worship served Anne's needs by removing gender as a requirement for ministry. She was an inner-circle woman in this system of lilies and thorns. Cotton's doctrine encouraged her to practice as preacher, prophet, and theologian, all roles denied to women. It did not allow her a pulpit, but it gave her power and access to power that she otherwise lacked.

But empowering women was not John Cotton's intention, conscious or otherwise. Like Winthrop and all his colleagues, he viewed women as inferior to and subject to men. Arriving in Massachusetts, he requested that women desiring church membership be examined in private only because public confession was "not fit for a woman's modesty."

Cotton's system worked for Anne Hutchinson, who was as particular about her priests as he was about his parishioners, but it did not suit all the congregants of Saint Botolph's. The thorns were naturally outraged at being excluded from the vicar's covenant of grace, and they went in protest to the bishop's court at Lincoln. The court suspended Cotton. The vicar appealed his suspension to a higher church court, at which with "pious subtlety" he presented himself as a preacher who could and would conform. Allowed to return to Boston, he continued to preach and worship as before, and his covenanted congregation flourished.

In 1618, to placate the thorns, Cotton had the church corporation add a second clergyman, Edward Wright, to minister solely to them. Every Sunday, on the broad stones outside the church's south door, the lilies and the thorns passed each other headed in different directions. After Wright completed the Apostle's Creed, at which the Anglicans stood, the Puritans filed in to hear Cotton preach, and the Anglicans quickly departed before the vicar's interminable sermon began.

To satisfy the authorities, Cotton furnished the church as they demanded, keeping the stained glass, the ornate tapestries, and the statues that Puritans disdained as idolatrous. He cleverly manipulated church routine, having Wright perform the ceremonies Cotton considered offensive. "The truth is," he explained, "the ceremonies of the ring in marriage, and standing at the creed, are usually performed by myself; and all the other ceremonies of surplices, cross in baptism, kneeling at the communion, are frequently used by my fellow-minister in our church." Meanwhile, Cotton administered church rites for his inner circle of true believers. For several years, these two congregations existed side-by-side in Saint Botolph's, largely due to John Cotton's "godliness" and personal appeal.

This delicate peace was shattered one night in April 1621 when men armed with hammers broke into St. Botolph's and destroyed its stained glass windows, tapestries, and stone statues. Out of deference to Cotton, the pulpit was not touched. Most offensive to the authorities, the vandals cut off the cross on the king's arms atop the mace that the mayor carried to church each Sunday and Thursday. The intruders were lilies, of course, inspired either by Cotton's invectives against "graven images" in church or by the scheduled sermon the next day by the prominent orthodox Anglican Robert Sanderson. In that sermon, which Sanderson delivered in the damaged nave on April 24, he said, "The right England Protestant . . . standeth in the middle between, and distinguished from, the Papist on the one hand, and the (sometimes styled) Puritan on the other"—a direct cut at Cotton. The vicar, for his part, was shocked at the violence that his passionate pursuit of reform had unleashed.

To the thorns, this mutilation of church art—especially the mayor's mace—was an act of sedition. They notified royal authorities, and a civil commission was soon appointed to investigate the crime. There was no evidence suggesting Cotton was involved. During the investigation the town clerk, who was Cotton's brother-in-law, testified, "Mr. Cotton never did connive at the cutting of those crosses." Nevertheless, Bishop Monteigne of Lincoln suspended him for nonconformity. But when the two men met in Lincoln to discuss the matter, Monteigne was so impressed with the vicar's piety and learning that he gave Cotton another chance. He could return to Saint Botolph's if he would conform by kneeling just once at the Eucharist, or he would show good reason why he refused. In Cotton's view, such kneeling was a sin against the second commandment—"Thou shalt not make for thyself a carved image. . . . Thou shalt not bow down to them, nor serve them . . . "—so he chose the second alternative. He sent the bishop this explanatory syllogism:

> Cultus non institutus, non est acceptus:
> Genuflexio in perceptione Eucharistiae est cultus non insitutus;
> Ergo, non est acceptus.

> *A practice of worship that is not officially established is not welcome:*
> *Genuflection upon receiving the Eucharist is not an officially established*
>   *practice;*
> *Therefore it is not welcome.*

Bishop Monteigne, too busy to trouble himself further with the matter of the damage to the church, let the matter drop. A few months later he was appointed Bishop of London and was succeeded in Lincoln by John Williams, who proved more tolerant of Puritans. Bishop Williams came to admire Cotton, finding him "unlike most Puritans" because he "did not appear to be a zealot but preached a more gentle species of Calvinism and pursued his nonconformity quietly." Cotton relaxed under Williams and even admitted in writing to his method of having another minister perform ceremonies he considered offensive.

While Lincolnshire was growing more amenable to Puritanism, the Church of England was tilting back toward Rome (away from Calvinist Geneva). In 1622 the hierarchy in London banned the non-conformist sermon practice of applying Scripture passages to modern times. Two years later all books on religion were required to be licensed by the church. In 1625, at the request of Prince Charles, who would soon become king, Bishop William Laud wrote in his diary a list of churchmen, placing next to each name either an *O*, for orthodox, or a *P*, for Puritan. The duke of Buckingham gave this list to King Charles soon after his coronation.

With King Charles and Archbishop Laud in power—the latter succeeded Monteigne as Bishop of London in 1628 and became Archbishop of Canterbury, or primate of England, in 1633—the church grew far less tolerant of Calvinism so that not even "doctrine remained to unite Puritan and bishop." King Charles had a Catholic wife, Henrietta Maria, of France, and decidedly nonpuritanical and nonevangelical tastes. He enjoyed the rituals of Anglican worship—the vestments, choir, and organ, the kneeling, crossing, and processing, and the candlelight, incense, and chanted prayers that derived from Catholic Rome. Instead of defacing art, he commissioned more, from the likes of Rubens, Raphael, and Van Dyck.

As the royal and ecclesiastic noose tightened around their throats, the Puritan divines gathered at Tattershall Castle, the home of Theophilus Clinton Fiennes, fourth Earl of Lincoln, to discuss their options. If church authorities summoned them to London, they had several choices. They could go to prison, enter the well-organized Puritan underground, become Separatist (leaving the state church, as the Pilgrims had done), or flee the country, usually to Holland, the West Indies, or—starting in the late 1620s—America.

Somehow, even as his Puritan peers were in exile in Holland or preparing to emigrate from England to America, Cotton's fame still flourished in England. "Of all men in the world I envy Mr. Cotton, of Boston, most," his colleague the Reverend Samuel Ward observed in 1629, "for he doth nothing in way of conformity, and yet hath his liberty, and I do everything that way, and cannot enjoy mine."

7

FROM BOSTON TO THIS WILDERNESS

In the first week of April 1630, as John Winthrop's fleet assembled near the Isle of Wight on England's southern coast, John Cotton made the long trip to Southampton to address the Massachusetts Bay Company as it prepared to set sail. This group, the largest body of colonists yet to leave for America, included many of Cotton's parishioners, among them the Dudleys and the Bradstreets, as well as the third Earl of Lincoln's daughter, Lady Arbella Clinton Fiennes Johnson, for whom the fleet's premier ship, the *Arbella*, was named. Hoping to entice Cotton to join them in Massachusetts, the leaders of the Bay Company had invited him to deliver their farewell sermon.

On the wooden dock at Southampton, the equable, black-robed minister stood before the emigrants and assured them that their leaving England was just and holy. "Tradesmen [here] no longer live one by another," he lamented, "but eat up one another." He admonished the emigrants to remain holy in the New World, which he said fulfilled the biblical prophecy "I will appoint a place for my people." Using the passage he chose for the occasion, 2 Samuel 7:10, Cotton exhorted the colonists not to separate from the Church of England but rather to extend it. Before closing, he encouraged their conversion of the "poor native." In exchange for the privilege of sharing the heathens' vast land, he said, "Feed them with your spirituals" and "make them partakers of your precious faith."

After the ships set sail for Massachusetts, Cotton returned contentedly to St. Botolph's to preach reform while seeming to conform. In 1631, though, disaster befell him and his wife. The couple contracted malaria, or tertian ague, which was common in the Fens, a lush breeding ground for mosquitoes. Gravely ill, the Cottons were moved to a hospital at a manor house of the fourth Earl of Lincoln. Over the subsequent year, John Cotton slowly recovered and his wife died. He presided over her funeral and burial, and then he began traveling around the country, consulting with other Puritan divines.

On April 25, 1632, John Cotton wed again, to a widow named Sarah Hawkridge Story, who had a little girl. Soon afterward, Cotton learned that Bishop Laud had sent a letter summoning him to the Court of High Commission to answer to the charge of nonconformity. Shedding his clerical garments, Cotton disappeared into the Puritan underground and was nowhere to be found when the court's messenger arrived in Boston. He remained in hiding for months, writing in September from London to his new wife, "If you should now travel this way, I fear you will be watched and dogged at the heels."

As for Cotton's future plans, he was unsure. His ministry in England had become a "torment," but he had never embraced the idea of emigrating. His colleagues advised him, "Fly for your safety." Always afraid of confrontation, he did not know what to do.

News of his predicament reached John Winthrop. Hoping to swell the colony, the governor wrote at once to invite the minister to Massachusetts. This invitation made up Cotton's mind. He wrote to Bishop Williams on May 7, 1633, "I see neither my bodily health, nor the peace of the church [of Saint Botolph's], will now stand my continuance there. . . . The Lord, who began a year or two ago to suspend, after a sort, my ministry from that place by a long and sore sickness, the dregs whereof still hang about me, doth now put a further necessity upon me wholly to lay down my ministry there, and freely to resign."

Before daybreak one morning in early June 1633, Cotton and his wife and her daughter were rowed from the Norfolk Downs out to the *Griffin*. Another noted Puritan divine, Thomas Hooker, who had also studied at Cambridge, was on board the ship as well. Commenting on this confluence, their colleague Thomas Shepard said, "I saw the Lord departing from England when Mr. Hooker & Mr. Cotton were gone." (Shepard followed two years later, sailing on the *Defense* in the late summer of 1635.) During the eight-week voyage, Sarah Cotton gave birth to her forty-eight-year-old husband's first child, a healthy boy they named Seaborn. To John Cotton, this happy event was a sign from God that he was pleased with their ocean crossing.

On September 4 the *Griffin* passed Lovell's Island at the mouth of the harbor of the new Boston, a wide pasture punctuated by three conical hills and a few trees on a peninsula, surrounded by marsh. Thinking of the tiered system of worship that had so suited him in his English church, Cotton composed a poem "upon his removal from Boston to this wilderness."

> *When I think of the sweet and gracious company*
> *That at* BOSTON *once I had,*
> *And of the long peace of a fruitful ministry,*
> *For twenty years enjoyed.*
>
> *The joy that I found in all that happiness*
> *Doth still so much refresh me*
> *That the grief to be cast out into a wilderness*
> *Doth not so much distress me.*

On the timbers of the town pier, which lay upon large rocks and wooden piles, Governor Winthrop and Deputy Governor Dudley stood waiting to greet the two eminent divines. In deference to Cotton's slightly greater eminence, they gave him a post in Boston and sent Hooker to preach in Newtown.

The following Saturday, John and Sarah Cotton were admitted to membership in the church, and their baby became the twenty-third person baptized in the meetinghouse of Boston. For Cotton's first sermon to the hundred-member congregation, he lectured on the subject of a true church using Canticle 6, or the sixth chapter of the Song of Solomon, which includes the lines, "My beloved is gone down into his garden, to the beds of spices, to feed in the gardens, and to gather lilies. I am my beloved's, and my beloved is mine: he feedeth among the lilies." A few weeks later Cotton was named teacher of the church, charged with preaching and supervising doctrine, preparing converts, and consoling and advising parishioners. The duties of the pastor, John Wilson, who had served since 1630, included presiding over services and administering sacraments.

In the meetinghouse that was the world's first congregational church, Cotton was now freed from the burden of preaching to the reprobate. Only the elect, as discerned by their peers, were allowed membership in this church. Over time, Cotton's sermons contained fewer references to his doctrine of conditional reprobation. In his theology based on the doctrine of free grace, he had to balance the contrary pulls of grace (which comes from God) and works (which are within human control). Once a person is justified by God's grace, the person's actions should, by definition, be good. At the same time, a true saint is overwhelmed by a sense of human helplessness. "When you look at duties," Cotton said to his congregation, "you are not able to do them, not able to hear or pray aright." In his view, human works are empty without God. After justification, he believed, the Holy Ghost becomes one with the saint, which led Hutchinson and no doubt many of his parishioners sometimes to feel powerfully close to God.

In response to Cotton's evangelical enthusiasm, a religious revival ensued. More conversions occurred in Boston in the six months after his arrival—sixty-three souls in all—than had occurred during the entire previous year, under the Reverend Wilson. As might be expected, Cotton encouraged making the standards for church membership even more restrictive. By the end of 1633 Massachusetts Bay ministers had agreed on two new requirements—soundness in doctrine, and evidence of good behavior. Cotton wished to add a third—candidates must testify publicly about their conversion experience and the working of grace in their soul. This was added in early 1636.

Only three months after Cotton's arrival, Winthrop exulted that "the Lord [gave] special testimony of His presence in the church of Boston, after Mr. Cotton was called to office there. More were converted and added to the church, than to all the other churches in the bay. . . . Diverse profane and notorious evil persons came and confessed their sins, and were comfortably received into the bosom of the church." The congregation welcomed his habit of fifth-day, or Thursday, lectures. They followed his lead in honoring the Sabbath for twenty-four hours, beginning at sundown Saturday. In a community "relatively devoid of pastimes," Cotton's sermons were great events. Parishioners could copy down his words and then discuss each sermon, in great detail, at home. They could lose themselves in weekly lectures, six or seven hours of preaching each sabbath day, and additional sermons on Fast Days and election days. After the difficulties of worshiping as they wished in England, Puritans could now indulge themselves in sermons, turning to their ministers and the Holy Spirit for relief from the hardships of the New World.

Each week, and often twice with Pastor Wilson away in England, Cotton obliged his parishioners by walking to the lectern of the meetinghouse of Boston, which still lacked a pulpit, and standing before them as an instrument of the Holy Spirit. He described how those whom God chose he justified and sanctified, giving them spiritual gifts that helped them live a godly life. Neither sanctification (the outward appearance of grace) nor justification (actually being saved) can come to one who was not elect from the beginning of time. All the elect, Cotton said, are sanctified, even if they sin. Instead of seeing the covenant as a sort of bargain, as many did, he preached the utter inability of humans to effect their own salvation. To argue otherwise, he thought, was to open the way for a Roman Catholic covenant of works. In the New World, he preached, the Mosaic Law and even the Gospel itself are "dead" as a means of salvation. Salvation is a completely inner experience, dependent on one's relationship with the Holy Spirit.

This doctrine had the potential to threaten civic and religious authority because it seemed to allow citizen-saints to act as the Holy Spirit dictated. Cotton's biographer Larzer Ziff explained the problem: "In a commonwealth where man's spiritual estate directly affected his civil estate, a doctrine which so distinguished between the Spirit and the word could be expected to find opponents."

But John Cotton, delighted with his situation in the Bible commonwealth and with his growing family, wrote to English friends to encourage them to emigrate. To remain in England, he suggested, was to become corrupt. On the September day in 1634 when the Hutchinsons' ship entered Boston harbor, he awaited the family on the dock. He was pleased to continue his spiritual collaboration with the woman who, he wrote not long after her arrival, was "the apple of our eye." Blessed with what he termed "a sharp apprehension, a ready utterance, and ability to express herself in the cause of God," Anne Hutchinson was "helpful to many to bring them off from their unsound [doctrinal] grounds and principles." Almost as though there had been no break in their shared work, Hutchinson began again to prepare souls for John Cotton to convert.

An even more distinguished arrival than the Hutchinsons, thirteen months later, was twenty-two-year-old Henry Vane, with whom Cotton felt so much immediate sympathy that he had the young aristocrat move into his house. A few months later, while still lodging with the Cottons (who now had a baby girl, Sarah, in addition to two-year-old Seaborn and the daughter of Mistress Cotton's first marriage), Vane arranged for a matching house to be built next door, with the same diamond-shaped windowpanes.

Within three weeks of his arrival, Henry Vane was admitted as a member of the Church of Boston, after reciting his account of being born again, which had occurred when he was fifteen. As he described it, a spring opened in the desert wilderness of his soul, and there came to him a "rich and free grace." For the first time ever, he felt joy. No longer was he moved by the Anglican worship of his father and the king. From then on, he enjoyed almost daily ecstasies of God's grace.

In light of Vane's and other dramatic conversions occurring in Hutchinson's male peers, it is notable that there is no record of her equivalent experience. She may have been born again, most likely in her late twenties. (A local Alford history infers that "Her religious conversion appears to have occurred during the 1620s," but there is no evidence of this occurrence.) Unlike Cotton and Vane, Hutchinson had parents and even grandparents who were already Puritan at her birth. While her male peers received this faith experience apart from—and sometimes in defiance of—their parents, she was bred on it. Vane, on the contrary, was a young man who abandoned his father's church and state and may have found in John Cotton a father figure.

Encouraged by Cotton, Vane began attending Hutchinson's meetings. Before long, he was given a special seat at her right hand, an honor extended to no one else. His notion of the "inner light of conscience" dovetailed with her ideas about revelation and the "indwelling of the spirit." The latter, which came from Cotton's sermons, was the idea that the Holy Spirit unites with the person of the believer, so that the justified person is of two bodies, not one. Vane also admired Hutchinson's analysis of sermons and of Scripture and her support of religious liberty.

He may have been the highest-status immigrant yet, but Vane was unlike most prominent colonists. At least a generation younger than they, he had been raised among Stuart courtiers in castles and manor houses. While other notable colonists had university or professional degrees, he had ended his formal education at sixteen when he dropped out of Magdalen College, Oxford, after a few months, during which he never even matriculated because he refused to swear the required oath of allegiance and supremacy to the church and crown. He spent the next few years traveling to France, Switzerland, Austria, and Holland on missions arranged by the court. In Rotterdam on royal business, he visited the Puritan congregation, then led by the Reverend Hugh Peter of Salem. At nineteen, Vane returned to London and told his father that England and its church were too constricting for him. He was interested in religious instruction and sermons, not ritual and liturgy. Distressed, his father asked Archbishop Laud to meet with young Harry and set him straight.

Vane and Laud's 1634 meeting was a disaster. If the young man's flowing locks were not enough to infuriate the archbishop, his refusal to take communion kneeling was. You must kneel at the Lord's Supper, the plump, red-capped, sixty-one-year-old archbishop insisted. But no, Vane replied. His God, unlike Laud's Aristotelian ideal, was a flame or a fountain—a "mysterium tremendum whose decrees inspired both love and fear, who arbitrarily sent or withheld his grace and who ministered without mediation to the individual soul. To kneel at that communion table would be to deny the God that whispered" in Vane's ear. The archbishop, who deplored the Calvinist doctrines of predestination, reprobation, and election, angrily dismissed the impudent young man.

Now, rejected by the hierarchies he despised, Vane was granted royal permission to do as he wished. The New World intrigued him, so he arranged to be sent for three years to New England as a representative of two lords who were Puritan patentees of Connecticut. A courtier observed that Vane "likes not the discipline of the Church of England; none of our ministers would give him the sacrament standing; no persuasions of our bishops nor authority of his parents could prevail with him; let him go." Vane's ambitious father hoped the experience would disabuse him of his Puritan fancies. To the Earl of Clarendon, the very notion of a privy counselor sending his son to New England for not kneeling at the Lord's Supper exemplified the "unnatural antipathy" developing between parents and children in England.

Two years before Anne's trial, in early October 1635, when Vane's boat, the *Abigail,* entered Boston harbor, Massachusetts Bay was splintered and anxious—a far cry from Winthrop's holy city upon a hill. Under Cotton, the Boston congregation had split doctrinally from the rest of the churches. Winthrop was sparring with Dudley, who had been elected governor over Winthrop in 1634 and deputy governor in 1635, when John Haynes became governor. Winthrop had lost power partly because Dudley and others considered him too lenient in enforcing discipline. In the case of the Reverend Roger Williams, who was soon to be banished, Winthrop had delayed action, angering his peers. In the coming years Williams and Vane would become enduring friends.

A distinctive but not handsome young man, Vane had almond-shaped eyes, a prominent nose, and full lips. His wavy brown hair fell to his shoulders, a style that offended not only his father and Laud but also most Puritans, who considered it ungodly. In Boston John Endicott was said to badger Vane to visit a barber. Vane's dandyish attire also challenged the Puritans of Boston, who in September 1634 had adopted a strict sumptuary code: "No person . . . shall hereafter make or buy any apparel . . . with any lace on it, silver, gold, silk or thread, under the penalty of forfeiture of such clothes. . . . All cutworks, embroidered or needlework caps, . . . all gold or silver girdles, hatbands, belts, rugs, beaver hats, are prohibited." And "if any man shall judge the wearing of any . . . fashions . . . or hair . . . to be uncomely, or prejudicial to the common good, . . . then [he] shall have power to bind the party so offending to answer it at the next court. . . ." As a high-status immigrant to Massachusetts, Vane had much more latitude in this regard than most.

Despite his foppish hair and dress, Vane initially delighted John Winthrop, who described him as "a young gentleman of excellent parts." If a privy councilor's son had come to New England, then more courtiers and aristocrats would surely follow, enhancing the colony's reputation, Winthrop reasoned.

Soon after his arrival, Vane determined to lessen the colonial conflict. Displaying an ambition reminiscent of his father, he assumed the role of guide and adviser. He arranged for a meeting between Dudley and Winthrop to air and resolve their differences. At this meeting, which was also attended by Governor Haynes and the Reverends Peter,

Cotton, and Wilson, Winthrop and Dudley both denied any bad feelings toward the other. Winthrop conceded that he ought to be stricter in the future with troublesome characters like Roger Williams. Vane got the credit for successfully arbitrating their dispute. As a result, the General Court ordered all disagreements in the colony to be submitted for arbitration to Vane and two elders. The next March Vane became not only a freeman but also head of a commission for military affairs, supervising the training and supply of the militia and conducting wars.

On May 25, 1636, at Vane's first annual election in Massachusetts, the ill-educated twenty-three-year-old aristocrat was chosen governor. Winthrop, who was elected deputy governor, neglected even to mention this election in his journal. Vane, in contrast, had the news of his election heralded by a "volley of great shot" from all fifteen ships at anchor in Boston harbor. Although he had refused to wear the college gown at Oxford, deriding it as needlessly formal, he now embraced the sort of pomp and ceremony that surrounded royalty in London and Vienna. He instituted the practice of having four colorfully uniformed sergeants bearing halberds and wearing plumed hats attend the governor of Massachusetts at all times. (A year later, when Winthrop returned to this position, he felt obliged to continue the habit, even after Vane's standard-bearers, among them Will's brother Edward Hutchinson, refused to stand for Winthrop.)

Despite Vane's glee at his rapid ascent to the zenith of colonial power, he realized that "tumultuous" issues faced Massachusetts. The religious divisions continued to cause irritation and anxiety among the settlers, a situation for which Vane was increasingly blamed, particularly by the orthodox ministers, who saw him as Hutchinson's friend. Then there were the French, who "continually encroach [and] gain all the trade," he complained in a letter to his father two months after the election. "The natives themselves are very treacherous, cruel, and cunning and let slip no advantages of killing and pilfering." And the charter, whose return the crown awaited, worried him. If the charter were to be revoked, he wrote, "much unsettlement is likely to grow amongst ourselves and great discouragement to the whole plantation. For those that are truly sincere, and are come out to advance the kingdom of the Lord Jesus, must either suffer in the cause or else labor for such retreat as God shall direct them to. In either of which cases I do not doubt but within two years this plantation, which is now flourishing, would become desolate, and either repossessed again with Indians or emptied by pestilence."

While young Vane worried over the colony's future, Hutchinson and other congregants of Boston appreciated the merging of church and state that came from having their governor and their favorite minister sharing roof and board. Cotton's congregation was emboldened to spread his word at military trainings, town meetings, and other gatherings. Members attended other churches, and after the pastor's sermon they would correct his doctrine in accord with Cotton's preaching. Proclaiming the error of seeing sanctification as a sign of justification, they warned others that they rested on a false sense of security, thinking they had nothing more to do now that they were in the New Jerusalem. Moral goodness, they warned, is not true godliness. The Holy Spirit must transform the heart to bring real reformation and "saving fellowship with Jesus Christ," in Cotton's words. They expounded on his ideas about revelation and the indwelling of the Spirit.

Winthrop and the orthodox ministers seized on this idea—the "indwelling of the Holy Ghost"—and attacked it. They argued that it was dangerous to encourage ordinary people to pursue prophecy and revelation. They feared the notion that the elect, in this union with Christ, could determine who else was saved. In a man, especially a man of the cloth, this could be justified, they felt, but in a woman it was heresy. The issue was of course blurry, as it often is in religion and politics. Indeed, in the fall of 1636, a year before Anne was brought to trial, when Winthrop and Vane engaged in a written debate on this matter, both agreed that the Holy Ghost does dwell in believers, although they could not agree exactly how. What struck Winthrop and the orthodox ministers as most offensive and potentially explosive was the alliance among Cotton—whom they could engage in polite doctrinal arguments—and Governor Vane and Mistress Hutchinson. This alliance, with its "potent party," was "an early outbreak of radicalism," according to historian David Hall, and "a frightening example of ideas about the discerning of visible saints carried to an extreme, for the Antinomians proposed that the indwelling of the Holy Spirit in the elect enabled them to discern who was truly worthy of church membership." It is worth noting that in opposing a covenant of works, Hutchinson actually suggested the opposite: that this life offers no clue to anyone's eternal prospects.

The orthodox ministers challenged her judgment in statements to the magistrates and to Cotton. They warned Cotton that his disciples, chiefly Hutchinson, were broadcasting outrageous opinions about the Holy Ghost. These doctrines dangerously emphasized a person's individual experience of God over clerical authority, they said. The Reverends Shepard and Hooker, of Cambridge, and Peter Bulkeley, of Concord, worried that Cotton's ideas about revelation could invalidate biblical law, and they requested he clarify his views. "All things are turned upside down among us," Winthrop noted in October. He feared ruptures in church and state and saw Mistress Hutchinson, whose theological errors he listed, as the root cause. He was also troubled that "there joined with her in these opinions a brother of her, one Mr. Wheelwright, a silenced minister sometime in England." Cotton remained exempt, apparently, from Winthrop's worry.

On October 25 Cotton, Wheelwright, the orthodox ministers, and Hutchinson met at Cotton's house for a "conference in private" to discuss the conflicts. Cotton smoothed over the doctrinal differences with his usual aplomb, conceding that sanctification might "help to evidence justification." On the indwelling issue, which Wheelwright affirmed, Cotton said that while "the person of the Holy Ghost and a believer were united," this does not imply that the justified person is godlike. The other ministers relaxed. Winthrop reported afterward that Cotton "gave satisfaction to them, so as he agreed with them all in the point of sanctification."

Five days later the Boston congregation voted to appoint John Wheelwright as its second teacher. Pastor Wilson was affronted, for the church already had two ministers, and Wheelwright was Hutchinson's brother-in-law. John Cotton naturally supported Wheelwright because they both preached an "unconditional covenant"—that people receive God's grace unconditionally, apart from their effort or works. But when Wilson objected strongly to Wheelwright, Cotton chose not to endorse the congregation's choice in public. On Saturday, October 30, at a gathering of the 150-member congregation, John Winthrop argued against adding a minister "whose spirit they knew not and one who seemed to dissent in judgment." Using the little-known unanimity rule, he prevented the appointment of Hutchinson's brother-in-law and had him sent ten miles south to Mount Wollaston, where a few Bostonians, who held farmland there, worshiped occasionally.

Winthrop urged Cotton to send female spies to Hutchinson's meetings. After doing so, the minister reported, "Some sisters of the church [went] on purpose to her repetitions [of sermons and Scripture] so that I might know the truth. But when she discerned any such present, no speech fell from her that could be excepted against."

As winter approached, Governor Vane grew more uncomfortable about his perceived role in the crisis. His opponents found him an easy target because he so often attended Hutchinson's meetings. Some of them whispered that Vane was a heretic. He felt "scandalous imputation brought upon himself, as if he should be the cause of all."

At the next General Court meeting, in early December, the young governor announced his wish to resign. Letters had come from England calling him home on urgent business. He "burst into tears," according to the court record, "and professed" he would risk the ruin of his "outward estate" rather than desert his people if he did not fear "the inevitable danger of God's judgments [that] were coming upon them for the difference and dissensions which he saw amongst them." Therefore, "he thought it was best for him to give place for a time."

Several other Hutchinsonians persuaded him to remain for the rest of his one-year term. Vane consented to stay and fight as an "obedient child of the church," but his power was compromised. In the wake of this shift, several magistrates charged Cotton with responsibility for the outrageous behavior of his congregation. The most noted minister in the colony was now suspect.

"About this time," Winthrop reported, "the rest of the ministers, taking offence at some doctrines delivered by Mr. Cotton, and especially at some opinions, which some of his church did broach, and for he seemed to have too good an opinion of, and too much familiarity with those persons, drew out sixteen points, and gave them to him, entreating him to deliver his judgment directly in them, which accordingly he did." In January 1637 Cotton gave "plain and short" answers to all the questions except Question Thirteen: "Whether evidencing justification by sanctification, be . . . a covenant of works," which required six pages to explain. He said, "I have spoken the more largely and distinctly" to this issue so that "I might avoid carefully all suspicion of ambiguity and obscurity." His answer, which in its defiant obscurity recalls his Latin syllogism of twenty years before, questioned the orthodox view that the pious man is the proper man. "Justifying faith cannot safely build or rest upon any ground, save only upon Christ and righteousness," Cotton wrote.

Hutchinson had been right, the other ministers realized: Cotton *was* charging them with preaching a covenant of works. This was not the answer that they and Winthrop had hoped to hear. "Dear Sir," they wrote in dismay to Cotton, "we leave these things with you, hoping that the Lord will honor you, with making you a happy instrument of calming these storms and cooling these hot contentions and paroxysms that have begun to swell and burn in these poor churches." Cotton replied with an even longer rejoinder denying that sanctification is evidence of justification.

The turmoil continued. At the close of the December court meeting, the Reverend Wilson delivered a "very sad speech" decrying the opinions that were causing the schism. Members of the Boston congregation moved to censure Wilson, but Cotton succeeded in stopping them. As in the old Boston, he seemed hardly touched by the divisions that roiled so many others. At the height of the crisis, in February 1637, Cotton reported in a letter to a friend in England that the two parties were not far apart: one is "advancing the grace of God within man, the other is advancing the grace of God toward man."

The Fast Day to resolve the conflict was January 18, 1637. The people of the colony sought God's protection in their various concerns: the difficulties of Protestant churches in Europe, especially England and Germany; the threat of Indian incursions; and the split of Massachusetts's largest church from all the others. Cotton gave the Fast Day sermon in Boston, on Isaiah 58:4: "Behold, ye fast for strife and debate, and to smite with the fist of wickedness: ye shall not fast as ye do this day, to make your voice to be heard on high." Then members of the congregation invited the Reverend Wheelwright to prophesy, to which Cotton consented. Wheelwright contradicted Wilson, blaming the troubles on the orthodox ministers' failure to maintain Christ properly in doctrine and worship. He stated that anyone who held sanctification as ground for salvation was wrong.

Demonstrating its vast power, which encompassed ecclesiastical as well as civic affairs, the Great and General Court of Massachusetts censured the Reverend John Wheelwright for this lecture at its next meeting, in March. Because of his views expressed while preaching, "Mr. Wheelwright was guilty of contempt [of state] and sedition." The court delayed punishing the minister, hoping that he might recant before its next meeting. But it did—for the first time—punish a Hutchinsonian for his religious views. Steven Greensmith of Boston was "committed to the marshall" and fined forty pounds "for affirming that all the ministers (except Mr. Cotton, Mr. Wheelwright, and he thought Mr. Hooker) did teach a covenant of works." In addition, "The Court did approve of [the Reverend] Mr. Wilson's speech."

At the general election on May 17, the magistrates and freemen of Massachusetts Bay gathered on the greensward of Cambridge Common. Each side—those who supported Vane (and Hutchinson and Cotton) and those who supported Winthrop and the orthodox divines—hoped to gain control of the colony. Several deputies from Boston were absent because they had not been informed of the meeting, which gave Winthrop an advantage. Governor Vane called the court to order and prepared to read aloud the petition in support of the Reverend Wheelwright, which several men of Boston had brought. Men from both sides began shouting, and some exchanged blows.

The Reverend John Wilson, of Boston, stepped into the fray, climbing a short way up an oak tree and ordering the freemen of Massachusetts to vote for their representatives. Winthrop quickly seconded the motion. Vane persisted in saying that he would now read the petition, but Winthrop stated that this was out of order until after the election of the deputies and magistrates. Winthrop turned to the crowd and asked the men to decide between him and Vane by a show of hands. The hands went up, and Winthrop won.

Still, Henry Vane refused to proceed until the petition was read. Nevertheless, Winthrop called for the election. The men of the colonial towns began choosing their deputies, who then voted for governor and deputy governor. At the conclusion of the voting, Winthrop and Dudley had been chosen to occupy the offices they had held at the colony's start. They took their oaths of office "for the year ensuing." They chose the loyal Reverend Wilson to "go forth with the soldiers against the

Pequots," and Captains John Underhill and Israel Stoughton to lead the troops, alongside the Connecticut troops under Captain John Mason.

The hapless Vane, now only a Boston deputy, finally read out the petition and the signatories' names. The mob, which was still divided, grew wild. When Winthrop requested Vane's four volunteer escorts, all men of Boston, to stand for him as the new governor, they all lay down their arms and refused. Not wishing to be upstaged, Governor Winthrop was thenceforth escorted by two male servants in feathered hats bearing halberds.

Over the long summer following the election, the Pequot War was finally won, despite the opposition of Hutchinson and many other Bostonians. By the end of July the Massachusetts and Connecticut forces had killed or left homeless all of the eight hundred inhabitants of the Pequot village near Saybrook, Connecticut. On August 3 a humiliated Henry Vane sailed for England, having stayed in Massachusetts for less than two of his appointed three years and leaving his followers with the empty promise that he would return, perhaps as a royal governor. Later that month the ministers met in Cambridge for a Religious Synod to agree on acceptable doctrine and to denounce the eighty-two errors held by Hutchinson that they had recorded in their meetings with her. The court banned her religious meetings. While women were allowed to meet "to pray and edify one another," when one woman "in a prophetical way" resolved questions of doctrine and expounded Scripture, the meeting was "disorderly."

When Hutchinson ignored this order, the General Court began to punish more of her allies and supporters. In response to the arrival of her husband's younger brother Samuel Hutchinson and other relatives on July 12, 1637, the court instituted the Alien Act—no one could stay in Massachusetts for more than three weeks without the court's permission—which kept more Hutchinsonians away. The Reverend Wheelwright was ordered before the court on September 26 and dismissed. On November 2, at the start of the General Court meeting that was still in session, the heretical minister, "being formerly convicted of contempt [of state] and sedition," was "disfranchised and banished, having fourteen days to settle his affairs."

On the same day—five days before the court called up Mistress Hutchinson—it discharged three Hutchinsonian deputies from Boston who had signed the "seditious libel called a petition" in support of Wheelwright: William Aspinwall, a notary, court recorder, and surveyor who was in his early thirties; forty-six-year-old John Coggeshall, the silk merchant; and Sergeant John Oliver, twenty-two. The court fined Oliver and Aspinwall and disfranchised Aspinwall and Coggeshall. It warned Coggeshall "not to speak anything to disturb the public peace, upon pain of banishment," and it banished Aspinwall for "seditious libel" and "for his insolent and turbulent carriage." Aspinwall had come from Lancashire to Boston in 1630 with Winthrop's party. He and his wife, Elizabeth, and their five children were friendly with the Hutchinsons and lived on the same side of Cornhill Road, slightly to the west, on land that extended north to the common.

Through it all, John Cotton avoided any censure. It was as though this remarkably even-tempered man was oblivious to the passion that his preaching could ignite. Just as he had not seen, until his church was vandalized, any warning signs among the worshipers at Saint Botolph's fifteen years before, he seemed unable mentally to register the profound colonial schism that his doctrine had aroused.

In the Cambridge courtroom, where he stood beside Mistress Hutchinson, John Cotton hesitated to respond to Winthrop's request to address the General Court. "I did not think I should be called to bear witness in this cause, and therefore did not labor to call to remembrance what was done."

He paused. Winthrop and the court waited. Cotton sought internally to find some place of comfort between the two opposing sides. He had experience of this kind, for he had previously fallen afoul of the authorities. Each time, though, he had slipped through the fingers of the law.

Watching the long-awaited encounter between Winthrop and Hutchinson's minister, the crowd in the meetinghouse grew still.

Finally Cotton said, "The elders spake that they had heard that she had spoken some condemning words of their ministry. They did first *pray* her to answer wherein she thought their ministry did differ from mine. How the comparison sprang, I am ignorant," he noted, "but *sorry I was* that any comparison should be between me and my brethren and uncomfortable it was." Winthrop was impressed, he confided later, that Cotton was "much grieved" at Hutchinson's comparisons between the ministers.

Cotton recalled her telling the other ministers "that they did not hold forth a covenant of grace as I did. 'But wherein did we differ?' [they asked.] Why, she said that 'they did not hold forth the seal of the spirit as he doth.' 'Where is the difference there?' said they. 'Why,' said she, 'you preach of the seal of the spirit upon a work and he upon free grace without a work or without respect to a work; *he* preaches the seal of the spirit upon *free grace* and *you* upon a *work*.'" At this, Cotton recalled, "I told her I was very sorry that she put comparisons between my ministry and theirs, for she had said more than I could myself, and I had rather that she had put us in fellowship with them and not have made that discrepancy.

"This was the sum of the difference [she found], nor did it seem to be so ill taken as it is," John Cotton added, "and our brethren did say also that they would not so easily believe reports as they had done, and withal mentioned that they would speak no more of it. And I must say that I did not find her saying that they were *under* a covenant of works, nor that she said they did *preach* a covenant of works." These words fell on Anne Hutchinson like a balm from heaven.

Desperate for a concession from the esteemed Cotton, the Reverend Hugh Peter urged his colleague to remember more. "Do you not remember that she said we were not sealed with the spirit of grace, therefore we could not preach a covenant of grace?"

Cotton demurred. The orthodox ministers began to argue about who had said what at the December meeting. Cotton begged to stay apart. To all their pleas, he said, "Under favor I do not remember that." Calmly and tactfully, he stood his ground without offending, as he had so many times before. In the face of his detachment, the other ministers disagreed among themselves.

Unbidden, Anne Hutchinson said, "My name is precious, and you do affirm a thing which I utterly deny."

Deputy Governor Dudley admonished her for forgetting John Wilson's notes of the meeting: "You should have brought the book with you." Hoping to salvage the case against her, he added, "They *affirm* that Mistress Hutchinson did say they were not able ministers of the New Testament."

"I do not remember it," the Reverend Cotton said once more.

With this testimony of Cotton's, the case against Anne Hutchinson could not stand. She had played her hand so well that only minor charges could be made. The judges could admonish her for her first two errors: passively supporting the signers of the Wheelwright petition, which she had not signed because a woman's signature carried no weight; and running Scripture meetings in a manner not "comely or fitting" for a woman. But without Cotton's assent, the third and most important charge, of traducing the ministers by usurping their powers without authority, would not hold.

This was Anne Hutchinson's moment of triumph. The men of power were arrayed before her—against her—yet she had won. Unlike her father, who was convicted of heresy and sent to jail, she stood her ground against the men in charge and won.

The end of her trial was near. It would not be long before she could return home, enjoy the warmth and comfort of her family, and throw herself once more into Scripture.

At this moment, Anne Hutchinson did something entirely in character. Raising her neck and leaning toward her gathered judges, she began to teach the men.

8

A FINAL ACT
OF DEFIANCE

"If you please to give me leave," the defendant told the assembled judges in the Cambridge meetinghouse, "I shall give you the ground of what I know to be true." Having denied teaching any men—and argued convincingly that her questionable statements were privileged because they were made in private—Anne Hutchinson began in public to teach.

"When I was in Old England," she started, leaping back nearly a decade in her journey of faith, "I was much troubled at the falseness of the constitution of the Church there. So far," she admitted, "as I was ready to have turned Separatist," like the earlier Plymouth settlers who had split from the English church. In 1607, when she was sixteen, they had come from Scrooby, eighty miles west of Alford, to the coast and tried to flee on ships. Caught by authorities, the Scrooby Separatists were imprisoned in Boston, Lincolnshire, and brought to trial. A year later they were allowed to move to Holland, from where they traveled to the tip of Cape Cod and then on to the more protected harbor at Plymouth.

Hutchinson, like Cotton and most of her audience in the meeting-house, finally rejected Separatism, but she remained unsettled about the quality of the preaching in the English Church, not unlike her father decades before. "Whereupon," she explained, "I set apart a day of solemn humiliation and pondering of the thing by myself, to seek direction from God." Her confidence in her ability "by myself" to solve such a problem was rare in a day when women were universally viewed as men's inferiors intellectually. As Hutchinson's younger contemporary Anne Bradstreet wrote,

> *. . . women what they are,*
> *Men have precedency and still excel.*
> *It is but vain unjustly to wage war,*
> *Men can do best, and women know it well,*
> *Preeminence in all and each is yours—*
> *Yet grant some small acknowledgment of ours.*

In the courtroom Governor Winthrop interrupted Hutchinson, noting that she had not been asked a question. There was no call for the defendant to speak her mind.

Hutchinson continued, undeterred, to describe her spiritual career and some of what she had learned when the Spirit of the Lord opened the Bible and thrust certain passages into her mind. "God did discover unto me the unfaithfulness of the churches, and the danger of them, and that none of those ministers could preach the Lord aright." Quoting 1 John 4:3, she said, "Every spirit that confesseth not that Jesus Christ is come in the flesh is not of God: but this is that spirit of Antichrist." While Puritans generally agreed that the Roman Catholic Church was the Antichrist, they used the term for all enemies of their faith.

Anne Hutchinson could freely quote the Bible in her own defense because she, like many of the men present, knew large portions of it by heart and regularly applied it to her daily life. "I marveled what this [passage] should mean," she went on, "for I knew that neither Protestants nor Papists did deny that Christ was come in the flesh. Who then was Antichrist?"

This style of tackling problems by analyzing Scripture was entirely familiar to her audience, many of whom employed it themselves in times of trouble or confusion. But her speech was out of order.

Winthrop was about to break in a second time when he thought better of it. A practical and politically astute man, he decided to wait and see where her statement might lead. A lengthy exploration of "God's dealing with her, and how He revealed himself to her, and made her know what she had to do," he realized, could achieve what he and the court up to now had been unable to do—convict her of threatening the stability of the state. Indeed, it was essential, in his opinion, that the court remove her from the colony. Years later, recalling this moment, he said that after "perceiving whereabouts she went, and seeing her very unwilling to be taken off," he "permitted her to proceed."

So Anne Hutchinson continued, lost in the moment, untroubled by the possible outcome of her words. She would describe to the court her scriptural method of resolving her spiritual troubles, as she had often been called to do for her followers at the meetings in her house. In a sense, she was pulling open the door to her parlor and inviting in the General Court. By doing this, she voided the very protection she had as a woman in the colony. Moreover, she assumed something not "comely or fit in her sex": a powerful, public role. She had acknowledged this proscription against women teaching in public when earlier she baited Winthrop, "Do you think it *not* lawful for me to teach women? And why do you call *me* to teach the court?"

Whatever force stole her wit and her caution, enabling her to teach the court, is not known. Surely she was tired. She may have been confused, angry, or even exhilarated by her success, which spurred her to pour out her truth for the world to hear.

Or perhaps she was aware that the world would listen to her as it had never listened before. For two days she had observed Simon Bradstreet and another state secretary scribbling her every word on parchment with a feather pen, an experience unknown to a woman of her time and place. The night before, she had read the transcript of her courtroom testimony. Consciously or not, she must have known these transcripts could be her legacy. Alone among the women of the day, she could leave a record of the workings of her mind.

There was and is no written account of most women's lives then, save their birth, marriage, and death dates, usually in parish records. Land deeds were signed only by husbands and, eventually, sons. Practically every historical document of the period was written by a man, quoting his or another man's words. In the paper record of early America, it is almost as though women did not exist.

Most of the words that Anne Hutchinson uttered are lost to history, as are all the words of the vast majority of her female contemporaries. Even Anne Bradstreet, who was then scribbling poems in her house not far from the courthouse, published nothing for another thirteen years, and then only across the ocean. She acknowledged this lack in a prefatory poem to "Short Matters," addressed to her children:

This book by any yet unread,
I leave for you when I am dead
That being gone, here you may find
What was your mother's living mind.

In a time when a woman's "living mind" was not considered worthy of public interest, the lure of speaking for posterity may have been too much for Anne Hutchinson to resist.

Hutchinson's trial transcripts run to roughly twenty thousand words—surely less than 1 percent of the millions of words she spoke to her husband, children, friends, and the many women she assisted in her work, but still a good deal of information by which to acquaint ourselves with her character and bent of mind. That we have this many words of Hutchinson's is a sort of miracle. It appears to be the result of a tactical error by the men in charge, for whom it would have been better, the historian Edmund Morgan noted, if Anne Hutchinson had never said a recorded word.

In part, Hutchinson felt a righteous generosity in offering her audience "the ground of what she knew to be true"—to share with them who she was and what she could do. A modern mind imagines her wishing, however naively, to be understood and accepted by the men who—she alone could see—were her peers. The literary scholar Lad Tobin described her speech as "a final act of defiance, as a final, definitive criticism of the limits and fallibility of male (and human) speech and understanding" and of our "false [sense of] personal power and control." Whatever the reason, she was going to explain to the judges of the General Court of Massachusetts how and why they came to be there.

"Now," she said confidently, "I had none to open the Scripture to me but the Lord, [who] brought to my mind another Scripture, 'He that denies the Testament, denies the death of the Testator,' from whence the Lord did give me to see that those who did not teach the New Covenant had the spirit of Antichrist."

Every one of her forty judges was silent. Seeing that Winthrop did not stop her, they watched her and listened, amazed. To a man they considered revelation through Scripture acceptable, indeed divinely inspired, but it was not a common occurrence for most of them.

Moreover, they did not expect to hear it recounted by a woman whom they also suspected of being the Antichrist.

Emboldened by the court's attentiveness, Anne Hutchinson went on. "Upon this [Scripture] he did discover the ministry unto me, and ever since—I bless the Lord—he has let me see which was the *clear* ministry and which was the *wrong*. Since that time, I confess, I have been more choice and more careful whom I heard [preach]. For after our teacher Mr. Cotton and my brother Wheelwright were put down, there was none in England that I durst hear." During the two years between Cotton and Wheelwright's departure from preaching in England and her decision to follow them, there were no ministers left from whom she felt she could learn. In her view, Jesus Christ spoke only through those two. She explained, "For the Lord has let me to distinguish between the voice of my beloved" Jesus Christ "and the voice of Moses, the voice of John Baptist, and the voice of the Antichrist, for all those voices are spoken of in Scripture."

Sensing skepticism in her audience about her claim to hear the actual voices of biblical figures, she added, "Now, if you do condemn me for speaking what in my conscience I know to be truth, I must commit myself unto the Lord."

Out of the stunned silence came the voice of the assistant Increase Nowell, of Charlestown. "How do you *know* that was the Spirit?"

She replied, "How did *Abraham* know that it was God that bid him offer his son, being a breach of the sixth commandment?"—"Thou shalt not murder."

"By an immediate voice," Thomas Dudley replied, meaning the direct voice of God, unmediated by Scripture or a minister.

"So to me," Anne Hutchinson said, "by an immediate revelation."

At the time, and in the minds of the men of the General Court, the only accepted mode of revelation was through Scripture or through a minister. Some ministers, of course, described hearing the actual voice of God. In 1634 Thomas Hooker, for example, who had led the Religious Synod the previous summer that had condemned Hutchinson's doctrine, had said, "It was revealed to me yesterday that England should be destroyed" by God unless its people reformed along Puritan lines. But for someone who was not a minister, especially a woman, to claim an immediate revelation was heresy.

"How!" Dudley exclaimed, both delighted at her admission and stunned at the arrogance of a woman who deigned to compare herself to Abraham. "An immediate revelation . . ."

"By the voice of *his own spirit* to my soul," Anne Hutchinson went on. She was admitting too much, as she may or may not have been aware. Some scholars see her as oblivious. Others sense that she knew there was nothing she could do or say to avoid banishment and that in stating her truth she might leave her voice for posterity. Based on the minor grounds for the banishment of men like Wheelwright, it seems likely that she would have been banished even if she had not taught the men. Colonial historian David Hall, who edited *The Antinomian Controversy*, the compendium of the major documents of these events, speculates that her judges "were just looking for some reason to get rid of her. Her outburst made it easy, but they would have succeeded anyway."

"I will give you another Scripture," Anne Hutchinson offered, moved by the spirit of the moment, "Jeremiah 46:27–28!"

But fear not thou, O my servant Jacob, and be not dismayed, O Israel: for, behold, I will save thee from afar off, and thy seed from the land of their captivity; and Jacob shall return, and be in rest and at ease, and none shall make him afraid. Fear thou not, O Jacob my servant, saith the Lord: for I am with thee; for I will make a full end of all the nations whither I have driven thee: but I will not make a full end of thee, but correct thee in measure; yet will I not leave thee wholly unpunished.

"Out of which," she cried, "the Lord showed me what he would do for me and the rest of his servants! And after that he did let me see the atheism of my own heart, for which I begged of the Lord that it might not remain in my heart."

In this speech she threw off the shield of her gender, which had protected her the day before, by acting as though she and her judges were equal. While a modern reader may see them as equal, this trial occurred nearly three centuries before women in America were permitted to vote.

Her feelings of anger and righteousness spilled over into apocalyptic language. "Therefore, I desire you to look to it, for you see this

Scripture fulfilled this day! And therefore I desire you, as you tender the Lord and the church and commonwealth, to consider and look what you do. You have power over my body, but the Lord Jesus hath power over my body and soul."

Revelation—receiving messages from God—was the issue in the courtroom, but the word is apt in its modern meaning too. In giving the court "the ground of what [she knew] to be true," Hutchinson shone a spotlight on her mind. Forgetting who and where she was—a defendant in a criminal proceeding—she lectured to her enemies and thus revealed herself.

"Then the Lord did reveal himself to me, sitting upon a throne of justice," she said, her anger rising, "and all the world appearing before him, and [He said that] though I must come to New England, yet I must not fear nor be dismayed. Then the Lord brought another scripture to me, Isaiah 8:9. The Lord spake this to me with a strong hand, and instructed me that I should not walk in the way of this people.

"I will give you one place more which the Lord brought to me by immediate revelations, and that doth concern *you all*. It is in Daniel 6," in which Daniel's godly worship and belief save him from certain death. "When the president [king] and princes could find nothing against Daniel, because he was faithful, they fought against him concerning the law of his God, to cast him into the lions' den. So it was revealed to me that they should plot against me," she prophesied. "But the Lord bid me not to fear, for he that delivered Daniel and the three children, his hand was not shortened. And see! This scripture [is] fulfilled this day in mine eyes!" Listening, the Reverend Thomas Weld found her "so fierce," he wrote later, that "instead of being like Daniel in the lion's den, she was rather like an antitype of the *lions* after they were let loose."

As she approached her conclusion, Anne's voice grew even stronger. "Therefore, take *heed* how you proceed against me," she warned the magistrates. "For you have no power over my body. Neither can you do me any harm, for I am in the hands of the eternal Jehovah my Savior. I am at his appointment. The bounds of my habitation are cast in Heaven. No further do I esteem of any mortal man than creatures in his hand. I fear none but the great Jehovah, which hath foretold me of these things. And I do verily believe that he will deliver me out of your hands," she said, coming to her climax with a brazen challenge. "I know that for this you go about to do to me, God will ruin *you* and your posterity, and this whole state!"

She posed herself as on God's side and against the state, while the magistrates saw themselves as with God and against her. Linking herself directly to God was heresy. While the Reformation had reduced the role of priest as mediator between human and God, most Protestants still saw ministers as necessary interpreters of God's word and believed that no man (and certainly no woman) could have direct communion with God or the Holy Spirit. It was permissible to call a storm a sign of God's anger or a safe trip a sign that he was pleased, but it was not acceptable to claim to hear God speak. Even John Winthrop believed he knew God's wishes—God had planned and approved of his coming to the New World to create a New Jerusalem, he was certain, and Winthrop himself had been chosen by God for this purpose—but the governor had never heard God's voice.

Either John Winthrop or Anne Hutchinson was deluded, he believed. It was imperative that the court punish her so the Lord would not in retribution punish the state.

Thomas Dudley asked the court, "What is the Scripture she brings?"

Israel Stoughton, one of the assistants, thought he saw the spirit of the Devil in the body of Anne Hutchinson. "Behold, I turn away from you," he said.

She replied, "But now, having seen him which is invisible, I fear not what man can do unto me."

"Daniel was delivered by miracle," Governor Winthrop told her. "Do *you* think to be delivered so, too?"

Nodding, she said, "I do here speak it before the court. I look that the Lord should deliver me by his providence" because he had said to her, "though I should meet with affliction, yet I am the same God that delivered Daniel out of the lion's den, [and] I will also deliver thee."

Thinking her damned for sure, Roger Harlackenden, an assistant from Cambridge, remarked, "I may read Scripture, and the most glorious hypocrite may read it and yet go down to Hell."

"It may be so," she agreed.

Sensing her peril, a magistrate named William Bartholomew, who had long been offended by her talk of prophecy and revelation, began to speak. He recounted that he and his wife, Mary, had hosted Anne and William Hutchinson in London before the two families sailed to America on the *Griffin*. On board the ship, he recalled, "when she came within sight of Boston, and looking upon the meanness of the place, she uttered these words: if she had not a sure word that England should be destroyed, her heart would shake. Now it seemed to me at that time very strange and witchlike that she should say so." Had she been a minister, like Thomas Hooker, prophesying the same thing, it would not have been strange at all; numerous Puritan divines—the word is from the Latin for "soothsayer" or "prophet"—felt certain that the world as they knew it was about to come to some apocalyptic end. But Hutchinson was not a divine, for no woman could be.

Witch hunting in America did not begin in 1690 in Salem Village. By 1630 it had been imported to the colonies from Europe, and twenty years later a wealth of documentation existed describing witch hunting. At least a hundred English settlers were convicted of or charged with witchcraft before 1690. Witches were commonly thought to be people—women, mostly—with satanic, or diabolical, powers, who repudiated religion and aimed to do ill. Just as God was in the soul of the saint, so the Devil abided within the witch. In the seventeenth century few challenged this view. Queen Elizabeth (who regularly consulted her court astrologer, Dr. John Dee) had passed statutes against witchcraft, as had her father, Henry VIII, and her successor, King James. Witches were linked to licentiousness and female sexuality; they had an extra nipple, it was said. They were seen as the cause of sudden, inexplicable, illnesses and deaths and various psychological disturbances. Anyone challenging the social order could be accused. According to the historian David Hall, *witch* was "a label people used to control or punish someone," and hunting witches reaffirmed the orthodox male authority whenever it was questioned, as by an Anne Hutchinson. Healers and fortune-tellers were often accused because of their social power. Women, especially those over age forty, were singled out and sanctioned disproportionately. The colonial laws against witchcraft arose from the 1604 English civil statute that defined it as a felony, punishable by hanging. Witchcraft was not considered a heresy, which was punishable by burning at the stake. As everyone in the Cambridge courtroom knew, the Devil often tempts women, but convicting a person of witchcraft required solid evidence.

Anne Hutchinson, asked to comment on Bartholomew's account of her alleged prophecy, denied it. "I do not remember that I looked upon the meanness of the place, nor did it discourage me, because I knew the bounds of my habitation were determined."

"I fear that her revelations will deceive," Bartholomew offered.

Winthrop asked him, "Have you heard of any of her revelations?"

"I remember as we were once going through [Saint] Paul's churchyard" in London, and she "was very inquisitive after revelations and said that she had never had any great thing done about her but it was revealed to her beforehand."

Anne repeated that she did not recall this.

Bartholomew quoted her saying "she was to come to New England but for Mr. Cotton's sake," which was true. He recalled her daughter Faith, then age seventeen, telling him aboard the *Griffin* that Anne "had a revelation that a young man on the ship should be saved" if he walked with God.

Eager to add his own shipboard experience of Hutchinson's heresies, the Reverend Symmes recounted her challenges to him. "Then, [she said to me,] what would you say if we should be at New England within these three weeks?" he quoted her. "I reproved her vehemently for it."

Frowning, John Endicott said, "She says she shall be delivered by a miracle. I hope the court takes notice of the *vanity* of it, and the *heat* of her spirit."

Thomas Dudley said, "I desire Mister Cotton to tell us whether you do approve of Mistress Hutchinson's revelations as she hath laid them down." The deputy governor was challenging her teacher to support her now.

"I know not whether I do understand her," John Cotton said, buying time. "But this I say: if she doth expect a deliverance in a way of *providence*," meaning in eternal time, "then I cannot deny it."

"No, sir," Dudley retorted, "we did not speak of that" sort of distinction.

"If it [her deliverance] be by way of *miracle*, then I would suspect it," Cotton conceded. A miracle was God inserting himself actively into the events of this world, while a providence could take place on the longer scale of eschatological time, including in the afterlife.

But "do you believe her revelations are *true?*" the frustrated deputy governor inquired further of Cotton, whom many present suspected of being the source of her heresies.

Cotton said quietly, "That she may have some special providence of God to help her is a thing that I cannot bear witness against." In his view, her revelations, however immediate they may have seemed to her, could be justified as true if they existed "in" or "through" or "with" Scripture, the word of God.

"Good sir," Dudley persisted, evidently irritated, "I do ask whether this *revelation* be of God or no?" In other words, Is God going to ruin every member of the court, all their descendants, and the state, as she prophesies?

"I should desire to know whether the sentence of the court will bring her to any calamity," Cotton replied, "and then I would know of her whether she expects to be delivered from that calamity by a *miracle* or a *providence* of God." Cotton turned to Hutchinson, according to Winthrop's journal, and asked her, "By a miracle do you mean a work beyond the power of nature, or only above common providence, for if you expect deliverance from this Court beyond the power of nature, then I should suspect such a revelation to be false."

She replied, "You know, when [revelation] comes, God doth not describe the way."

Changing his terminology, Cotton said to her, "Do you mean a deliverance from the sentence of the court or from the calamity of it?"

According to the trial transcript, Anne Hutchinson told her teacher and the court, "By a *providence* of God, I say, I expect to be delivered from some calamity that shall come to me." She was not claiming a miracle, only that God in his providence would protect and deliver her.

"This case is altered," Governor Winthrop announced, confident that he had heard enough about her "bottomless revelations" to move the question to a vote. "The ground work of her revelations is the *immediate* revelation of the spirit and not *by* the ministry of the word. This is the means by which she has very much abused the country that they shall look for revelations and are not bound to the ministry of the word!" The issue was no longer just her assault on the ministers; it was that she professed direct revelation from God, which Winthrop viewed as an ecclesiastical crime. The governor was relieved finally to have found—actually, received from her—a charge against her that, at least in early America, could stick. Pointing at Anne Hutchinson, he cried, "*This* has been the ground of all these tumults and troubles. *This* is the thing that has been the root of all the mischief."

"We all consent with you," most of the judges cried out.

Thomas Dudley judged that the time had come to raise the frightening outcome of religious extremism that had afflicted Germany a century before. In 1534 radical Protestants called Anabaptists had taken over the city of Münster. The siege of the city had ended in a bloodbath as the orthodox Protestants slaughtered the radicals. These Anabaptists emphasized the "light within" rather than clerical authority in judging the veracity of religious experience. Another extreme Protestant sect, the Family of Love, or Familism, centered in Holland, was associated with the concept of "free grace," or salvation unleashed from works. Familism was founded in the sixteenth century by a Dutch mystic named Hendrik Nichlaes who claimed to receive revelations from God. According to David Hall, Familists "were popularly (and incorrectly) supposed to believe in 'free love' between the sexes." In actuality, they preferred the "spirit" to the "letter" of the Bible, they denied original sin, and they believed that women and men are equal before God. "Familists laid themselves open to the accusation of advocating free love by insisting that marriage and divorce should be a simple declaration before the congregation of the church," the historian Selma Williams observed. Moreover, they "denied the immortality of the soul and therefore the existence of heaven and hell, or afterlife." While the Familists and Anabaptists neither preached nor supported promiscuity, they were, at least in the minds of the orthodox Puritan magistrates in Cambridge, purveyors of licentiousness and free love.

Dudley suggested that Hutchinson subscribed to one or both of these sects. "These disturbances that have come among the Germans have been all grounded upon revelationship," he said, "and they have stirred up their hearers to take up arms against their prince and to cut the throats one of another. Whether the Devil may inspire the same in their hearts here I know not, for I am *fully* persuaded that Mistress Hutchinson is deluded by the Devil, because the spirit of God speaks truth in all his servants."

"I am persuaded," Governor Winthrop said, "that the revelation she brings forth is delusion."

"We all believe it!" more than thirty magistrates cried. "We all believe it!"

Moving swiftly, Winthrop noted that "the court hath thus declared itself," having heard "what she by the providence of God hath declared freely without being asked." And "they would now consider what is to be done to her."

9

NOT FIT FOR
OUR SOCIETY

Even after the Great and General Court of Massachusetts voted over-whelmingly to convict Anne Hutchinson, several men stood to speak on her behalf. Thirty-nine-year-old William Coddington, the wealthiest man in Boston, who had lost his magistracy the day before because he supported her, declared, "I do not, for my own part, see any equity in the court in all your proceedings." Stating what now seems obvious, Coddington went on, "Here is no law of God that she hath broken, nor any law of the country that she hath broke. Therefore I would entreat you to consider whether those things you have alleged against her deserve such censure as you are about to pass."

William Colburn, a prominent merchant who was the town assessor, added, "I [too] dissent from censure of banishment."

Ignoring these men, Governor Winthrop returned to the issue of the oath, which no longer seemed necessary now that he had convinced most of the judges that the defendant was guilty of claiming false revelations. But Winthrop wanted to strengthen his case. He predicted that the ministers' objections to the oath would be less strenuous now. "We desire the elders to take their oaths," he said, prompting "a great whispering" among the ministers. Some drew back; others stepped forward.

Gamely, the Reverend John Eliot said, "If the court calls us out to swear, we will swear." Winthrop declared that two ministers would be sufficient. Eliot and Weld raised their hands and took the oath—"I swear to tell the truth and nothing but the truth as far as I know; so help me God"—and repeated what they recalled her saying about the inadequacies of their preaching: they preached a covenant of works, they were not able ministers of the New Testament, and they were not sealed with the Spirit.

John Cotton saw that his disciple was doomed. As if in a flash, he saw clearly what before had been obscure: she was proud, too sure of her own election. He remembered worrying on occasion that she strengthened her faith through private meditations, apart from the public ministry, and that she was more censorious of others than a servant of God should be. Earlier that year, he remembered, he had "dealt with Mistress Hutchinson of the erroneousness of these tenets and the injury done to myself in fathering them upon me." She so "clearly discerned her justification" that she had to work to avoid pride, he later explained. She was "puffed up with her own parts," overly confident of her salvation. In describing her thus, Cotton might have been describing himself, since he had deigned to distinguish between "lilies" and "thorns."

"I remember," Cotton said in the courtroom, joining the chorus of her challengers, "she said she should be delivered by God's providence, whether now or at another time she knew not."

This may have shocked Hutchinson, who had anticipated his continuing support. After all, he and she had shared evangelical work, preaching God's word and saving souls, for more than two decades. She had never strayed from his doctrine, she felt, and always saw her views as consistent with his.

But the ministers were not entirely surprised by Cotton's shift. Nine weeks earlier, in late August, they had reconciled with him. At the Religious Synod in Cambridge, at private meetings of which Hutchinson was unaware, they had persuaded Cotton to abandon his grievances. Near the end of the synod, at which the ministers had condemned eighty-two errors, there were only five points remaining between Cotton and Wheelwright and the rest. In a spirit of reconciliation, Cotton had conceded on these. Wheelwright's refusal to concede had led to his banishment, while Cotton's compromises had brought him back into communion with most of his colleagues. As he had done in England, according to the historian Janice Knight, Cotton relied on "the wisdom of strategic self-revisions [and] outward compliance [to] secure an essential freedom of opinion." In this way Cotton "kept his pulpit, chastening his rhetoric without revising the substance of his own doctrine."

In the courtroom, the Reverend Hugh Peter publicly welcomed Cotton back into the fold. "I profess I thought Mr. Cotton would never have took her part."

Seeing even Cotton distance himself from her, Governor Winthrop determined to read the verdict. "The court hath already declared themselves satisfied concerning the things you hear, and concerning the *troublesomeness* of her spirit and the *danger* of her course amongst us, which is not to be suffered. Therefore, if it be the mind of the court that Mistress Hutchinson for these things that appear before us is *unfit for our society*, and if it be the mind of the court that she shall be banished out of our liberties and imprisoned till she be sent away, let them hold up their hands."

All the magistrates but three—Colburn, Coddington (whose vote should not have counted, as he had been removed from the court), and William Jennison, a deputy from Watertown—raised their hands, according to the transcript. Unlike her father's judges at Saint Paul's, these magistrates had a public vote. In this early approximation of democratic justice, the Great and General Court of Massachusetts found Anne Hutchinson guilty as charged and "not fit for our society."

Winthrop did not define her crime, which appears to have been beside the point. As the literary scholar Lad Tobin noted, even before her judges had "settled on a charge, they were certain of the verdict . . . guilty." The journal kept by the legally trained governor suggests that the court considered her guilty of two crimes. The first was heresy—the ecclesiastical crime for which her father was imprisoned, a half century earlier, by a Church of England court—on account of her revelations. In deeming her a heretic, they neglected to specify which doctrine of the Church of England she had violated. These doctrines had been established, in 1571, under Queen Elizabeth, as the Thirty-Nine Articles of Religion, not one of which refers to revelation. Hutchinson's second crime was sedition, or resisting lawful authority, because she had questioned and criticized the colonial ministers.

English common law had a shadowy role in these proceedings. While it underlay much of the judges' thinking, it did not bind them as it would have in English courts. As Francis Bremer explained in his biography of John Winthrop, the governor actively opposed the idea of creating a fixed code of colonial laws. He disagreed with Dudley and others who saw codification as a way of ensuring social stability and bringing colonial life into accord with the mandates of the Bible. Winthrop's opposition reflected "his background in the common law, the proper administration of which was, to Englishmen like himself, the essence of the 'ancient constitution,' which at this time was seen as a framework setting forth the obligations and responsibilities of the subject more than as a guarantee of rights," according to Bremer. Winthrop "expressed a preference for judging cases according to circumstances and allowing the law to develop through the accumulation of such precedents," as in the common-law tradition. He also argued that a code of colonial laws was prohibited by the charter, which required making "no laws repugnant to the laws of England." Bremer notes, "Much of what was done in New England was, indeed, repugnant to the laws of England, but as long as that practice was customary and not mandated by state, the letter of the charter provision was not violated." Even in the Bible commonwealth, Winthrop was able to exploit his extensive training in English common law.

"Mistress Hutchinson," he called out, "the sentence of the court you hear is that you are banished from our jurisdiction as being a woman not fit for our society, and are to be imprisoned till the court shall send you away."

Stricken but not silenced, Anne Hutchinson inquired, "I desire to know wherefore [why] I am banished."

"Say no more," Winthrop commanded her. "The court knows wherefore and is satisfied."

In Nathaniel Hawthorne's version of the foregoing event, "Mrs. Hutchinson" in *Tales and Sketches*, "the excitement of the contest" makes Anne Hutchinson's heart "rise and swell within her, and she bursts forth into eloquence."

> She tells them of the long unquietness which she had endured in England, perceiving the corruption of the church, and yearning for a purer and more perfect light, and how, in a day of solitary prayer, that light was given; she claims for herself the peculiar power of distinguishing between the chosen of man and the Sealed of Heaven, and affirms that her gifted eye can see the glory round the foreheads of the Saints, sojourning in their mortal state. She declares herself commissioned to separate the true shepherds from the false, and denounces present and future judgments on the land, if she be disturbed in her celestial er-

rand. Thus the accusations are proved from her own mouth. Her judges hesitate, and some speak faintly in her defense; but, with a few dissenting voices, sentence is pronounced, bidding her go out from among them, and trouble the land no more.

In seventeenth-century Cambridge, the judges filed out of the meetinghouse, and the crowd dispersed. Outside, on the market square, Anne's supporters gathered around her and Will. No one knew where she would have to go or when.

Anne and Will retraced their steps of two mornings before, traveling home on foot across fields of ice and snow. They passed the cow common and exited the town gate. The ox pasture and planting field to the right were fallow and coated with frost. The couple followed the Indian path across the fields of Cambridge, north of the marsh bordering the river, heading toward Charlestown and its ferry landing, the route to Boston.

Scrub grass covered the gently rolling landscape, on which few trees grew. The Hutchinsons passed land farmed by their neighbors on Shawmut to supplement their house gardens. To the south were the Great Marsh and the Charles River. At a deserted Indian village, untilled fields and scattered corpses and skulls testified to the plague of smallpox imported by their countrymen a decade or more before the Hutchinsons arrived.

The sun was near the horizon when they reached the Charlestown dock. Will called for the ferryman. Thomas Marshall, a stocky, irascible widower in his forties, emerged from a shed carrying a long wooden oar. They gave him two shillings for their passage. He rowed them across the choppy mouth of the Charles toward Shawmut. To the east, the sea was wrinkled and cold. The ferry landed, and the Hutchinsons walked the last mile to their house. It was "by duskish" before they arrived home.

At the meetinghouse in Cambridge, the magistrates met privately after the trial to decide what to do with Mistress Hutchinson. Having won the "first great struggle for control" of Massachusetts, these men would show "little mercy to the vanquished," observed David Hall, the colonial historian. For Winthrop and his allies, the conflict that had roiled the colony for more than a year was over. They would move quickly to solidify their power and further reduce Hutchinson's. That night, one imagines, Winthrop and Dudley and the orthodox ministers slept better than they had in months.

In the next few weeks the General Court removed all Hutchinsonians from power. On November 15 Will's brother Sergeant Edward Hutchinson was jailed for a night, disfranchised, fined, and "discharged from any public office" for "using contemptuous speeches" and signing the Wheelwright petition. The same day the court disfranchised, fined, and "discharged from any public office" Sergeant William Baulston for signing "the seditious libel called a remonstrance or petition." (Only Anne's relative was sent to jail.) The top three Antinomians, Hutchinson, Wheelwright, and Aspinwall, were already banished. Eight other men close to her—Coggeshall; Baulston; Edward Hutchinson; the blacksmith, Richard Gridley; the ferryman, Thomas Marshall; William Dyer; William Dinely; and Captain John Underhill—were disfranchised for signing the petition and lost their "public places." Ten other signers acknowledged their "sin," had their names scratched off the remonstrance, and so remained freemen.

Five days later every man who had signed the petition was disarmed. Even the Pequot War hero Captain Underhill had to turn in his sword. They were ordered to surrender "all such guns, pistols, swords, powder, shot, and match as they shall be owners of, or have in their custody, upon pain of ten pounds for every default." Disarming a man was a severe punishment, especially as the court had just ordered in March that because of increased fear of natives on account of the Pequot War all men over eighteen had to carry muskets "furnished with match, powder, and bullets." Of the seventy-five men disarmed now, fifty-eight were from Boston, five from Roxbury, two from Charlestown, five from Salem, three from Newbury, and two from Ipswich. After the disarmament order, thirty-five more petition signers acknowledged their fault and were allowed to keep their guns: "If any that are to be disarmed acknowledge their sin in subscribing to the seditious libel, or do not justify it, but acknowledge it evil to two magistrates, they shall be thereby freed from delivering in their arms."

"In what amounted to a coup," according to the historian Janice Knight, "the Winthrop party thus guaranteed against their possible ouster by election or by violence. Truly extraordinary by any standard, these tactics of exiling the opposition, restricting new settlement, and limiting eligibility for public office to those residing in the Bay for at least one year (meaning that only survivors of this partisan scrutiny would be allowed the privileges of freemanship) ensured that the party elected in 1637 would hold power for a good time to come."

Finally, the Massachusetts court determined to build the colony's first college as a way of minimizing Hutchinson's threat. "The college," which would later be named for the wealthy newcomer John Harvard, "is ordered to be at Newtown," the court stated on November 15. At a college, orthodox ministers would be able to indoctrinate young men before they fell under the Antinomian spell. While the court had discussed the prospect of a college for some months, there was now a pressing need to begin construction.

Just over a year earlier, in August 1636, Governor Vane and the court had granted four hundred pounds toward the creation of a college so that the first graduates of Boston Latin could continue their study. Boston Latin School, founded in 1635, was just above the Hutchinson and Winthrop houses, on School Street, at a corner of what is now Boston's Old City Hall. A year later, just days before Hutchinson's trial, the court—"dreading to leave an illiterate ministry"—appropriated further funds for the college that did not yet exist. In a nod to Newtown, which through the efforts of Pastor Shepard had avoided all Hutchinsonian doctrine, the college would be located there. Modeled on such English colleges as Emmanuel College, Cambridge, it would offer Traditional Arts, Philosophies, and Learned Tongues. Newtown itself they renamed Cambridge.

The first college building, of timber, clay mortar, and thatch, was erected in the spring of 1638. Meanwhile, a sickly, Cambridge-educated immigrant named John Harvard bequeathed half his estate, roughly seven hundred pounds, and his extensive library to the fledgling Congregationalist college. Harvard, the son of a butcher and tavern owner in London, had arrived in Boston in 1637, at age thirty, and fallen ill. He died at home in Charlestown on September 14, 1638, after which the college was named Harvard in honor of his large gift.

But Anne Hutchinson was the true midwife of Harvard. "As a result of her heresy," the Reverend Peter Gomes, Plummer Professor of Christian Morals at Harvard, wrote in *Harvard Magazine* in 2002,

the colony determined to provide for the education of a new
generation of ministers and theologians who would secure New
England's civil and theological peace against future seditious
Mrs. Hutchinsons "when our present ministers shall lie in the
dust," as the inscription on the [college's] Johnston Gate puts
it. At Harvard we may seek her memorial in vain, but without
her it is difficult to do justice to the motivating impulse of our
foundation. Inadvertent midwife to a college founded in part to
protect posterity from her errors, Anne Marbury Hutchinson,
ironically, would be more at home at Harvard today than any of
her critics.

Five days after "ordering" the college, the General Court created
Harvard's first board of overseers, or trustees. The first board comprised six politicians (Winthrop, Dudley, Bellingham, Humphrey, Harlackenden, and Stoughton) and six clergymen (Cotton, Weld, Wilson,
Davenport, Shepard, and Peter).

In the minds of the ministers, the college allowed them to fulfill
their essentially pedagogical role. Puritan worship was in part an at-
tempt to restore the early primitive Christian church of the Acts and
Epistles, which followed closely the gatherings of Jews with their rabbi,
or teacher. Samuel Eliot Morison described this form of worship in *The
Founding of Harvard College:* "Neither the weekday lectures nor the
Lord's Day assemblies of the Puritans were services of worship, as worship is understood by Catholics; they were, literally, meetings of the
faithful to offer up prayers in matters of common concern, and to hear
the Sacred Scripture read, interpreted, and expounded by an expert."
That description applies also to Anne's religious meetings—the problem
the ministers were struggling to rectify. She functioned as a teacher,
rabbi, or minister—something no woman could do. Morison continued,

Glorifying God by the singing of psalms was incidental; even
the Lord's Supper was not conceived of as a sacrament or act of
worship, but as a commemorative observance. Hence the teaching function, implicit in every Christian ministry, was explicit
and almost exclusive in the Puritan ministry. And in those simple days teachers were supposed to know the subject they pro-

fessed, not merely to be trained in teaching methods. Hence no amount of godliness, goodwill, or inspiration could compensate for want of learning. Down to the American Revolution and beyond, only a "learned" minister could qualify for a Congregational church in the Puritan colonies. He must be "learned" not only in the Sacred Tongues, but in the vast literature of exegesis and interpretation that had grown up around the Scripture. There was nothing more dangerous and detestable, in the eyes of orthodox Puritans, than an unlearned preacher presuming to interpret Scripture out of his own head.

How much more "dangerous and detestable," then, if that "unlearned preacher" were a woman.

Before concluding their November 1637 General Court meeting, the men ordered that a summary of the trial just concluded be written in the court record. Omitting her first name, they wrote, "Mrs. —— Hutchinson, the wife of Mr. William Hutchinson, being convented [brought into court] for traducing the ministers and their ministry in the country, she declared voluntarily her revelations for her ground, and that she should be delivered and the Court ruined, with their posterity, and thereupon was banished, and in the meanwhile was committed to Mr. Joseph Weld (of Roxbury) until the Court shall dispose of her."

A few days later Anne was told she could remain in Massachusetts for the winter, under house arrest, in Roxbury, two miles from her home. The court had two reasons for letting her stay. Her innate feminine weakness was one. Williams and Wheelwright could be sent into the woods at any time of year, but a woman could not. The second reason was that she was now a heretic. As such, she had to be dealt with also by her church, the self-acknowledged church of saints.

That church, in communion with all the churches of Massachusetts Bay, would try her on the third lecture day—Thursday—in March 1638, the first month in which winter might be expected to loose its clutch, allowing ministers and elders from outlying towns like Salem and Ipswich to attend. The ministers would admonish her, hoping to cleanse her of her sin. If she could not be cleansed, they would consider excommunication, the process by which the church of saints removed those who were not worthy of membership.

In the meantime, over the winter, the ministers might soften Anne Hutchinson's heart, convince her to recant, and thus end the matter without having to carry out this dire punishment. Her jailer during the winter would be Joseph Weld, a brother of the Reverend Thomas Weld, one of her most vituperative challengers, who was eager to start convincing her of the errors of her ways. Born in England in 1595, Pastor Weld was a former Separatist who had gone to Holland before coming to Massachusetts in 1632. He and his brother Joseph owned extensive tracts of land in Roxbury, the town just southwest of the Shawmut Peninsula, on the mainland below the slender neck of Boston. The Reverend Weld was accumulating land in Roxbury at such a rate that by 1652, when he was away in Cromwellian England as a colonial emissary, he held "eight parcels" in Roxbury amounting to nearly five hundred acres, including "two acres of land with his dwelling house, barn and other outhouses, as well as yards, gardens and orchards," fifteen acres of "meadow and marsh," and thirty-two acres of "upland and marsh."

During Anne's stay at the Welds', her husband was expected to pay for her upkeep. "The town of Roxbury is required to take order for the safe custody of Mrs. Hutchinson," the court record stated, "and if any charge arise, to be defrayed by her husband." She could not work, "walk abroad," or entertain visitors except her immediate family, who in winter could make the two-mile trip only occasionally, with difficulty.

In the long view of history, the just-concluded trial was "the least attractive episode" in John Winthrop's entire career. "In nearly every exchange of words [Anne Hutchinson] defeated him, and the other members of the General Court with him," Edmund Morgan concluded in *The Puritan Dilemma*, his study of Winthrop.

> There was no jury, and no apparent procedure. The magistrates (and even some of the deputies) flung questions at the defendant, and exploded in blustering anger when the answers did not suit them. Even Winthrop was unable to maintain his usual poise in the face of Mrs. Hutchinson's clever answers to his loaded questions.

Morgan noted that the governor fought Hutchinson "by fair means and foul. . . . Anne Hutchinson was his intellectual superior in everything except political judgment, in everything except the sense of what was possible in this world." This seems apt, for her greatest concern was not this world but the next. At the same time, she and Winthrop both seemed to lack the wisdom that Learned Hand, the great twentieth-century judge, described as "the spirit which is not sure it is right"—a lack that appears to have been endemic among Puritans.

To their credit, both Winthrop and Hutchinson behaved during the trial in a manner consistent with their previous goals and behavior. Winthrop may have been blundering, shortsighted, harsh, and even cruel, but his actions were entirely consistent with his life's goal—ensuring the security of Massachusetts. Nothing mattered more to him than the colony's survival. It was, after all, God's will, and anything that threatened it had to be removed. He had repeatedly compromised in pursuit of this goal, suppressing his differences with politicians such as Dudley and Vane. In Hutchinson's trial, while he did not serve the goals of fairness or (to use a modern term) civil rights, he showed himself as he was, a man deeply concerned with the practical matter of creating a new country in line with his understanding of the common good.

Anne Hutchinson too proved consistent to her life's goal. Her focus all along was the salvation of the soul—not the commonwealth, which she now saw as doomed. Throughout her career as nurse, mother, and wife, she aimed straight at God, who was the center of her life. Every day she strove to do his work, studying his words and living in his way, and her behavior in court was entirely consistent with this.

The "saintly" John Cotton was less consistent with his previous goals. He had spent decades encouraging his best pupil to evangelize and explicate for private audiences his radical ideas about grace, and then he hesitated hardly a day before joining the chorus of accusers when she was publicly attacked. At least in the courtroom, John Cotton was a man who served and saved himself.

Nathaniel Hawthorne is said to have modeled the Reverend Arthur Dimmesdale, in *The Scarlet Letter*, on John Cotton, and the vivid character may illuminate the elusive man. Dimmesdale's voice, Hawthorne writes, "was in itself a rich endowment; insomuch as that a listener, comprehending nothing of the language in which the preacher spoke, might still have been swayed to and fro by the mere tone and cadence.

Like all other music, it breathed passion and pathos, and emotions high or tender, in a tongue native to the human heart, wherever educated."

Scholars have anguished over Cotton, whom they describe variously as an honorable man, a scoundrel, and finally—David Hall's word—an "enigmatic" man. Everett Emerson, a biographer of Cotton, noted that many believed "he failed his follower Anne Hutchinson because he was not willing to become a martyr for his dedication to the power of the Holy Spirit." In contrast, the historian Daniel Boorstin noted that had Cotton and her judges treated her differently, "they might have merited praise as precursors of modern liberalism, but they might never have helped found a nation." Edith Curtis, a biographer of Hutchinson, concluded that "John Cotton provoked bitterness, for he saw the light, considered the effect, and then deliberately helped to put it out."

But there is no doubt as to how the defendant acquitted herself. "The record of [Anne Hutchinson's] trial, if it is proper to dignify the procedure with that name," Edmund Morgan observed, "is one of the few documents in which her words have been recorded, and it reveals a proud, brilliant woman put down by men who had judged her in advance. The purpose of the trial was doubtless to make her conviction seem to follow due process of law, but it might have been better for the reputation of her judges if they had simply banished her unheard."

Fortunately for us, they did not. By trying Hutchinson and carefully recording and saving her extensive testimony, the judges inadvertently gave her what few women of her time enjoyed: a lasting voice. The trial that led to her imprisonment also enables her to speak to us, nearly four centuries hence.

10

THE HUSBAND OF MISTRESS HUTCHINSON

The morning after the trial, Anne and William Hutchinson awoke in the second-floor bedchamber of their own house to the normal sounds of a market day. There was the clanking of carts rolling up and down the rutted main road that lay between them and the Winthrops' front door, the market vendors' faint shouts, and the raucous caws of the harbor gulls scavenging among the stalls.

Outside was an ordinary Thursday, but inside the house was quieter than ever before. There was none of the usual morning mayhem: the giggles accompanying the games that Mary and Katherine orchestrated for the littler ones in the bedchamber next door; the shouts of young William and Samuel wrestling below; or the thuds as the older boys piled the mattresses that lay each night on the parlor floor. This morning, every member of the family was afraid.

As for Anne, as she faced the day, how much sweeter the innumerable pleasures of her domestic life must have seemed now that they would soon be gone! The excitement and bustle of her children, with their clever questions and their sparkling eyes. The fruits of her gardens, which only now, after three harvests, were taking on a life of their own. The close reading of Scripture and sermon she shared with her followers in the parlor. The luxury of lolling in bed with Will on the rare morning that the little ones left them alone. . . .

There would be no lolling in bed this morning, no wrapping her arms and legs around the sweet man beside her on the two mattresses piled on the floor. Will Hutchinson, now fifty-one, had tousled gray hair and a salty beard, and his efforts to be a loyal follower to her surely showed on his face. The trial had been tiring; exhausting was the prospect of a winter in which to find and create a new home for his family. Only three years before, he had traversed the ocean for Anne and supervised the construction of this wonderful house. Now he had to do it again, under duress, with an even larger family and an absent wife.

If Anne "had rather been a husband than a wife," in the words of the Reverend Peter, then Will was in many respects the ideal Puritan wife—kind, devoted, constant, and remarkably fertile. Nathaniel Hawthorne imagined that the husband of "Mrs. Hutchinson" must "have been (like most husbands of celebrated women) a mere insignificant appendage of his mightier wife." Indeed, colonial leaders sometimes wondered what was lacking in the man. Winthrop described Will Hutchinson as "a man of very mild temper and weak parts, and wholly guided by his wife." These statements speak more of Winthrop's and Hawthorne's mistrust of female power than of anything in Will, who left far fewer recorded words than did his wife. Survived by neither diary nor letters, Will marked his simple, solid signature on a few land deeds and other legal documents. The quotations attributed to him in other men's journals number fewer than fifty words. Whatever the essence of his character, his marriage to Anne was one of the great pairings in history, sustaining both partners remarkably for more than forty years.

William Hutchinson was born in Alford, Lincolnshire, on August 14, 1586, the first child of a wealthy young textile merchant, Edward Hutchinson, and his wife, Susan. The boy's paternal grandfather, John Hutchinson, had been mayor of Lincoln, the county's largest town. A hill town founded by the Romans in the first century CE, Lincoln was (and is) overseen by the vast Gothic cathedral that was until 1549 the tallest building in Europe. Saint Hugh's body and the heart and viscera of Queen Eleanor of Castile, wife of Edward I, are interred beneath its nave. Mayor John Hutchinson's son Edward married Susan in 1585 and settled thirty-six miles from Lincoln in her hometown of Alford, then a village of several hundred souls and roughly seventy thatched houses set around a large market square. Edward Hutchinson opened a textile store on the square, where on Tuesdays and Fridays the market was held. A stone's throw away, across the main road that ran just north of the square, was Saint Wilfrid's Church, where Francis Marbury preached to the townspeople, including Will and his ten younger siblings.

Will Hutchinson was five years older than Anne Marbury, but they grew up together, meeting at Sunday services, the market, the biannual fair, and the occasional mystery play at her father's church. With their siblings and friends they explored the fields surrounding Alford and the adjacent Wolds, which are crisscrossed with walking paths. Both families inhabited the thatched mud-and-stud houses that were common in Lincolnshire before brick was widely available. These wood frame houses had walls of wattle and daub—a mixture of the hair of a horse, goat, or cow, lime, and mud plaster. The upright timbers stood on staddle stones, which prevented the earth's dampness from rising into the wood. Each roof was thatched with marsh reeds and straw, which was always a fire hazard. Most mud-and-stud houses had a chimney lined with brick, one or two fireplaces, two stories (often with dormers on the second floor), and multiple chambers, or rooms. The Marbury house likely had three rooms, and that of the Hutchinsons, several more. Edward Hutchinson made good money importing and selling fine cloth, while Francis Marbury's income was limited to his church and school salaries and small allowances. Both families kept animals, including chickens, pigs, sheep, and cows, but the Hutchinsons could afford far more, including a large herd of sheep and several horses. Like the Marburys, the Hutchinsons were nonconformist Christians, preferring less adornment and better preaching in church. Around the age of six, William and his younger brothers went to the Reverend Marbury's grammar school.

An amiable, easygoing youth, Will was apparently drawn to Anne's fire and light, her mix of virtue and passion. She was the perfect complement to his calm, passive nature. According to local history, the couple was sufficiently close by the time the Marbury family left for London, when Anne was fourteen, that Will was heartbroken. Now nineteen, he had completed grammar school—he knew some Latin and possibly Greek and could write—and was working alongside his father. His position as a clothier enabled him to justify occasional trips to London, the center of trade in a nation whose leading industry was cloth manufacture. As often as possible during Anne's years away, Will made the 140-mile trip to London on horseback, which took at least three days.

London's textile market, Cheapside, was a short walk north of the Reverend Marbury's church. In addition to purchasing fine cloth from the far reaches of the world, Will could escort Anne on a tour of such pleasures of post-Elizabethan London as street jugglers, tumblers, and balladeers. Will wore the relatively drab attire and plain black felt hat of Puritans, but many men of London preferred leather jerkins with pinked decoration, doublets, and hats with feathers, and they carried daggers and swords in leather scabbards. To country people like Will and Anne, this was a new and fascinating world.

Some of the fascination verged on disgust. The Marburys' church was so close to the Thames that in certain weather the noises of the sinful south side were audible: the roar of the drunken crowd at the bull run and the bearbaiting ring; the screams emanating from William Shakespeare's open-air Globe Theatre, which in warm months ran plays every afternoon except Sunday (when the predominant sound was the ringing of hundreds of church bells); and the cries of the vendors at Borough Market. A theater, to a Puritan, was a monument to folly, a den of iniquity, and a hotbed of drunkenness, prostitution, and the heresies uttered on the stage. The Marburys doubtless avoided Shakespeare's plays, several of which were performed for the first time during the family's years in London. However, the playwright regularly passed Saint Martin in the Vintry on his daily walk from his apartment on Muggle (now Monkwell) Street, well north of the river, to his work on the south side and back again. In a 1603 sermon at Saint Paul's cross, during an outbreak of the plague, a Puritan preacher said that "the cause of plague is sin, and the cause of sin are plays, so the cause of plague is plays."

For the Marburys, pleasure was found in arguing over Scripture. They gathered at the table in the single room of their new home, the vestry extending south from the altar, from which it was separated by a heavy wooden door. This large room contained a fireplace, a privy, a cupboard, and a wooden table, which they pushed aside at night to place mattresses on the floor. Led by the vigorous, demanding Reverend Marbury, who was known as "crusty, disputatious, and strongwilled," Anne "mastered all the fine points of Anglican and Calvinist theology. She read her father's books of theology and sharpened her native intellectual ability through regular discussions with her father and siblings," according to a local Alford history. "She was remarkable for her nimble wit, her strong assertiveness in debate, her bold presentation of her own position, and her genuine compassion in helping other women both by medical care and by psychological and spiritual counseling." She found time to assist her mother in bringing babies into the world and was thus trained as a nurse and midwife. "She had good reason to learn all she could about health care, for the body, she believed, was the temple of the soul, and for the reborn it became the dwelling place of the Holy Spirit. Physical birth and spiritual rebirth were logically connected in her thinking." Now the oldest child at home (her surviving older sisters, Susan and Mary, had moved away), she no doubt assisted at the births of her younger siblings Thomas, in 1607, Anthony, in 1608, and Katherine, in 1610.

While Anne was in London, William entered his twenties and discovered, to everyone's surprise but his, that there was no one else he wanted to marry. He had to convince his parents, whose reluctance arose from her family's lack of money. Where the Hutchinsons had wealth in abundance, the Marburys had wit, and for Will and Anne this proved a good match.

Francis Marbury's death early in 1611, which was heralded by the peculiar tolling of the five (rather than the usual six) bells of Saint Martin in the Vintry, threw his family into disarray. After his burial, Anne and her mother and her ten younger siblings still at home—ranging from sixteen-year-old Francis to baby Katherine, who was less than a year—needed quickly to vacate the vicarage for the new rector's family. The Marburys spent the following year camping out at Saint Mary Woolchurch Haw and Saint Mary Woolnoth, a combined parish a few blocks north, alongside that church's minister and his family. This was tight quarters even by London standards. Seven months after Francis's passing, death struck again. Anne's nine-year-old brother, Daniel, was buried that September just west of the Vintry parish at Saint Peter, Paul's Wharf, "in the churchyard at the further end by the bones."

The family began to disperse, although Bridget remained in London for several years, and then she moved to Hertfordshire. Francis's will, which he had signed on January 30, 1611, gave each of his surviving children 200 marks—nearly 140 pounds—when they came of age. At age twenty-one, they could remain with their mother or "receive their portions and dwell where they would choose."

Will Hutchinson soon asked twenty-year-old Anne for her hand. The couple was married at Saint Mary Woolnoth in August 1612, less than a month after her twenty-first birthday. Anne wore a bone corset and her best dress. After the simple wedding ceremony, the church warden penned in his ornate script, "On the ninth day of the same month were married William Hutchinson of Alford in the country of Lincoln, mercer [merchant], and Anne Marbury daughter of Francis Marbury, minister, per license," meaning that banns had not been read three times in a church, in this case because the couple presently lacked a home parish.

The Alford to which Anne returned after a seven-year absence was much the same as it had been when she was a child. The preacher at Saint Wilfrid's Church was now George Scortreth, one of Lincolnshire's "wonderfully" verbose lecturers, who had been appointed upon Marbury's move to London. An ordained clergyman with a master's degree, Scortreth was "a moderate man, and popular with all parties." In 1617, upon the death of Vicar Joseph Overton (who had served through Marbury's years there), Scortreth became vicar of Alford, where he remained until his death in 1645. "As early as 1614 many of the [local] lecturers refused to pray for the king, and, like the Reverend John Cotton, had quite disregarded the liturgy of the Church of England." Scortreth, who would baptize Anne and Will's children in Alford, was more moderate than Cotton, for he used the orthodox Book of Common Prayer.

Another change in Alford was the grand new manor house rising up alongside the main road just west of the church and the market square. It was Alford's first building with an exterior of brick. With eight or nine spacious rooms, it was far larger than any other dwelling in the town, including those of well-off gentry like the Hutchinsons. According to local history, a relative of Sir Robert Christopher, the seventeenth-century knight entombed in marble beside the altar of Saint Wilfrid's church, built the manor house for the combined manors of the tiny towns of Rigsby, Ailby, and Tothby. Its main timbers were felled in 1611, according to modern dendrochronology, so the house was under construction as Anne and Will began their married life.

The couple furnished for themselves a cozy mud-and-stud cottage, in which they anticipated growing old. They had the money for fine carpets, a four-poster bed with feather-stuffed pillows (rather than straw pallets on boards), pewter dishes, Chinese pottery, and silver spoons. Will's textile business, which he eventually inherited from his father, prospered. Widely respected, he was asked to serve as a governor of the local grammar school. From 1623 until 1632 he appears in town records as a "prominent resident" and "chief citizen," as had Francis Marbury for the years 1595 to 1605. Will enjoyed farming and kept a large herd of sheep. He had several house servants and farm laborers, and eventually two unmarried female cousins, Anne and Frances Freiston, moved in to help care for the family.

Anne also earned money working as a midwife and healer, for which she grew a large herb garden. While every woman then grew and distilled herbs for daily use, mostly medicinal, a midwife had more expertise than most. She made syrups, decoctions, lotions, and tonics from the simples (herbs used individually for their curative powers) and worts (those used collectively) in her garden. Among these were betony (to reduce labor pains), columbine (to speed delivery), horehound (to ease labor), tansy (to prevent miscarriage), pennyroyal (to induce abortion), comfrey (to relieve nursing sores), stinging nettle (to increase the flow of breast milk), lady's mantle (an aid to conception and healthy pregnancy), the towering angelica (to ward off the plague), lemon balm (to "purge melancholy," making it, along with lavender, gillyflowers, and thyme, an early antidepressant), clary (its seeds were crushed into a paste to extract thorns), borage (to fortify the heart), heartsease (against syphilis and epilepsy), elecampane (for coughs), garlic (to relieve aches and pains), bugle (to cure nightmares), feverfew (to reduce fever), herb Robert (a diuretic), monkshood (to exterminate rats and other vermin), spearmint ("friendly to a weak stomach"), and sage (to quicken the memory). Like Will, Anne spent much of the year outside, planting in spring, weeding in summer, and harvesting in fall.

In the early 1620s, as a natural extension of her nursing and her efforts to educate her children in Scripture and theology, she began running meetings similar to those she would run in Massachusetts. She gained wide respect among local women for her thoughtful analysis of Ecclesiastes, the letters of the apostle Paul, and the book of Revelation, as well as of recent sermons. She brought to these conventicles some of the exegetical skills her father had used while composing sermons. While a woman could never climb to a pulpit and preach, she could teach the Bible at home, to her children or an audience of her female neighbors. Will was happy to go along with these meetings. While Anne found her greatest solace in the company of Christ Jesus, Will was most comfortable with her.

Throughout their marriage, Will and Anne had children at a remarkable rate. Roughly every eighteen months for the twenty-two years following her wedding, Anne gave birth. In a time when one in two infants did not survive his or her first year, the Hutchinsons had fifteen sons and daughters who lived well past infancy. In the same parish record book that contains her birth—"1591, July, Anna filia Francesci Meurberi bapt. 20th day," on a page notably faded by multiple examinations over four centuries—are the records of the births of her first fourteen children:

Edward, "filius Gulielmi Hutchinson,"
baptized June 28, 1613

"Susanna, filia Gulielmi Hutchinson"—Susan—
baptized September 4, 1614

Son Richard on January 8, 1616

Daughter Faith on August 14, 1617

Bridget on January 15, 1619

Francis on December 24, 1620

Elizabeth on February 17, 1622

William on June 22, 1623

Samuel on December 17, 1624

Anne on May 5, 1626

Mary on February 22, 1628

Katherine on February 7, 1630

William on September 28, 1631[1]

Susan on November 15, 1633[2]

---

[1] Named for his deceased brother of the same name, who died of unknown causes between 1626 and 1629

[2] Named for her deceased older sister

Anne's fertility did not go unnoticed by her peers, who saw it as a sign of good health and hygiene and also of a sexually fulfilling marital relationship. In seventeenth-century England, it was a truth universally acknowledged that conception cannot occur if the woman does not "delight in the acting thereof." In England and most of Europe at the time, a "properly consummated sexual relationship was deemed crucial to successful matrimony, and the birth of children confirmed the existence of such a relationship," according to the historian Mary Beth Norton. Conversely, "the absence of children called into question the character of a marriage and, in particular, the husband's ability to satisfy his wife sexually."

The couple's days were taken up with chores. For Anne, there was always a baby on the way, a baby just born, or a toddler still nursing. Instead of diapers, she wrapped a cloth around a baby's waist or, in warm weather, left it naked until it learned to sit on a chamber pot. Will grew food for the family and livestock, and Anne took charge of feeding and clothing the family. As her mother had done, she assigned chores to her children over the age of three or four. The cows had to be milked and the butter churned. The exterior of the house needed to be whitewashed yearly and the reeds in the roof occasionally tightened or replaced. The fields needed to be planted and tended and the crops harvested. The sheep had to be fed, moved (to shine up their coats), shorn, and eventually slaughtered.

On free afternoons Anne and Will took the children on long walks to neighboring villages, churches, or up into the Wolds. On gray days the clouds often parted to reveal a blue and gold sky like those that Dutch painters were capturing in oils. A favorite destination of the Hutchinsons was Rigsby Wood, two miles above Alford to the west. In May, when the bluebells bloomed, the wood provided a carpet of purple for the family's picnics. The village of Rigsby—now a tiny Norman church in a churchyard of battered gravestones and, in spring, daffodils and rabbits—was in 1086 the site of the first church in this region. From this hillside on the edge of the Wolds one can see Alford amid the flat farmland that extends to the North Sea. Beside this churchyard a sign, "Public footpath to Alford," marks the Hutchinsons' route. Beyond such local trips, the Hutchinsons did not travel, except to Saint Botolph's to hear John Cotton preach.

During the 1620s they also grew close to the Reverend John Wheelwright, who served at the village of Bilsby, one mile northeast of Alford. Wheelwright married Mary Hutchinson, William's youngest sister, in 1629, when he was thirty-seven and she was twenty-three. The two couples shared not only kinship but also the religious conviction that humans depend only on God's free grace, not on their own works. Wheelwright, known for his godly, "modest" sermons, was Anne's favorite preacher after Cotton, who was far less accessible at twenty-four miles away. Even in winter weather the Hutchinsons could travel the mile up the Bilsby road to the medieval church in which their brother-in-law preached.

Wheelwright, the only son of a farmer and his wife in Cumberworth, several miles east of Alford, had likely attended the Reverend Marbury's grammar school around the turn of the seventeenth century. At age nineteen Wheelwright went to Sidney Sussex College, Cambridge, where he became a close friend and wrestling buddy of Oliver Cromwell, the Puritan who led England after its civil war. Before being presented to Bilsby in April 1623, Wheelwright received his master's degree, served as a deacon in Peterborough, and took Holy Orders. He had four children with his first wife, Mary Storre, a minister's daughter, who died in May 1629. The first child of his second marriage, a girl he baptized Katherine on November 4, 1630, would grow up to become Katherine Nanny Naylor, of Boston, Massachusetts, whose backyard privy—a stone-lined chamber dug into the ground for use as an outhouse and for trash disposal—was in the late twentieth century excavated by archeologists as part of Boston's Big Dig, the modernization of its downtown highways.

The contents of this privy, on display at the Massachusetts Commonwealth Museum, or the "Big Dig Museum," in Dorchester, provide detailed information about the lifestyle of early Boston settlers such as the Hutchinsons and Wheelwrights. Finds include imported ceramic tableware, good English pottery, keys made of iron, belt buckles, a candle sconce, early-seventeenth-century fireplace tiles decorated in a Chinese style, pewter spoons and knife blades (forks were not used for eating until 1690), leather shoes, a sewing kit, and a tiny brass bucket used as a pincushion. The privy contained more than a quarter of a million pits and seeds (mostly from cherries, some of them preserved, and including thirty-two varieties of plums), the skull of a pig and other animal bones, the wings of granary weevils (flour-eating bugs), coriander and other herbs, pollen from corn and wheat, and parasite eggs. The people who used this privy ate pulpy stews and pottages, fruit pies in abundance, fresh eggs, salted or pickled fish, and freshly killed game (duck, pigeon, chicken, squirrel, hare, venison, beef, and mutton), and they sometimes—based on the evidence of the parasite eggs—suffered from gastrointestinal distress.

Katherine Wheelwright Nanny Naylor's birth in Bilsby, England, in November 1630, happened during the darkest days that neighboring Alford had known. The town was quarantined; one-fourth of its inhabitants were dead or dying of the bubonic plague. This bacterial infection (by the organism *Yersinia pestis*), spread by way of flea-infested rats, was also known as the Black Death because of the dark hemorrhages it caused under the skin. It killed nearly one in three Europeans between the fourteenth and seventeenth centuries—more than thirty million people.

The plague had arrived in Alford in June 1630, when the Hutchinsons felt blessed to have eleven healthy children, from seventeen-year-old Edward down to their own little Katherine, age four months. In July, to prevent the disease from spreading outside Alford, the market was canceled and the town isolated. This was standard procedure during epidemics. In London, for instance, the Black Death shut down every theater and stopped all construction for three miles outside the city walls.

Treatments for the plague—all ineffectual until the advent of antibiotic drugs—included refraining from bathing (on the theory that this shrinks pores, rendering one less susceptible); breathing pleasant odors (posies or incense of juniper, laurel, pine, beech, lemon leaves, and rosemary), and loud noises. So the people of Alford bathed less often than their usual few times a year. (Even the most privileged Queen Elizabeth said that her habit was to take a bath once a month whether she needed it or not.) And the ringers of Saint Wilfrid's spent hours every day in the bell tower pulling the cords of its bells, which were usually rung only before church services, drowning the townspeople in sound.

Anne Hutchinson threw herself into the care of the sick. No family in town could avoid exposure, and several of her children contracted the plague. Those who remained healthy shared in the regular two-mile pilgrimage up to Miles Cross Hill to collect the bread and other food that inhabitants of neighboring villages left for them at the plague stone. The base of a medieval high cross, the stone is about two feet square, with rounded edges and a shallow indentation on top, into which the people of Alford poured vinegar, their only disinfectant. In exchange for goods they received there, the people left money at the stone, which was taken away by their neighbors when they next came. This way, the affected and unaffected towns could assist each other while avoiding physical contact. The plague stone, which was later moved into the village of Alford, remains there today, in the garden of Tothby House, as a sort of monument.

The Alford parish register starkly outlines the disease's effect. During the 1620s, before the scourge struck, the average annual number of deaths in Alford was 19. In 1630 there were 131 burials, and 19 more deaths occurred in just the first two months of 1631. In a period of eight months, the plague had killed nearly one in four of Alford's 600 inhabitants. Thirty-five years later, the Great Plague of London wiped out a somewhat lower proportion of the population—69,000 of the city's 460,000.

The first victim of Alford's "Incipit pestis," as Vicar Scortreth defined the cause of death, was Mary Brown, buried on July 22, 1630. A family named Brader suffered six deaths in twelve midsummer days: two daughters on July 24, the father the next day, and then three sons, on July 29, August 3, and August 4. The disease reached its height in mid-August. On the twentieth of the month, the vicar presided over five funerals at Saint Wilfrid's Church. Two weeks later he had to bury his own daughter Rebecca. Twenty-five other Alfordians died in September, and nine more the next month.

The Hutchinsons lost two daughters, sixteen-year-old Susan on September 8, and Elizabeth, who was eight, on October 4. Like the rest of the victims, the Hutchinson girls were cremated and their remains buried in the churchyard without headstones. The outbreak finally ended in February and the quarantine was lifted in March.

Following this great loss, according to a local history, "For twelve months Anne withdrew from her neighbors seeking solace from her religious beliefs." The following autumn she gave birth to a boy whom they baptized William on September 28, 1631. The birth of this second William is evidence that the family had also lost a son, the William born in 1623. There is no record in Alford of this child's death, which occurred between the ages of three and six. (Six weeks before Anne delivered the second William, a first cousin of hers in Aldwinkle, Northampton, had a son, John Dryden, who would become the poet laureate of England.)

During Anne's period of isolation, William's father, Edward Hutchinson, died, on Saint Valentine's Day 1632, and was survived by his wife, Susan. On June 7 of the same year, in Berkhamstead, Hertfordshire, Anne's youngest sister, twenty-two-year-old Katherine, who had been an infant at their father's death, married a shoemaker named Richard Scott.

At this point Anne and Will may have thought that their sadness was over. But in 1632 John Wheelwright was silenced and deprived of his living in Bilsby for what the church termed "the irregularity of simony." Given that Wheelwright is unlikely to have bought or sold church offices or preferments—the usual definition of simony—a local historian theorized that "he had made himself so unpopular with the authorities that they were glad to get rid of him on any pretext." Wheelwright went into hiding. He likely served Puritans privately as a "bootleg" preacher, but his whereabouts were unknown until early 1636, when he sailed to Massachusetts with his wife, children, and mother-in-law, Susan Hutchinson, and moved temporarily into Anne and Will's Boston house.

Cotton, who had ceased to preach when he contracted malaria in 1631, also went underground in the spring of 1632 when he learned that Laud was summoning him to London. Cotton decided late that year to emigrate, although he did not resign at Saint Botolph's until the following May. During that winter or spring he may have invited the Hutchinsons to join his pilgrimage. Whether or not he did, they were in no position to move. They had recently lost three children, and Anne was pregnant with their fourteenth child, due in November 1633. Their oldest son, Edward, just twenty, and Will's youngest brother, twenty-six-year-old Edward, and his wife, Sarah, did sail to America on the same ship as the Cottons, but it is not clear if they knew of Cotton's plans until they encountered him on board. Unlike Anne's mother and most of her siblings, who remained in England, many of Will's siblings and even his widowed mother emigrated.

During the "much troubled" period after Cotton's departure, Anne Hutchinson recalled later, "The Lord did discover to me all sorts of ministers, and how they taught," and "thenceforth I was the more careful whom I heard" preach. "For after our teacher Mr. Cotton and my brother Wheelwright were put down," she would tell the Massachusetts court, "there was none in England that I durst hear." To a woman like Anne, the lack of a spiritual teacher was a great hole.

As was her custom when faced with a crisis or dilemma, she opened the Bible at random in the hope of receiving divine guidance. Her eyes fell on a passage in Isaiah, chapter 30 verse 20, which it "pleased God to reveal himself to me in." The passage reads, "Though the Lord give thee the bread of adversity, yet thine eyes shall see thy teachers. Thy teachers shall not be removed in a corner any more, but thine eyes shall see thy teachers." And then it was revealed to her that she should "go thither also" to the New World, "and that there I should be persecuted and suffer much trouble."

That November she gave birth to a girl who was baptized Susan, after her deceased older sister, on the fifteenth. Soon afterward, the family began arranging to remove to a new continent. Will sold his Market Square textile business to Anne's younger brother John Marbury. As required, Will paid in advance the standard price for a ticket to America, a hundred pounds per person. The family packed only those belongings they could easily carry, leaving behind large items such as bureaus and the four-poster bed. Unlike many families, they could afford luxurious building supplies such as windowpanes for the house they would build in the colony.

At the same time, authorities were closing the borders to prospective emigrants on suspicion that the Massachusetts colonists opposed the English king and church. Laud temporarily prevented several ships of Puritans headed for the colony from leaving the harbor. A few months before the Hutchinsons planned to sail, the archbishop set out guards to catch any man or woman trying to slip away to Massachusetts. If caught while attempting to flee, the Hutchinsons would be prosecuted.

In June 1634, just before their scheduled departure, the king's council ordered the Massachusetts court to return the 1629 charter to England because various factions were pressing claims to land held by the settlers. The Massachusetts magistrates delayed action, explaining they had to wait until their next meeting, in September. Each time they met, they delayed action. King Charles, diverted by other matters in England and, later, political conflict in Scotland, neglected to pursue the matter of the Massachusetts charter.

In the late spring of 1634 Anne, Will, ten of their children, Anne's twenty-four-year-old sister, Katherine Marbury Scott, and her husband, and William's two spinster cousins, Anne and Frances Freiston, set off for London on horses and horse-drawn carts. They traveled three days. In the city they boarded with the Bartholomews and succeeded in eluding the authorities. A few days later they continued east to Thamesside, where they boarded the *Griffin* for the ocean voyage.

Ten weeks later, as the ship sailed into Boston harbor, a familiar dark figure in a skullcap, his gray hair flowing in the salty wind, waited to greet the new immigrants on the pier. Walking up from the dock onto the meadow with the three hills that was now their home, John Cotton pointed out the rustic meetinghouse where he lectured, the marketplace and adjacent town spring, and the "best quarter" of town in which they would live, all within a few hundred yards. Instead of traveling twenty-four miles to hear Cotton preach, the Hutchinsons could now walk a short distance up the road. Cotton's superior, the Reverend John Wilson, was back in England for at least a year, so Cotton was presently Boston's principal pastor, lecturing every Thursday and Sunday for as many hours as he was moved.

By the mid-1630s, Massachusetts Bay Colony and Plymouth Plantation made up one of the largest European outposts in North America. Massachusetts had roughly five thousand English settlers, mostly from Lincolnshire and East Anglia, in nearly twenty townships from Cape Ann to Cape Cod, including Charlestown, Roxbury, Dorchester, Medford, Watertown, Newtown, Newbury, Ipswich, Salem, Saugus, Marblehead, Weymouth, and Hingham. The colony's population would grow to more than ten thousand by 1640, when political change in England caused Puritan emigration to decline dramatically.

Boston, with roughly 20 percent of the colony's population, was its largest town. It was growing rapidly when the Hutchinsons arrived and already had more than a hundred houses. The previous owner of the half-acre plot that Will purchased on the rocky meadow overlooking the sea was apparently Isaac Johnson, the husband of the Lady Arbella Clinton Fiennes Johnson for whom Winthrop's 1630 flagship was named. To this plot Will Hutchinson "added certain property purchased of John Coggeshall" so that the Hutchinson land was bounded on the west by "land allotted to Thomas Scottow," on the north by "the lot of Samuel Cole," on the east by modern-day Washington Street, and on the south by School Street.

For two months the Hutchinsons lodged with friends and relatives who had preceded them. Will and his older sons supervised the construction of their house by laborers, whom he paid slightly more than two shillings a day. It faced east, so the view would take in the salt marsh below, the town pier, and the harbor with its many islands. The house was ready by November—none too soon on a promontory afflicted with biting ocean winds and temperatures far lower than Lincolnshire's.

The Hutchinson house, one of the largest on Shawmut, had a timber frame, a central chimney, overhanging gables, several dormers, at least two stories (there may also have been an open attic), and glass windows. The roof was of boards, chinked with mud plaster and covered with thatch. The walls were made of sawed logs and plaster. The kitchen, buttery (pantry), hall, and parlor were on the first floor. The parlor, where Anne held her meetings, was also the bedroom for the family's two male servants and the older boys, who slept on mattresses that they laid out each night across the wooden floor. The kitchen was the warmest, busiest room, for the hearth glowed all day long and through many cold nights. The children ate and studied at wooden benches, which were dragged into the parlor for use by those attending Anne's meetings. At mealtime the women set the food on a long table of boards near the fireplace, around which various kettles, skillets, and pots hung. The second floor of the house had at least two bedchambers. Anne and Will and the baby occupied the master bedroom, above the kitchen. The other bedroom served the girls, the younger boys, and the adult female relatives, on bed ticking laid out across the floor. Rugs and blankets kept the family warm during the cold months. The house was crowded with people and awash in odors—smoke from the fire; drying rosemary, spearmint, and lemon balm; chamber pots not yet emptied; and perishable foods.

Outside, the men dug a privy, which they enclosed with a wooden shed. Every few years they moved the shed, covered the hole with dirt, and dug a new privy in another part of the yard. The Hutchinsons created an orchard from cuttings they had brought from England, which they grafted onto native crabapple trees. They planted Indian corn, peas, barley, carrots, parsnips, onions, turnips, pumpkins, cabbages, lettuces, and other greens, as well as a garden of herbs. Anne dried the herbs on an *I*-shaped wooden frame, laced with twine, that hung from the main beam of the house's second floor. The family kept a few pigs, sheep, and chickens in the yard, but most of their cattle and swine grazed on the six hundred acres of pasturage that the court granted Will on Mount Wollaston, ten miles south, in modern-day Quincy, below the mouth of the Neponset River. Will Hutchinson's farmland, which was "betwixt Dorchester bounds and Mount Wollaston river," extended from the height of Mount Wollaston, now known as Wollaston Heights, to the shore, which is now Wollaston Beach. John Winthrop held land of roughly the same size in Medford, to the north, as did Thomas Dudley, in Cambridge.

In early Boston every man was a farmer in addition to his other work. Except on the Sabbath—twenty-four hours starting at sundown Saturday when the taverns were closed and people did not work—he had almost constant labor fencing land, building structures, and clearing roads. His wife worked too, in the gardens or house, where she cooked at the fire, made soap from boiled ashes, or potash, and cared for the children. The settlers planted in spring, tended fields in summer, and harvested crops and threshed wheat in fall. For entertainment they had skates and sleds, but they avoided swimming, which was not yet considered recreation. The men occasionally hunted. Will continued to sell silks and other fine textiles, which he stored and displayed in a shed that he built beside the house. "For even the wealthiest," according to Larzer Ziff, "a day in the Massachusetts Bay settlement was a day of toil."

At the same time, Will's wallet had expanded just by crossing the sea. At home he was a wealthy member of the gentry, but here he was effectively an aristocrat. Besides his six-hundred-acre farm, he owned an entire island in the harbor, where in some seasons he grazed his sheep. "Taylor's Island is granted to Mr. William Hutchinson," the July 8, 1635, court record states, "to enjoy to him and his heirs forever." In the New World, of course, thousand-acre farms and complete islands were here for the taking, at least by prosperous men. "The founding gentry of Boston," according to the literary scholar Andrew Delbanco, "acted quickly to reestablish their wealth in land; grants of hundreds of acres were made . . . to such leading families as the Haughs and Bellinghams and Hutchinsons and Keaynes. Pastor Wilson of the First Church was soon in possession of a six-hundred-acre tract (even as he declared that 'a man that has competency, may not pray for more enlargement in the world'), and Winthrop himself obtained an expanse of outlying farmland which can only be explained by the prospect of speculative gain."

The new land was both abundant and wild. The air was clean, and fresh milk cost only a penny a quart. Currants, blueberries, raspberries, and plums were free. Indian corn grew everywhere. The sea was filled with edible delights: crabs, eels, mussels, oysters, lobsters, sturgeon, and cod. Fowl and deer roamed on endless parks of free land, more abundant even than on the lands of the king.

In addition to these natural differences between New England and old, there were artificial ones. The settlers chose not to re-create here many aspects of life that "were commonplace in much of Europe," according to David Hall. There were no "popish" bishops, no processions of clergy, no altars, no formal liturgy, no tithes paid to clergy, no prayers for the dead, no saint's days, no elaborate weddings, no Christmas celebrations, no carnival before Lent, no godparents or maypoles, no sacred places, no relics, no fairy tales, no ballad singing, and no dancing on Sundays. Henry James added, in an essay on Hawthorne, that early America distinguished itself from England in having "No sovereign, no court, no personal loyalty, no aristocracy . . . no diplomatic service, no country gentlemen, no palaces, no castles, nor manor, nor old country houses, nor parsonages, nor thatched cottages, nor ivied ruins; no cathedrals, nor abbeys, nor little Norman churches. . . ."

With these agreeable subtractions, the Hutchinsons successfully approximated their comfortable former life. As at Alford, they assumed leading roles in community life. Anne and Will both testified convincingly—he in public before the church, and she in private in writing, which the minister read to the congregation, according to custom—that they had experienced saving grace and were thus elect. Will was accepted as a member of the church of Boston on Sunday, October 26. She followed a week later, the delay due to Symmes's concerns about her portentous strivings and disrespect during the voyage. Anne quickly gained the trust of many women as their midwife. Within six months of their arrival, the adult men of the family—Will and his sons Richard, nineteen, and Francis, fourteen (the age allowable under the law that lowered the official age of adulthood to sixteen)—took the freeman's oath, which entitled them to vote in the annual elections for the court. (Their son Edward had already taken the oath.) Two months later, at the May 1635 General Court meeting, Will was elected to the board that regulated taxation and was made a deputy from Boston and thus a magistrate of the court, the highest power in the land.

Two and a half years later, in November 1637, the colonial world to which Anne and Will awoke every morning had changed. She was banished, with her entire family—and as a result many other families felt as though they were banished. For her stalwart supporters, such as the Coddingtons, Coggeshalls, and Dyers, there was never any question whether they would follow her. If the Hutchinsons had to leave Massachusetts, they would too.

A few days after Anne returned from her trial in Cambridge, it was time for her to leave. Outside the house, a cab and horse awaited her on the rutted dirt road that ran through the center of the settlement, dividing Winthrop's land from Hutchinson's. Anne bade her family farewell and boarded the carriage for the trip to Roxbury, where she effectively would be out of their reach. She carried only her Bible, her *Herbal*—a guide to medicinal plants—and sufficient clothes for the winter.

The cart headed southwest. The driver, she observed, kept a gun at his feet, as required by the March 1637 decree aimed at protecting the colonists from the natives. But Anne had no fear of the natives. She believed that the true threat was in and among themselves, in the hearts and minds of those who preached a covenant of works, for they could kill the soul while the natives could destroy only the body. In her attitude toward Indians, Hutchinson was somewhat rare. Even the Reverend John Cotton, who in 1630 at Southampton wharf had admonished the settlers of Massachusetts Bay to "feed the natives with your spirituals," came after a few years in America to a much altered opinion of its native people: "Blast all their green groves and arbors."

The cart that carried Anne Hutchinson to Roxbury followed the single road—now known as Washington Street—along the spine that connected Shawmut to the mainland. Blueberries and other bushes covered the uneven landscape, which as it approached the coastline abounded in swamps. Looking out to the right, or northwest, Anne saw cows grazing on the common space that John Cotton and others had created in 1634 from parcels of the departed Reverend William Blackstone's solitary farm. Just below this common, on the edges of the great marsh that is now Boston's Back Bay, were fish weirs, set out by natives. To her left, stretching out to the horizon, was the vast harbor of her adopted home. The sea shimmered, making the harbor islands into dark spots.

The first town on the mainland was Roxbury, a cluster of wood houses and a meetinghouse set on a hillside above the intersection of Cornhill Road and the Roxbury road, near modern-day Dudley Square. The cart stopped at the house belonging to Joseph Weld, and she was let out. She was hardly two miles from Boston. But to Anne Hutchinson it seemed far from home.

11

AN UNEASY AND
CONSTANT WATCH

"The prisoner," as John Winthrop took to calling Anne Hutchinson that winter, saw little of her children during her house arrest. One-year-old Zuriel; Susan, age four; six-year-old William; seven-year-old Katherine; Mary, nine; ten-year-old Anne; thirteen-year-old Samuel; and Francis, seventeen, stayed in the house on Shawmut with their father, his cousins Anne and Francis Freiston, and several servants. The older siblings—Richard, Edward and his wife, and Faith and Bridget and their husbands—often visited, as did their young aunt Katherine Scott. But the children saw their mother only rarely on account of the winter weather, which that year was particularly harsh.

It was the court's intention to isolate the prisoner and reduce her support. Winthrop was determined that no one should be inspired by her or spread news of her. Still, she caused the governor to worry. "She began now to discover all her mind to such as came to her," he wrote of her confinement, "so that her opinions came abroad, and began to take place among her old disciples, and now some of them raised up questions—which the elders, finding to begin to appear in some of their children, they took much pains both in public and private to suppress."

The ministers, who had agreed among themselves to make the trip to Joseph Weld's house in Roxbury as often as possible during her imprisonment there, came at least once a week, alone or in pairs. Thomas Weld, one of her strongest opponents, who lived nearby in Roxbury, came frequently. He had suggested his brother as her jailer in order that he might have more access to the prisoner and opportunity to reform her. Another forceful opponent of Antinomianism, Thomas Shepard, came as often as he could manage from Cambridge, and even Hugh

Peter made the trip from Salem every few weeks. John Eliot, who seemed less forceful than the rest, came several times a week because he lived in Roxbury.

The ministers had two purposes in coming. They preached God's word so she might see the light and recant her obnoxious opinions. In addition, they recorded those "errors, taken from her own mouth," to present as evidence at her church trial in the spring. After each visit, the ministers dutifully added to the list they were compiling, "proved by four witnesses," themselves. By the time of the trial in March 1638, this list would contain nearly thirty errors.

When the ministers challenged her doctrine, she repeatedly associated herself with the colony's most respected minister, saying, they reported, that she "held nothing but what Mr. Cotton held" and "Mr. Cotton and she were both of one mind." To this, the Reverend Weld, for one, told her she must have changed. He showed her papers written by Cotton "expressly *against* some of the opinions she held," but "she affirmed still that there was *no* difference between Mr. Cotton and her."

Apart from these missionary visits, which Hutchinson did not welcome but could not refuse, she spent the winter largely alone. She was isolated from her "scholars," as Weld mocked her followers, much as her father had been isolated from his students and congregation during his three years of house arrest. Through the short, cold days and long, cold nights of her imprisonment, Anne Hutchinson studied Scripture, sang psalms, meditated on God's word, and watched her belly swell as it had done fifteen times before. This time, though, she was more tired than ever before, including the awful summer when she had tried to save her daughters from the plague. This sixteenth pregnancy was not like the rest, she was sure. But even the midwife did not know how or why.

In the midst of this late pregnancy, she was welcoming grandchildren. Edward's firstborn, Elishua, had arrived just before her trial. A month later, without benefit of Anne's assistance, her eighteen-year-old daughter Bridget delivered her first child, a boy named Eliphal Sanford, who was baptized in Boston on December 9. Bridget's husband, John Sanford, whom she married in 1636 after his first wife died, was an educated Englishman about ten years her senior who had arrived in Boston in 1631. Prior to that, he was employed by the Winthrop household in England, "often acting as a purchasing agent for John Winthrop." A respected citizen of Boston, Sanford was disarmed along with other prominent Hutchinsonians on November 20, 1637, and relieved of his official duties in Boston, which in his case included serving as a select-man, a member of the committee regulating cattle, a surveyor of ord-nance and ammunition, and cannoneer of the fort. But Anne could not see her new grandchildren unless they were brought to her, which in winter was impossible.

Snow and ice closed down Massachusetts Bay before Christmas, which fell on a Monday that year. While many holy days were cele-brated with great fanfare in the Church of England, Christmas was largely ignored here, except for a church prayer service and sometimes a Fast Day. Puritans considered decorations, gifts, and parties to be pagan idolatry.

The General Court next convened on January 8, 1638, in Boston, now that most local Hutchinsonians had been dismissed, disfranchised, or otherwise removed. At that meeting, as an apparent award for hav-ing removed himself from the continent, Sir Henry Vane was granted in absentia two hundred acres of land at Running Marsh, which is now called Revere. At the same time, Governor Winthrop received one hun-dred fifty acres bordering Vane's land—perhaps to keep tabs on Vane should he reappear, as promised. Vane, Winthrop could now write, "showed himself a true friend to New England, and a man of noble and generous mind."

Governor Winthrop continued during Hutchinson's internment to gauge her moods, although he no longer could spy her comings and goings from behind the windowpanes of his house. In conversations with the ministers, he took note of her inability to repent and reform. "She thought it now needless to conceal herself any longer," he ob-served. It was even clearer to him now that "The root of all [the trou-bles in the colony] was found to be in Mistress Hutchinson." She was surely allied with Satan, who never "would lose the opportunity of so fit an instrument."

The snow was so deep that winter that most settlers rarely ventured outside except to attend church and cut more firewood. One January day, when Boston's supply of wood had fallen dangerously low, about thirty men set out in fair weather for Spectacle Island to gather and cut more wood. The weather turned—the wind rose, the temperature dropped, the snow fell, and "the bay was all frozen up, save a little channel," Winthrop noted in his journal—so the men were stranded for two days on the island without fire or food. Several lost fingers and toes. One man died.

Sometime that winter John Cotton decided to remove himself from Massachusetts. Anne had turned Separatist, he believed, and the Boston church she had so influenced was growing Separatist too. He envisioned feeling more at home among the settlers of New Haven, Connecticut, whom his old friend John Davenport was about to join. The Reverend Davenport was now lodging with the Cottons, as he had since his arrival the previous June from London, where he had preached at St. Stephen's Church. Born in England in 1597, Davenport had also traveled to Holland. Now he and a wealthy London merchant named Theophilus Eaton planned to purchase land from the Indians in modern-day New Haven and form a settlement named Quinnipiac, or "long water," in April 1638. Like Cotton, the future minister of New Haven saw himself as part of the Church of England in the New World.

Cotton's plan instilled terror in John Winthrop's heart. Should word reach England that the esteemed Cotton was leaving Massachusetts Bay, emigration would surely slow or stop. If King Charles heard of further dissension here, he could send a ship to retrieve the charter, as he had threatened. Winthrop resolved to prevent Cotton from departing the colony. In every discussion of the controversy, the governor took the minister's side. Winthrop informed people that Hutchinson and her followers had "abused" the Reverend Cotton and made him their "stalking horse," the creature behind which hunters hide, under cover, while pursuing their prey.

Cotton cooperated by playing down the intimacy that he and Hutchinson had enjoyed. "Mistress Hutchinson seldom resorted to me," he said of their relationship of two decades, "and when she did come to me, it was seldom or never (that I can tell of) that she tarried long. I rather think that she was loath to resort much to me, or to confer long with me, lest she might seem to learn somewhat from me." Whether Cotton stayed or left Massachusetts, he knew that his name could no longer be linked with hers.

Unlike the previous winter, when the conflict between the Hutchinsonians and the orthodox was raging, Massachusetts was now quiet, fearful, and vigilant. In the forced calm the members of the General

Court kept "an uneasy and constant watch" that more Hutchinsonian ideas not arise. Helen Campbell, a biographer of Anne Bradstreet, observed in 1891, "Freedom had ended for any who differed from the faith as laid down by the Cambridge Synod, and but one result could follow. All the more liberal spirits saw that Massachusetts could henceforth be no home for them, and made haste to other points."

The magistrates continued to consolidate their power. Perhaps as a reward for their work in unifying the colony, the General Court granted its leaders Dudley and Winthrop each a thousand acres of additional land. These grants, first made at the November court session at which Hutchinson was tried, were clarified six months later, on May 2, 1638, when the court convened again in Cambridge. "It was ordered by this present Court that John Winthrop, Esquire, the present Governor, shall have 1200 acres of land, whereof 1000 was formerly granted to him, and Thomas Dudley, Esquire, the Deputy Governor, his 1000 granted to him by a former Court, both of them about six miles from Concord northwards; the said Governor to have his 1200 acres on the southerly side of two great stones standing near together close by the river," and "the Deputy Governor to have his thousand acres on the northerly side of the said two great stones."

As for the Hutchinsonian men who were now out of power, they gathered secretly throughout the winter of Anne's imprisonment to discuss creating a new settlement that might allow them freedom of conscience. Most of these meetings were held in William Coddington's large house on Shawmut, which was then the only brick structure in the town. In the Coddingtons' parlor, Will Hutchinson and his wife's most devoted male followers studied maps of the American coastline. Their requirements were good soil for farming, easy access to fresh water and wood, and an easier climate than Boston's. They decided to head south to Long Island or New Jersey.

But the banished Reverend Roger Williams, who had settled Providence Plantation two years before, urged them to try Aquidneck Island, which met all their requirements. (Aquidneck was the native name of the island that Europeans, starting with Giovanni da Verrazzano in the early sixteenth century, called Rhode Island, which now contains the towns of Portsmouth, Middletown, and Newport.) Other than Williams's plantation sixteen miles north by water and the encampment at modern-day Cumberland, Rhode Island, of the solitary Reverend William Blackstone, who had been forced from Beacon Hill in 1634 by Boston's rapid population growth, this region had no English settlers. Best of all, from Will Hutchinson's perspective, the island of Aquidneck was only forty-five miles southwest of Boston. This was a boon to a man who, initially at least, had to leave most of his children and his incarcerated wife in Massachusetts.

February 2 was Candlemas (forerunner of Groundhog Day), a religious festival associated with early spring, although the official start of spring (and of the new year, by the English calendar) would not arrive until Lady Day, on March 25. With the hope of spring in the air, Will and more than a dozen other men prepared to sail to Providence Plantation and then on to their new land. While still in Boston, on March 7, they signed an agreement to become joint proprietors of Rhode Island:

> We whose names are underwritten do solemnly in the presence
> of Jehovah incorporate ourselves into a body politic and as He
> shall help, will submit our persons, lives and estates unto our
> Lord Jesus Christ, the King of Kings, and Lord of Lords, and to
> all those most perfect and most absolute laws of His given in
> His Holy Word of truth, to be guided and judged thereby.

Forty-year-old William Coddington, whom they chose as their sole magistrate, signed first. John Clarke, the twenty-eight-year-old minister who, some believe, penned the document, signed second. Will Hutchinson, whose wife's ordeal had inspired them, put his name third. Will was not interested in being a magistrate: it was not in his nature to lead a coalition, although by virtue of being her spouse he was a central figure. John Coggeshall signed next, and then the crusty William Aspinwall, who became the new settlement's first secretary and is the other candidate for transcribing this document, known as the Portsmouth Compact. The names of Anne's two sons-in-law appear: John Sanford, the husband of Bridget, and Thomas Savage, who had married Faith. "Edward Hutchinson Jr." was her oldest son, and "Edward Hutchinson Sr." was Will's younger brother, who later would move, with his wife and two sons, from Rhode Island back to England, where he died in 1669. William Dyer, Mary's husband, and William Baulston also signed. Henry Bull, who was illiterate, signed with an X, and someone else wrote, "his mark." Randall Holden, who would represent these nineteen men at the purchase of the land they would occupy to the south, signed last.

After signing the solemn compact, Will Hutchinson added, to the right of the formal text, in an angled script that made clear this was a gloss,

Exodus 24:3, 4, 7: And Moses came and told the people all the words of the Lord, and all the judgments: and all the people answered with one voice, and said, All the words which the Lord hath said will we do . . . and be obedient.

2 Chronicles 2:3: And Solomon sent to Huram the king of Tyrus, saying, As thou didst deal with David my father, and did send him cedars to build him an house to dwell therein, even so deal with me.

2 Kings 11:17: And Jehoida made a covenant between the Lord and the King and the people, that they should be the Lord's people: between the King also and the people.

These scriptural references and the religious language of the Portsmouth Compact may seem to suggest that these men aimed to create yet another church, to compete with those of Massachusetts, but this was decidedly not their intent. The Rhode Island historian Samuel Arnold explained, regarding the Portsmouth Compact,

So prominent indeed is the religious character of this instrument that it has by some been considered, although erroneously, as being itself "a church covenant, which also embodied a civil compact." Their plans were more matured than those of the Providence settlers. To establish a *colony* independent of every other was their avowed intention, and the organization of a regular *government* was their initial step. That their object was to lay the foundation of a Christian *state*, where all who bore the name might worship God *according to the dictates of conscience*, untrammeled by written articles of faith, and unawed by the civil power, is proved by their declarations and by their subsequent conduct.

These men were determined, following Anne Hutchinson's and their experiences in Massachusetts, to guarantee freedom of conscience in Rhode Island. One of their first written rules upon arriving was "No person within the said colony, at any time hereafter, shall be in any wise [ways] molested, punished, disquieted or called into question on matter of religion—so long as he keeps the peace." These first Rhode Islanders valued religious liberty, a freedom that, in large part because of them, the constitutions of Rhode Island and the United States would later proclaim.

A few days later, in the still-bitter March, the men packed building supplies on a ship that they hired to sail them around the tip of Cape Cod. Edward Hutchinson went with his father, leaving his wife and baby in the family's house on Shawmut. The men traveled first to Providence Plantation, where the Reverend Williams arranged a meeting between them and the Narragansett *sachems*, or chieftains, Miantonomo and Canonicus.

On March 24, 1638, one day before the start of spring, the eighteen "purchasers of Rhode Island" gave the Narragansett sachems forty fathoms of white wampum beads, ten coats, and twenty hoes as a "gratuity" in exchange for the slender, fifteen-mile-long island of Aquidneck. The marks of Miantonomo, Canonicus and his son, and two other Indians, and the signatures of Randall Holden, the twenty-six-year-old Bostonian who represented the Hutchinsonian men, and the Reverend Roger Williams appear on the land deed. Although the sachems did not share the English settlers' concept of ownership, they agreed to instruct their people to vacate the island before the next winter. Of the transfer, Roger Williams later noted in a self-congratulatory mode, "It was not price nor money that could have purchased Rhode Island. Rhode Island was obtained by the love and favor which that honorable gentleman Sir Henry Vane and myself had with the great sachem Miantonomo."

The new proprietors of Rhode Island continued south on ships to their new home between the Sakonnet River and Narragansett Bay.

After exploring the land, which was level and boasted fertile soil, the men agreed to make their settlement on the flat northeastern end, which had a fine natural spring and a pleasant saltwater cove surrounded by marsh. The Indians called this place Pocasset, which the English made into Portsmouth, after the port from which some had sailed. They pitched tents and built huts to live in while they cleared land. As winter became early spring, the men chose two- to three-acre house lots between the cove and the spring and began framing simple houses. Amid their labor, they awaited their founder, who languished in her Roxbury jail.

12

A SPIRIT OF
DELUSION AND ERROR

As Will Hutchinson began building their new home, forty-five miles away on Aquidneck Island, Anne learned that she would be allowed to return to their house in Boston for a few days before her second trial. The location of this trial, just up the road from her house, was the simple structure of timber, clay, and thatch in which for three years she had prayed and worshiped and sung psalms—the Boston meetinghouse. Winthrop and the court had sufficiently reduced her "potent party" in Boston to permit a trial of Hutchinson to be held in her town.

In the few days before she was to depart Joseph Weld's house, she eagerly awaited the trip by coach back along the muddy road to her own house. The Welds had the challenge of scheduling her trip to avoid the spring tide. Each spring, according to a seventeenth-century ditty, "The rocky nook, with hilltops three, looked eastward from the farms, and twice each day the flowing sea took Boston in its arms," turning the Shawmut Peninsula briefly into an island, as Winthrop had first imagined it, from Charlestown, when he named it Trimountaine.

Having traveled from Roxbury back to Boston, Anne was again at home with her family for a few days in the second week of March. She still felt ill from the pregnancy, which was now visible to all, but she enjoyed the reunion with her many children and her new grandchildren. Much of the family's time during these few days was taken up with packing to move. It seemed inevitable that the Hutchinsons would be forced again to leave behind many of their belongings.

The General Court convened in Boston on March 12, 1638, three days before she was to be brought to trial by her church. At this meeting the court banished the midwife Jane Hawkins, whom Anne had assisted at the Dyers' sad delivery in October. Hawkins, who had come to

America in 1635 from Cornwall, England, with her husband, Richard, was ordered to disappear by May or else the magistrates would "dispose of her. In the meantime, she is not to meddle in surgery, or physics, drinks, plasters, or oils, nor to question matters of religion, except with the elders for satisfaction."

To Winthrop, Mistress Hawkins's attendance at Mistress Hutchinson's meetings proved her a "rank Familist." Hawkins's other crimes included giving barren women fertility potions of herbs, being "notorious for familiarity with the Devil," and occasionally falling into trances in which she spoke Latin. Men of the period tended to view midwifery, a realm of power from which they were excluded, with suspicion. English law prohibited midwives from using witchcraft, charms, or sorcery; administering herbs or potions to induce abortion; allowing a woman to deliver a child in secret; and baptizing infants. At a conference on religion at Hampton Court in 1604, King James I, upon being told that some midwives actually baptized, "grew earnest against the baptizing by women."

"About Mrs. Hutchinson," the March 1638 Massachusetts court record continues, "It is ordered that she shall be gone by the last of this month; and if she be not gone before, she is to be sent away by the counsel, without delay, by the first opportunity; and for the charges of keeping Mrs. Hutchinson, order is to be given by the counsel to levy it by distress of her husband's good." In addition, her son, "Edward Hutchinson, Junior, is bound in forty pounds" that no one "shall come to Mrs. Hutchinson [without the court's permission]; and [after the trial] she is to remain at Mr. Cotton's until further order."

The court also ordered another Fast Day. "The 12th day of April should be kept a day of humiliation in the several churches, to entreat the help of God in the weighty matters which are in hand, and to divert any evil plots which may be intended, and to spare the way of friends which we hope may be upon coming to us."

Three days later, on the morning of Thursday, March 15—the third lecture day of the month—Anne Hutchinson rose from her bed, dressed warmly, and had her morning meal of corn mush and baked fruit. Her son Edward and her son-in-law Thomas Savage prepared to accompany her, not only to support her but also because as male church members they were entitled to participate in matters before the church. With these two young men, who were now twenty-four and twenty-nine, Anne Hutchinson stepped out her front door onto Cornhill Road. Directly across the road was John and Margaret Winthrop's front door. Turning left, the Hutchinsons walked slowly up the icy dirt road toward the austere meetinghouse, which had no carvings or spire, as befitted the children and grandchildren of reformers who had smashed religious art in trying to free their Christianity from any pagan or Roman influence. Anne and her sons each carried a copy of the Bible.

That lecture day, as always, the saints of Boston gathered "by ten of the clock in the morning"—a banging drum announced the hour—to hear a reading from Scripture and, often, the second sermon of the week, usually by Wilson or Cotton. Today's gathering was larger than usual, for it included not only the Boston congregation but also ministers from most churches of Massachusetts Bay and many other elders of the colony.

Anne Hutchinson and her sons arrived a few minutes late. When she entered the church, the Reverend Wilson was reading a Scripture passage he had chosen for the occasion. Staring as her son and son-in-law took their seats on benches in the family's place at the front of the church, the minister intoned, "We have heard this day *very sweetly* that we are to cast down all our crowns at the feet of Christ Jesus." The minister warned the members of his congregation to cut their ties to Anne Hutchinson so as to strengthen their bond with God. "So, let everyone be content to deny all relations of father, *mother*, sister, brother, friend, and enemy, and to cast down all our crowns, and whatsoever judgment or opinion that is taken up may be cast down at the feet of Christ. And let *all* be carried by the rules of God's word, and tried by that rule, and if there be any error let no one rejoice! None but the devils in Hell will rejoice! But in all our proceedings this day let us lift up the name of Christ Jesus and so proceed in love!"

Hoping to avoid any censure on account of Hutchinson's tardiness, Thomas Oliver, the seventy-year-old surgeon and church elder married to Anne's friend Anne Oliver, stood. "I am to acquaint all this congregation that whereas our sister Hutchinson was not here at the beginning of this exercise, it was not out of any contempt or neglect to the ordinance, but because she hath been long [under] durance," or imprisoned. The few eyes that had not already noted the pale face and swollen abdomen of the woman at the center of the proceedings did so. "She is so weak," Oliver continued, "that she conceives herself not fit nor able to have been here so long together." He held up a piece of paper that his wife had given him, from Anne. "This she sent to our elders."

Thomas Leverett, one of the three men who had defended Hutchinson during her November trial, asked the members of the Boston congregation, who would have to decide Hutchinson's ecclesiastical fate, to gather in one area. They should "draw as near together as they can, as they may be distinguished from the rest of the congregation, that when their consent or dissent is required to the things which shall be read, we may know how they do express themselves. . . ."

Leverett and Oliver were both ruling elders of the church, charged with handling disciplinary matters. According to the church covenant, members were required to "walk . . . according to the rule of the Gospel, and in all sincere conformity to His holy ordinances." Members who violated these rules could be admonished—temporarily prevented from receiving the Lord's Supper—and then, if repentance did not follow, they would be cast out. Any known evildoer or heretic had to be expelled. The congregation of the church could excommunicate a member, unlike in England and Rome, where only a bishop had this power. In other respects, however, excommunication was "wholly derivative," according to the historian David C. Brown: "The Congregationalists simply adapted a centuries-old disciplinary system which had been painstakingly developed by their Catholic and Anglican forebears."

The Puritan process of excommunication was as intense and public as that leading to admission to the church, only in reverse. Based on contemporary accounts, redemption (justification) involved, first, a response to the Word, then a sense of remorse, humiliation, and repentance, then the arrival of the Holy Spirit bringing saving grace, followed by the transformation of the soul by faith, justification, sanctification, and assurance of eternal redemption. Puritan divines broke down the process of receiving saving grace into steps: preparation, conviction, humiliation, a will and desire to believe, and, finally, assurance, or the "grace to endeavor to obey His Commandments by a new obedience." In excommunicating a person, the congregation had to make a similar judgment in reverse, determining if the member in question were still worthy of being in communion with the church.

Leverett turned to Hutchinson and held up the stack of papers gathered by the ministers. "Sister Hutchinson, here are diverse opinions laid to your charge by Mr. Shepard and Mr. Frost [Edmund Frost, a ruling elder of the Cambridge church] and Mr. Weld and Mr. Eliot, and I must"—for he did not wish to—"request you in the name of the church to declare whether you hold them or renounce them as they be read to you."

He read them out, starting with, "That the souls of all men by nature are mortal." This first error, to which the ministers would devote much time, was known to all as "mortalism." It was the idea that the soul of an elect person dies with the body and is then resurrected, with the body, after death. The orthodox view was that the soul is immortal and cannot die. An error related to this was "That our [physical] bodies shall not rise with Christ Jesus at the last day."

The next error dealt with the question, raised by Hutchinson and Vane and others, of whether the Holy Ghost dwells in the body of a justified person. Leverett read to her, "Those that are united to Christ have two bodies—Christ's and a new body—and you knew not how Christ should be united to our fleshly bodies."

He went on, "That the resurrection mentioned in 1 Corinthians 15 is not of our resurrection at the last day, but of our union to Christ Jesus. . . . That in Christ there be no created graces, nor in believers after union. . . . That there is an engrafting into Christ before our union with him, from which we may fall away. . . . That union to Christ Jesus is not by faith. . . . That you had no Scripture to warrant Christ being now in Heaven in his human Nature. . . . That the disciples were not converted at Christ's death."

Before continuing with this list, one must remember that these errors, which were the focus of her lengthy church trial, were not, finally, its point. The entire controversy, according to historian David Hall, was "not about matters of doctrine but about power and freedom of conscience." Moreover, according to Charles Francis Adams, author of the first major study of the Hutchinsonian controversy, published in 1892, the many documents of theological controversies "may, so far as the reader of to-day is concerned, best be described by the single word impossible." Adams concluded that the ministers' language during this controversy was "a jargon which has become unintelligible"—an overstatement that may reassure readers of the transcript of Hutchinson's church trial.

The abstruse theological discussions in which the clergymen and Hutchinson engaged are worth exploring if only because they represent the usual form of discussion between Anne Hutchinson and John Cotton as well as among the ministers of the colony. In a community devoted to evangelical preaching, people cited Bible passages at will, from memory, and discussed the resurrection of the body and the evidence of justification in the casual manner that people now chat about sports scores or new films.

Leverett continued reciting her errors. "That there is no kingdom of Heaven but Christ Jesus. . . . That the first thing we receive for our assurance is our election."

Some errors dealt with the controversy over the covenant of grace: "That sanctification can be no evidence of a good estate. . . . That Abraham was not in saving estate until he offered Isaac and so, saving the firmness of God's election, he might have perished eternally for any work of grace that was in him. . . . That a hypocrite may have the righteousness of Adam and perish. . . . That we have no grace in ourselves, but all is in Christ, and there is no inherent Righteousness in us."

Others involved Hutchinson's claims of revelations: "That your revelations about future events were as infallible as the Scriptures themselves. . . . That you were bound to believe them as well as the Scriptures, because the Holy Ghost was the author of both."

Some of the errors involved Hutchinson's perceived lawlessness: "That we are not bound to the [earthly] law, not as a rule of life. That not being bound to the law, no transgression of the law is sinful."

Having recited all the errors on the ministers' lists, Leverett repeated in a quiet voice, "It is desired by the church, sister Hutchinson, that you express whether this be your opinion or not." He gazed at the floor, finding himself unable to look at her.

"If this be error, then it is mine and I ought to lay it down," she replied. "If it be truth, it is not mine but Christ Jesus', and then I am not to lay it down." Even in her distress and humiliation, she was as sharp as ever—admitting nothing, denying nothing, and defining herself alongside God and Christ.

In the silence that followed, she asked a question. "I desire of the church to demand, by what rule of the Word these elders [did] come to me, in private, to desire satisfaction in some points" of doctrine, "profess[ing] in the sight of God that they did not come to entrap nor ensnare me, and now ... bring it publicly unto the church, before they privately dealt with me? For them to come and inquire [of me] for light, and afterwards to bear witness against it, I think is a breach of church rule." Lacking sufficient witnesses to make any accusation against the ministers, she pointed out the deviousness of their tactics. She had in mind Matthew 18:15, "Moreover if thy brother shall trespass against thee, go and tell him his fault between thee and him alone." She intimated a zone of privacy for conversations and beliefs, which the ministers violated when they cited publicly the errors she had expressed privately. At the time, of course, no such zone existed, and ministers and government officials had multifarious powers and prerogatives that today are divided among police officers, legislators and other elected officials, clergy, parole boards, and judges.

In the ensuing lengthy debate, Hutchinson's question was not answered. Cotton, however, invited his "brother" Shepard to "give God glory and speak." The Reverend Shepard recalled visiting Hutchinson three times during her incarceration. The first time, he questioned her about "some speeches she used in the court." The second time, he said, "I came not to entrap her. But, seeing the fluentness of her tongue and her willingness to open herself and to divulge her opinions and to sow her seed in us that are but strangers to her," he recorded her words. He explained, "I account her a very dangerous woman, to sow her corrupt opinions to the infection of many." At his third visit, "I told her I came to reduce her from her errors and to bear witness against them. Therefore, I do marvel that she will say we bring it into public before I dealt with her in private."

"I did *not* hold diverse of these things I am accused of," Hutchinson said, "but did only ask a question."

Shepard warned, "The vilest errors that ever were brought into the church were brought by way of questions!"

"Brother, we consent with you," Cotton assured him. "Therefore, sister Hutchinson, it will be most satisfactory to the congregation for you to answer to the things as they are objected against you in order."

"I desire they may be read," she said, and so Cotton now read the list that Leverett had already read. At least an hour passed. A lengthy discussion of mortalism followed. After Cotton read this error—"The souls of all men by nature are mortal and die like beasts"—he corrected it by saying, "The spirit ascends upwards, so [as in] Ecclesiastes 12:7," which reads, "Then shall the dust return to the earth as it was: and the spirit shall return unto God who gave it." He added, "The soul of man is immortal."

"Every man consists of soul and body," she replied, almost as though they were alone in his parlor, discussing Scripture, as they often had. "Now, 'Adam dies not, except his soul and body die.' And in Hebrews 4 the word [spirit] is lively in operation, and divides between soul and spirit: so then the spirit that God gives man, returned to God indeed, but the soul dies, and that is the spirit Ecclesiastes speaks of, and not of the soul. Luke 19:10." For each chapter and verse citation, Hutchinson and Cotton both knew the exact scriptural words. Some in the meetinghouse were not so skilled, and many did not follow their meaning. John Winthrop himself had admitted in his journal less than a year before that these doctrinal errors were so murky as to be understood by hardly anyone: "No man could tell (except some few, who knew the bottom of the matter) where any difference was" between the theological arguments.

Cotton said to Hutchinson, "If you hold that Adam's soul and body dies and was not redeemed or restored by Christ Jesus, it will overthrow our redemption," adding, "1 Corinthians 6, end of the chapter."

"I acknowledge I am redeemed from my vain conversation and other redemptions," she replied, "but it is nowhere said that he came to redeem the seed of Adam—"

The Reverend Wilson interrupted their dialogue. "I desire that you would seriously consider of 1 Corinthians 6, at the end, 'the spirit of God needs no redemption.'"

"I speak not of God's spirit now," Hutchinson said. "My main scruple [concern] is how a thing that is immortally miserable, [the corporeal body], can be immortally happy," or eternally saved.

"He that makes miserable can make us happy," the inscrutable Cotton replied.

"I desire to hear God speak this and not man," Hutchinson retorted. "Show me where there is any Scripture to prove it that speaks so!"

Ten minutes into their dialogue, Hutchinson queried Cotton in a familiar manner. "Do you think man's natural life is gone into heaven, and that we shall go into heaven with our natural life?" She was suggesting that the physical body is not resurrected—a natural corollary to the Reformed belief, accepted by all present, that the Lord's Supper is not the actual body of Christ but its spiritual presence.

"Sister, do not shut your eyes against the truth," Cotton said reprovingly. "All these places [in Scripture] prove that the soul is immortal."

"The spirit is immortal, indeed, but prove that the soul is," she challenged him. "For that place in Matthew which you bring of, 'casting the soul into hell' is meant of the spirit."

"These are principles of our Christian faith," he answered ominously, "and *not* [to be] denied."

Hutchinson was trying to find words for concepts that cannot be clearly defined. As she knew from her study of Scripture, these matters could not finally be fixed or classified. What is the nature of the soul? How does God choose those whom he elects? How do they know they are saved? For her, unlike for her judges, truth was fluctuating. In reading Scripture, she could approach God's meaning more closely than before but never attain complete comprehension of his word. But to the ministers, who wished to fix the truth as defined by God and Jesus Christ, her shifts and alterations were both maddening and suspect. The literary scholar Lad Tobin attributes this difference to gender: "Because the [male] elders saw God in the Law and in the Word, their root metaphors focused on maintaining the covenant and on the idea of the commonwealth as a family; because Hutchinson saw God in the spirit and in inspiration, her root metaphors focused on an individual's intimate relationship with Christ, the indwelling spirit. In Hutchinson's language," Tobin added, "we see (and the elders heard) a consistent emphasis on intimacy, inspiration, and moments of light." Moreover, she questioned whether anyone can "interpret with absolute certainty individual passages of Scripture." Unlike her judges, she suggested that words do not have set meanings, that there is a gap between speaker and listener, and that human understanding always "falls short of absolute truth."

"The sum of her opinion," John Cotton concluded in the meeting-house of Boston, "is that the souls of men by creation are no other or better than the souls of beasts, which die and are mortal, but are made immortal by the redemption of Christ Jesus, to which hath been answered that the soul *is* immortal by creation, and the souls of the wicked [are] cast into Hell forever, and the souls of the godly are kept in a blameless frame unto immortal glory."

Sensing Cotton's impatience, Leverett asked if the Boston congregation was prepared to vote on this error. Anne's son-in-law Thomas Savage stood up to request more time for the parties to come to agreement regarding this error. He and many present recalled that Governor Winthrop had invoked the church's unanimity rule eighteen months before to forestall the appointment of John Wheelwright as the second teacher of this church. This rule, which was not applied uniformly, stated that the church not act without the consent of every member. Seeing that the whole "church is not accused of this opinion, but one party," Savage asked that "the church may have time first to consider of it." Savage, a twenty-nine-year-old merchant, had been born in Somerset, England, sailed from London to Boston in the spring of 1635, been admitted to this church the following January, made a freeman that April, and married Anne's daughter Faith in 1637.

The Reverend Wilson tried to counter Savage by raising the ancient Israelites' response to blasphemy: "They did rend their garments and tear the hair of their heads in sign of loathing! And if *we* deny the resurrection of the body, then let us turn epicures: Let us eat and drink and do anything, for tomorrow we shall die." Referring to the prophet Elijah's defeat of Queen Jezebel, Wilson cried, "And when all the priests of Baal pleaded for Baal, and Elijah *proved* the Lord to be God, if anyone had a scruple and was not satisfied but [believed] Baal was still God, should one man's scruple hinder all the rest of the congregation [from crying] out that the Lord is God! The Lord is God! And the Lord *only* is the Lord!"

Governor Winthrop joined his longtime ally. "The whole congregation but one brother"—Thomas Savage—"is sufficiently satisfied with what hath been already spoken to this point to be sufficient. Therefore, let us proceed to the next."

The Reverend Cotton looked at Hutchinson's son-in-law Savage and said, "We are *not* to hear what natural affection will say. For we are to forsake father and mother, wife and children for Christ Jesus.

1 Corinthians 5:12." He questioned the Hutchinsons' catechism: "I am sorry to hear *any* of our brethren to be so brought up that they should not hear of the immortality of the soul."

The Reverend Wilson raised the controversy over the indwelling of the Holy Spirit. "I look at this opinion to be dangerous and damnable," he cried, flushing, "and no less than Sadduceeism and atheism, and therefore to be detested!"

"If error be the thing you intend," Hutchinson replied, "then I desire to know *what* is the error for which I was banished [in November], for I am sure *this* is not [the error], for then there was no such expression from me on this." Indeed, no one had raised any of these doctrinal issues, such as the resurrection of the body and soul or the indwelling of the Spirit, at her November trial.

An unidentified supporter of Wilson's called for a show of hands. Most of the saints of Boston, according to the transcript, "did express themselves satisfied with what hath been spoken and by lifting up of their hands did show their dislike of it and did condemn it as an error."

"This question of the immortality of the soul is an ancient heresy," remarked John Davenport, the English minister who was staying with Cotton while awaiting the best time to travel southwest to a fledgling settlement that he would call New Haven. "They that speak for the mortality of the soul speak most for *licentiousness* and sinful liberty. Therefore, I think there should be no scruple" about "casting out" offenders and heathens from the church.

During the hours of testimony, Hutchinson made some concessions to her inquisitors. At one point when Davenport tried to clarify something for her, she said gratefully, "I thank the Lord I have light. And I see more light a great deal by Mr. Davenport's opening of it."

At other times, she resisted their pressure to change her views. Davenport tried to get her to concede that "the coming of Christ to the soul in Thessalonians is *not* meant to be Christ's coming in union" with us. She replied, "I do not acknowledge it to be an error, but a mistake. I do acknowledge my expression to be erroneous, but my judgment was not erroneous, for I held before as *you* did but could not express it so." She listed her references: "John 12, 1 Corinthians 4:3, 1 Corinthians 15:37–44, on having two bodies, and 1 Corinthians 4:16."

Cotton said, "You *say* you do not know whether Jesus Christ be united to our fleshly bodies. There lies the scruple and the absurdity of it! Therefore, remember, both soul and body are united to Christ."

Occasionally she returned to her familiar role as his student, as when she asked him, "I desire you to speak to that place in 1 Corinthians 15:37–44 for I do question whether the same bodies that die shall rise again."

Davenport seemed to encourage her, asking after he explained something, "Therefore, are you clear in that place?"

"No, not yet," she replied.

At one point, the Reverend Peter Bulkeley entered the fray. Bulkeley, now fifty-five years old, had come to Boston a year after Anne, had founded Concord, where he preached, and, with Thomas Hooker, had run the Cambridge Synod, which established orthodox colonial doctrine. "I desire to know of Mistress Hutchinson whether you hold that foul, gross, filthy, and abominable opinion, held by Familists, of the *community of women*," meaning a community in which women have power over men. This was the same fear that Winthrop had expressed prior to the court trial, that Hutchinson would "establish a community of women," with their "abominable wickedness."

It is not clear that the ministers actually believed Hutchinson was a Familist or a believer in free love. These terms were useful against her, so Winthrop and the orthodox ministers portrayed her this way. In a letter to Cotton in 1634, Shepard had referred to her obliquely: "Familists do not care for word of ordinances but only the spirit's motion. They will profess that there they meet with the [Holy] Spirit and their superlative raptures." Shepard added, "Jezebel, Revelation 2, who hath her depths, calls herself a prophetess, 'tis her glory to interpret scripture. . . ." In response, Cotton had denied knowledge of any Familism in his flock, a denial that Shepard seemed to accept.

Now, in response to the Reverend Bulkeley's charge of Familism, Anne Hutchinson said hotly, "I hold it not!" Of course she was not a Familist. To address this accusation and that of subscribing to the indwelling of the spirit, she said, "I do *not* believe that Christ Jesus is united to our bodies."

"God forbid," Wilson gasped, as if even to state the heresy in denying it was an offense.

The Reverend Davenport ignored her denial and echoed the Reverend Bulkeley's concern. "If the resurrection be past, then marriage is past, and then if there be any union between man and woman it is not by marriage but in a way of community," or what is now called free love.

Repelled by the suggestion that she questioned the sacred vow of marriage, Hutchinson said, "If any such practice or conclusion be drawn from it, then I must leave it, for I abhor that practice."

"The Familists do not desire to evade that question, for they practice the thing," Winthrop offered. "And they bring this very place [in Scripture] to prove their community of women and to justify their abominable wickedness. It is a *dangerous* error."

Leverett pleaded on her behalf. "But our sister doth not deny the resurrection of the body."

"No," she sighed. But most everyone in the room acted as though Leverett had not spoken, or if he had his words were not true. In this church trial, unlike the civil trial the previous November, Anne had little success in undercutting the many misrepresentations of her beliefs and attacks on her character. Moreover, she was already convicted as a heretic and banished, so she had less stature. In addition, the ministers whom she had criticized were anxious to shore up their egos by attacking her. They bullied her at times. The Reverend Peter asked her, "Do you think the very bodies of Moses, Elijah, and Enoch were taken up into the heavens, or no?"

"I know not that," she admitted.

"These are opinions that cannot be borne!" Davenport cried. "They shake the very foundation of our faith and tend to the overthrow of all religion. They are not slight matters [but are] of great weight and consequence."

"We *much* fear her spirit," the Reverend Eliot agreed.

Sensing that his moment had arrived, the Reverend Wilson said, "If the church be satisfied with the arguments that have been propounded—that they are convinced in their judgments that these are errors, let them express it by their usual sign of holding up their hands—and that they look at them as gross and damnable heresies." Many members of the Boston congregation, except Anne's sons and several women, raised their hands. As all were aware, Hutchinson's strongest supporters were gone to Rhode Island, and any additional support she might enjoy had been suppressed.

Wilson continued confidently, "And because it is very late and many things yet to go over, the church thinks it meet to refer further dealing with our sister till the next lecture day."

Edward Hutchinson, Anne's oldest son, rose from his bench to object to the church acting without unanimity. "I desire to know by what rule *I* am to express myself in my assent or dissent when yet my mother is not convinced. For I hope she will not shut her eyes against any light."

"Brother," Wilson cautioned him, "you may as well question whether God will confess you before his Father which is in heaven, when you *deny* to confess *his* truth before men though against your own mother."

Davenport seconded this warning. "You are *not* to be led by natural affection, but to declare your opinion for the truth and against error, though held by your own mother. The question was not whether the arguments were weighty enough to convince your mother, but whether *you* have light enough to satisfy your conscience that they are errors."

"Then I consent to them, as far as I know, that there *is* a resurrection," Edward replied, not knowing how else to support his mother.

Thomas Shepard broke in. "If there be *any* of this congregation that do hold the same opinions [as she does], I advise them to take heed of it, for the hand of the Lord will find you out! And for Mistress Hutchinson, she hath often boasted of the guidance of God's spirit and that her revelations are as true as the Scriptures. But she hath already confessed her mistake in the two first points by the light she hath received from Mr. Davenport. Now, then, her spirit hath led her into some errors. Therefore, I hope she will see the rest to be errors, and know it is not God's spirit but her own spirit that hath guided her hitherto—a spirit of delusion and error!" Shepard was expressing powerful emotions that had possessed him for two years, fueling countless letters and sermons. "I know not wherein I might show more love to her soul than in bringing her to her own congregation to answer to these dangerous and fearful errors which she hath drunk in. . . . For she is of a most dangerous spirit, and likely with her fluent tongue and forwardness in expression to seduce and draw away many—especially simple women *of her own sex.*" As he suggested, a "fluent tongue," "forwardness in expression," and many of Anne's other virtues were permissible only in men.

The Reverend Wilson called for a vote on admonition. "If the church be satisfied with what hath been spoken, and that they conceive we ought to proceed to admonition, we will take their silence for consent. If any be otherwise minded, they may express themselves."

The moral high point of the church trial occurred now, near the close of the first day, when Thomas Savage stood again for his mother-in-law. "For my part I am not yet satisfied," the brave young man began. "Neither do I see any rule why the church should proceed to admonition, seeing that in the most churches there hath been some errors or mistakes held. Yea, and in this very Church of Corinth there were many unsound opinions, and in particular some amongst them that held this very opinion about the resurrection as appears by Paul's arguments in the fifteenth chapter" of the apostle's First Epistle to the Corinthians, some of whom believed that "there is no resurrection of the dead." Savage continued, "Yet we do not read [in 1 Corinthians 15] that the church did admonish them for it. Indeed, in point of fact, as in the case of incest, the church proceeded to excommunication because it was gross and abominable, but not for opinion. Now, my mother not being accused for any heinous fact, but only for opinion—and that wherein she desires information and light, [rather] than peremptorily to hold—I cannot consent that the church should proceed yet to admonish her for this."

Two and a half centuries later, the historian Charles Francis Adams would remark, "Thomas Savage, who had recently married Faith [Hutchinson], did himself infinite credit by rising and courageously protesting against the admonition about to be bestowed; and, as a result of so doing, he had the honor of being himself admonished together with her he so manfully fought to protect."

In the meetinghouse, John Cotton addressed Thomas Savage. "Your mother, though she be not accused of anything in point of fact or practice—" and he interrupted himself to add, "Neither, for my own part, do I know there is any cause. Yet," he continued, "she *may* hold errors. Therefore, I see not but the church may proceed to admonition." He admitted that he had no choice but to proceed, even without cause.

At this point in the trial, according to David Hall, there was nothing that the ministers, magistrates, or even Hutchinson herself could say or do to change the course of events. She was out of place and had to be removed.

Lowering his voice for emphasis, Cotton told Savage, "You do a *very* evil office—out of your natural, not religious, affection—to hinder the church in her proceeding, and to be a means to harden your mother's heart in these dangerous opinions, and so keep her from repentance."

Seeing nothing else to say or do to help his mother-in-law, Savage took his seat.

Another daring soul took his place. Lieutenant Edward Gibbons was a merchant who had arrived in Boston in 1630 and strongly supported Hutchinson, Cotton, and Vane. Known as "a man of resolute spirit, bold as a lion, very generous and forward to promote all military matters," Gibbons would become commander of the Suffolk regiment of the militia in 1644, then a major general, and, finally, captain of the Ancient and Honorable Artillery Company. "Admonition," he said, "is one of the greatest censures that the church can pronounce against any offender, and one of the last, next to excommunication, to be used against impenitent offenders. Seeing that God hath turned her heart about already to see her error, or mistake as she calls it, in some of the points, had not the church wait a little longer to see if God will not help her to see the rest? Then the church may have no occasion to come to this censure."

Faced with this compassion for Hutchinson, the Reverend Symmes took aim. "I am *much* grieved to hear that so many in this congregation should stand up and declare themselves unwilling that Mistress Hutchinson should be proceeded against for such dangerous errors." He scanned the room, considering how to raise the community's dread of losing its foothold on the continent. "I fear that if by any means *this* should be carried over into England—that in New England and in such a congregation there was so much spoken, and so many questions made about so plain an article of our faith as the resurrection is—it will be one of the greatest dishonors to Jesus Christ, and of reproach to these churches, that hath been done since we came hither."

Thomas Oliver, the church elder, asked whether unanimity was necessary to censure Hutchinson, given that her sons, at least, appeared unlikely to consent. "I desire to be satisfied in one thing: how the church can, or whether it may, proceed to any censure when all the members do not consent thereto—or whether the church hath not power to lay a censure upon them that do hinder the church's proceedings." Recalling "the pattern of the primitive churches of Jesus Christ," he said, "All things in the church should be done with one heart and one soul and one consent: any and every act done by the church may be as the act of one man."

The Reverend Cotton replied, "If the church do take pains and do bring arguments such as satisfies the whole congregation to be sufficient, if yet some brethren will persist in their dissent—upon no ground or out of natural affection—then the church is not to stay her proceeding for that."

"The church is satisfied," Davenport said. "I perceive none doth oppose the church—some, only two or three which are tied to her by natural relation—for these others that have spoken, they did propound it but as scruples, and they have received satisfaction. Therefore, I see nothing that may hinder."

Now, according to the trial transcript, "the whole church by their silence consented to the motion, and so they proceeded to admonition." This consent was not only silent but also not the "whole church," according to Thomas Leverett. Although Cotton later recalled that "the whole body of the church (except her own son) consented with one accord," Leverett said that many other men objected to her censure. Their voices were not recorded, and also not recorded were the voices of the many women present and the men who had already been disfranchised, disarmed, and banished from the colony.

Church elders Leverett and Oliver asked Cotton to give the admonition "as one whose words by the blessing of God may be of more respect and sink deeper, and so was likely to do more good upon the party offending than any of these. And it was also left to him to do as God should incline his heart, whether to lay any admonition [also] upon her two sons."

Before he began, the Reverend Cotton took a breath deep enough to carry multiple clauses. "I do in the first place bless the Lord, and thank in my own name, and in the name of our church, these our brethren, the elders of other churches, for their care and faithfulness in watching over our churches, and for bringing to light what ourselves have not been so ready to see. . . ."

"I confess," he went on, blithely assuming responsibility for the church's predicament, "I have not been ready to believe reports, and have been slow of proceeding against any of our members. . . . But now, they have proceeded in a way of God, and do bring such testimony as doth evince the truth of what is affirmed, [so] it would be our sin if we should not join in the same."

Turning to Edward Hutchinson and Thomas Savage, who sat at the front of the men's side of the meetinghouse, Cotton said, "In the first place, I shall direct my speech and admonition to you that are her sons. Let me tell you *from the Lord*, though natural affection may lead you to speak in the defense of your mother and to seek to keep up her credit and respect—yet in the cause of God you are neither to know father nor mother, sister nor brother. Yea, you must cast down your mother's name and credit, though it be the chiefest crown that either yourselves or your mother hath, at the feet of Jesus Christ and let that be *trampled* upon, so His crown may be exalted!"

Raising his voice ever so slightly, he said, "I do *admonish* you both, in the name of Christ Jesus, and of his church, to consider how ill an office you have performed to your mother—to harden her heart, and nourish her in her unsound opinions, by your pleading for her, and hindering the proceedings of the church against her, which God hath *directed us* to take to heal her soul, and which God might have blessed and made *more* effectual to her had not *you* intercepted the course.

"Instead of loving and natural children," he told Hutchinson's son and son-in-law, "you have proved *vipers to eat through the very bowels of your mother*—to her ruin, if God do not graciously prevent. Take heed how by your flattery or mourning over her, or your applauding of her when you come home, do hinder the work of repentance in her. But look up to Christ Jesus, and address yourselves to her with all faithful and gracious counsels, that you may bring her to a sight of these evils in her, and to reduce her from them. *Then* shall you perform the parts of faithful children indeed, and the Lord will bless you," he prophesied. "If you do otherwise, the Lord will bring you to an account for it."

Done with the sons, he turned to the women's side of the meetinghouse, where some women of Boston, including Mary Dyer, sat on benches alongside the wives of the assembled ministers and magistrates. Some of these women silently condemned the proceedings.

Others would follow Anne Hutchinson to Rhode Island. "To the sisters of our own congregation," Cotton said, "many of whom have been seduced and led aside by her, I admonish you in the Lord to take heed that you receive *nothing* for truth which hath not the stamp of the word of God. Let me say this to you all, let *not* the good you have received from her in your spiritual estates make you to receive *all* for good that comes from her. For, you see, she is *but* a woman."

This was, indeed, a problem. Historians argue over the degree to which gender affected this case—the literary scholar Lad Tobin called Anne's gender her trial's "root cause"—but all agree that, had Hutchinson been a man, she would have had a public forum for her intellectual gifts, either in government or, more likely, the ministry. As it was, she had to preach and lead in private and against the law. The reason, according to Cotton, was that a woman "is more subject to error than a man." In *Singing of Psalms a Gospel-Ordinance*, he wrote, "It is not permitted to a woman to speak in the church by way of propounding questions though under pretence of desire to learn for her own satisfaction; but rather it is required she should ask her husband at home." Recalling what seemed to him Hutchinson's deception, Cotton added, "For under pretence of questioning for learning sake, she might so propound her question as to teach her teachers; or if not so, yet to open a door to some of her own weak and erroneous apprehensions, or at least soon exceed the bounds of womanly modesty."

For a minister to attack a convicted heretic on the basis of her gender seems, at the very least, overkill. The ministers aimed their antagonism at her character and her sex because she threatened their notions of "the family, the state, the religion, and the status hierarchy," according to the historian Lyle Koehler. Thus they "managed to salve the psychological wounds inflicted by this woman who trod so sharply upon their male status and their ministerial and magisterial authority." Her pride and aggressiveness seemed to them the work of Satan rather than "the more human desire for equal opportunity and treatment" that Hutchinson "never hesitated to assert by example in the intellectual skirmishes she had with her accusers throughout her trials." The oppression of a male-dominated society "could not destroy her self-respect," her ability to ally herself with God, and her skill at debating religious matters with the authorities, be they ministers or magistrates.

In the meetinghouse, the Reverend Cotton continued, "And many *unsound* and *dangerous* principles are held by her. If you have drunk in any evil or poison, make speed to vomit it up again, and to repent of it, and do not harden her in her way by pitying of her or confirming her. But pray to God for her, and bear witness against any unsound thing she held forth."

Now he turned without apparent emotion to his former disciple and dear friend, who was now weakened by her imprisonment, her unsettled pregnancy, and the disruption of her family life. It was necessary, he felt, to establish distance from her. Distance, it now seemed, was the only politic stance. Placing his palms together, he prayed, "The Lord put fit words into my mouth, and carry them home to your soul for good."

She sat on her bench, hardly ten feet away, quietly observing the minister whom she for more than twenty years had followed and served.

"It is true," he began, seeming to take her side, "when you came first over into this country, we heard of some opinions that you vented upon the seas in the ship" about which the authorities needed to be reassured before admitting her to church membership. "Since then, you have been an instrument of doing some good. The Lord hath endowed you with good parts and gifts fit to instruct your children and servants, and to be helpful to your husband in the government of the family." In addition, she had prepared many souls for Cotton to save, and she had spread, especially among women, his condemnation of the covenant of works. "You have been helpful to many to bring them off from building their good estate upon their own duties and performances or upon any righteousness of the law."

Just as a few saints of Boston began to suspect that he might not admonish Hutchinson after all, he switched his tone. "Yet notwithstanding" all this, he said, "we have a few things *against* you, and in some sense *not* a few, but such as are of great *weight* and of a heavy nature and *dangerous* consequences. Therefore, let me warn you and *admonish* you in the name of Jesus Christ to consider of it seriously—how the dishonor you have brought unto God by these unsound tenets of yours is *far greater* than all the honor you have brought to Him. And the *evil* of your opinions doth outweigh all the good of your doings." He begged her to "consider how many poor souls you have misled," and "that by this one error of yours, in *denying* the *resurrection* of these very *bodies*"—a view associated with the Family of Love—"you do the uttermost to raze the very foundation of religion to the ground, and to destroy our faith!" While it is unlikely that Hutchinson ever denied the resurrection of the body, this was indeed the sole error the ministers had mentioned that merited excommunication for heresy, for it was a denial of a fundamental belief of English Calvinism as stated in the Thirty-Nine Articles of Religion.

John Winthrop, who could not but enjoy the Reverend Cotton's assault on the "obstinate" Mistress Hutchinson, noted later how Cotton "remembered her of the good way she was in her first coming, in helping to discover to diverse [people] the false bottom they stood upon, in trusting to legal works without Christ." Then, according to the governor, Cotton "showed her how by falling into these gross and fundamental errors she had lost the honor of her former service, and done more wrong to Christ and his church than formerly she had done good."

Cotton's litany continued: "Yea, if the resurrection be past, then you cannot evade the argument pressed upon you by our brother Bulkeley and others, that *filthy* sin of the community of women—and all promiscuous and *filthy* coming-together of men and women without distinction or relation of marriage—*will* necessarily follow!" He was saying that her doctrine guaranteed a community of men and women joined in sexual relationships outside marriage—a notion that everyone present, including Hutchinson, found abhorrent.

Noting her look of horror, Cotton prophesied, "And though I have not *heard*—neither do I think—you have been unfaithful to your husband in *his* marriage covenant, yet that *will* follow upon it! Yours is the very argument that the Sadducees bring to our savior Christ against the resurrection, and that which the Anabaptists and Familists bring to prove the lawfulness of the common [sexual] use of all women, and so more dangerous evils and filthy uncleanness and other sins will follow than you do now imagine or conceive!"

Sexual expression in Puritan New England was restricted to marriage. To maintain social control, the ministers forbade and punished sexual activity outside marriage and any other sexual behavior that might damage the structure of the family. Adultery was a capital offense, the General Court decreed in 1631. The death penalty was not actually imposed in most cases of adultery that came before the Massachusetts court, but offenders usually received a severe whipping or a symbolic hanging—sitting for an hour on the gallows with a rope around the neck—and were then banished. As for other sexual crimes, all "unnatural filthiness [is] to be punished with death, whether sodomy, which is carnal fellowship of man with man, or of woman with woman; or buggery, which is carnal fellowship of man or woman with beasts or fowls." These words, which the court had made law in 1635, were penned by Cotton himself, after he was asked to write the first code of colonial laws.

Hearing him describe sins of which she could not even conceive, Anne Hutchinson said, "I desire to speak one word before you proceed. I would forbear [wait], but by reason of my weakness I fear I shall not remember it when you have done."

Grimly, he replied, "You have leave to speak."

"All that I would say is this, that I did not hold any of these things [opinions] before my imprisonment." Despite all he had prophesied, she still deflected his reproach. Even the attacks of her minister did not shake her great faith in God. She believed, as the apostle Paul described in 2 Timothy 4:17–18, that "The Lord stood with me, and strengthened me . . . and I was delivered out of mouth of the lion. And the Lord shall deliver me from every evil work, and will preserve me unto his heavenly kingdom."

Before replying, Cotton considered how his fellow ministers, some of whom still suspected he had supported her all along, would respond. "I confess I did not know that you held any of these things, nor hear, till here of late. Maybe it was my sleepiness, and want of watchful care over you." Seeming to steel himself, he said, "But you see the *danger* of it, and how God hath left you to yourself to fall into these dangerous evils. For I have often feared *the height of your Spirit* and being *puffed up with your own parts!*" It was all her fault. She was too proud. Exhibiting the very vice for which he was calling down the wrath of God, he said, "Therefore, it is just with God thus to abase you, and to leave you to these desperate falls, for the Lord looketh upon all the children of pride and delights to abase them and bring them low."

Again he listed all the offensive views she was said to hold—"the mortality of the soul by nature," "that Christ is not united to our bodies," and "that the resurrection spoken of at his appearing is meant of his appearing to us in union." If these were all true, he asked, "What need we care what we speak, or do, here—if our souls perish and die like beasts?"

She shook her head, for she believed none of them.

"Nay," he said, "though you not hold them positively, if you do but *make a question* of them, and propound them as a doubt for satisfaction, yet others that hear of it will conclude them positively. And they will think, *Sure there is something in it if Mistress Hutchinson makes a question of it*—if those that have great parts of wisdom and understanding, and such an *eminent* Christian makes a question of them—then there is something that needs further inquiry."

Summoning his most vivid apocalyptic imagery and self-righteousness, Cotton said, "And so your opinions fret like a gangrene and spread like a leprosy, and infect far and near, and will eat out the very bowels of religion, and hath so infected the churches that God knows when they will be cured! Therefore, that I may draw to an end"—he raised his arms toward heaven—"I do *admonish* you and also *charge* you in the name of Christ Jesus, in whose place I stand, that you would sadly consider the just hand of God against you, the *great hurt* you have done to the churches, the *great dishonor* you have brought to Jesus Christ, and the *evil* that you have done to many a poor soul. And seek unto Him to give you repentance, and a heart to give satisfaction to the churches you have offended hereby, and bewail your weakness in the sight of the Lord, that you may be pardoned. And consider the great dishonor and reproach that hereby you have brought upon this church, how you have laid us *all* under a suspicion of holding and maintaining errors. And take heed how you did leaven the hearts of young women with such unsound and dangerous principles, and labor to recover them out of the snares which you have drawn them to. And so the Lord carry home to your soul what I have spoken in his name!"

Cotton nodded to Shepard. To ensure that no one would leave the meeting doubting that Hutchinson had lied, Shepard said, "*Lest* the crown should be set on her head in the day of her humiliation, I desire leave to speak *one* word before the assembly breaks up." He turned to Cotton and said, "It is no little affliction nor grief to my spirit to hear Mistress Hutchinson interrupt you, by speaking in the midst of her censure, unto which she ought to have attended with fear and trembling. But it was an astonishment to me to hear that she should thus *impudently*," like Francis Marbury, "affirm so horrible an untruth and falsehood in the midst of such a solemn ordinance of Jesus Christ and before such an assembly. Yea, in the face of the church to *say* she held none of these opinions before her imprisonment, when she *knows* that she used this speech to me, when I was *with* her and *dealt* with her about these opinions, and she had fluently and forwardly expressed herself to me, yet she [even] added [that] if I had but come to her before her restraint she would have opened herself more fully to me and have declared many other things about these very opinions. Therefore, I am sorry that Mistress Hutchinson should so far forget herself. It shows but little fruit of all the pains taken with her. This makes me *more* to fear the unsoundness of her heart than all the rest."

"It was the same grief also to myself," the Reverend Eliot affirmed, to which other ministers nodded. In their joint disgust, the ministers were counting on the human tendency to believe what one is told, especially if the teller has authority. If they pinned on her labels of "free love" and "Familism," "libertine" and "seductress," few colonists would rise in response to the question, Who will support Mistress Hutchinson now?

While reformation was one goal of the church's process of examination, reforming Hutchinson was no longer the point. Her judges were making an example of her before the entire church and most of the elders of the colony. Their trial was itself a performance, with the goal of further shrinking her influence. She seemed beyond reform, but she could be forever an example of how not to behave in Massachusetts. Through her, they might frighten others, especially women and the defiant merchant class of men that supported her, into submission. The literary critic Susan Howe wrote that Hutchinson served as "the community scapegoat," the sacrificial animal that the ancient Jews used to bear away their sins.

Anne Hutchinson was not a feminist, in the modern sense, but her gender was a central issue for the men. The religious doctrine that so frightened them was for her "simply an ideology through which the resentments [she] intuitively felt could be focused and actively expressed," observed Lyle Koelher. "Her feminism," such as it was, "consisted essentially of the subjective recognition of her own strength and gifts and the apparent belief that other women could come to the same belief." Her rebellion was in no way directed self-consciously against her status or toward its improvement. A woman of her time, she accepted the gender hierarchies of the seventeenth century. There is no evidence that she questioned the rightness of having her husband and sons sign deeds and documents on her behalf or of having her husband, rather than herself, become a member of the government. Our modern concept of equal rights would likely shock her, although one imagines her ultimately embracing it.

In regard to Anne Hutchinson's failure to reform even under the threat of banishment and excommunication, it is essential to note that she could not reform while maintaining any public power or voice. Unlike her father, who in exchange for outward conformity to Anglican authorities was allowed to return to his pulpit and his teaching, she had neither pulpit nor public place from which to teach. On the one occasion when she did teach in public, during her second day before the General Court at Newtown, she was banished. The moment she opened the door to the parlor that served her as both classroom and meetinghouse, she was finished as a preacher and teacher. For a woman in colonial Massachusetts, to conform to the status quo was to be silent and passive. This was not an option for Anne Hutchinson.

Her fundamentally Calvinist doctrine—that in a sinful world Christ redeems people without their merit and then in some way joins with them—challenged colonial society at its very foundation. According to the literary scholar Amy Schrager Lang, Hutchinson and her followers "rejected the colonists' view of themselves as a chosen people, bound by covenant to fulfill God's work in the New World, and offered in its place the notion of a mystical community of the elect. The system of reward and punishment adduced from the Law and embodied in temporal authority" was, for Hutchinson, irrelevant. She was "free of the sometimes productive, sometimes disabling anxiety characteristic of the Puritan saint. Election is, for him, a condition of self-abnegation, his individuality no longer individual, his labors at an end, his destiny secure." To such a Puritan saint, Hutchinson seemed "to indulge the furthest extremes of self-assertion." Her claims to "invisible witness, absolute assurance, and exemption from the Law could only seem like sheer arrogance. Abandoning the social for the teleological, then, the Antinomian elevates the self to a new status precisely by insisting on the dissolution of the self in Christ." By losing herself in Christ, she became far more powerful than Winthrop, Cotton, and Wilson could abide.

In the meetinghouse of Boston, the hour grew late. "Sister Hutchinson," the Reverend Wilson cried, "I require you, in the name of the church, to present yourself here again the next lecture day, this day seven-night, to give your answer to such other things as this church or the elders of other churches have to charge you withal concerning your opinions, whether you hold them or no, or will revoke them."

The prisoner indicated her assent. "The court had ordered that she should return to Roxbury again," Winthrop observed, "but upon intimation that her spirit began to fall, she was permitted to remain at Mr. Cotton's house (where Davenport was also kept)" for the following week. Now that her removal from the country was so near, there was no need to return her to Roxbury, but she could not be allowed the freedom to stay at home.

At twilight Anne walked the short, familiar route from the meetinghouse to the house at the foot of Pemberton Hill where John and Sarah Cotton lived with their four children: four-month-old Elizabeth, two-year-old Sarah, four-year-old Seaborn, and Sarah Cotton's first daughter. Located at modern-day Pemberton Square, facing Government Center, the house overlooked the harbor from a higher vantage point than Hutchinson's, through the diamond-shaped windowpanes that distinguished it from every other house on Shawmut except the matching house that Vane had built next door.

It was Cotton who, intimating Anne's falling spirits, had requested her week's incarceration here. He felt that he and Davenport had much work to do on her soul. He was troubled by her doctrinal questions, her persistence in the face of his reproach, and his own credibility in the eyes of his brother divines. His judgment was sorely compromised in Massachusetts because of his connection with Hutchinson. Looking back on more than twenty years of friendship with her, he recalled that "she did much good in our town," and "found loving and dear respect both from our church elders and brethren." But he believed that she had duped him twice. First, she lied in telling him and many others that her beliefs and his were the same. While at one time true, he felt, this was now false. Her second deceit was that she at some point changed her theological views. "This change of hers," he explained in defending himself, "was long hid from me."

In part to cleanse himself of her stain, he hoped still to convince her to recant her views, to repent, to renounce her powers of prophecy, to try persuasively to undo everything she'd done, to show submissiveness, and to beg his and the country's forgiveness. Her banishment now seemed inevitable, but at least she might be shown the error of her ways.

13

A DANGEROUS
INSTRUMENT OF
THE DEVIL

On the morning of Thursday, March 22, 1638, Anne Hutchinson did not arrive late to the lecture-day service, as she had the week before. She filed into the meetinghouse of Boston alongside most of the women of the congregation, who were followed by the men of this church and many other churches of Massachusetts Bay Colony. Unlike most lecture days, elders and men from other towns had traveled to Boston to attend the conclusion of the trial of Anne Hutchinson by her church. It was essential, in the opinion of the leaders, that "the face of the country" be present at such an important event.

The Reverend John Cotton began the second day of the trial with a brief Scripture reading. Then he nodded to Thomas Leverett, his old friend from Lincolnshire, who rose from his bench.

"Sister Hutchinson," Leverett said, "an admonition was passed against you, and you are now to make answer to other things laid to your charge. But first, I would have the members of our own church draw near to express their consent or dissent to the things in hand which doth most concern them." Again there was a shuffling as the Boston congregation clustered together so their raised hands could be seen more easily.

Leverett again read the errors laid to Hutchinson's charge, most of which she had now rejected, either on the previous lecture day or in discussions with Cotton during the week. In the presence of her congregation and all the ministers, Hutchinson confessed her errors. She listed them one by one, conceding, "I do acknowledge I was deeply deceived; the opinion was very dangerous. . . . I acknowledge my mistake. . . . I acknowledge—and I do thank God—that I better see that Christ is united to our fleshly bodies.... I acknowledge that there is grace created in Christ Jesus as Isaiah 11:2, 2 Peter 4:24, Colossians 3:10.... I do see good warrant that Christ's mansion is in heaven as well as his body. I have considered some Scriptures that satisfy me that the image of Adam is righteousness and holiness.... I acknowledge that to be a hateful error which openeth a gap to all licentiousness. And I believe if we do anything contrary to the law it is a grievous sin." Under Cotton's coaching, she was bowing to the law and to the orthodox authorities. She handed over a paper to this effect, which she had written with Cotton, and signed.

Noting that there were still more errors, Leverett said, "Have you any answer to the rest?"

As Cotton had instructed her, she apologized for her November prophecy of the colony's doom. "For the Scriptures that I used at the court in censuring the country," she said, "I confess I did it rashly and out of heat of spirit and unadvisedly, and have cause to be sorry for my unreverent carriage to them, and I am heartily sorry that anything I have said has drawn any from hearing any of the elders of the Bay."

But to a few errors, she could only say truthfully, "I never held any such thing."

The Reverend Wilson said, "There is one thing that will be necessary for you to answer to. You denied you held none of those things but since your durance whereas he"—Shepard—"alleged to you that you expressed the contrary."

"As my sin hath been open," she said, "so I think it needful to acknowledge how I came first to fall into these errors. Instead of looking upon myself, I looked at men." This is both a pointed reference to Cotton's flaws—a nod to how he disappointed one who had trusted him—and also an indication of Hutchinson's great confidence in herself. She had a pioneering sense of her self and her destiny, which is extraordinary in a woman of the seventeenth century, to whom so little authority was allowed. Hutchinson's desire to look within for guidance is characteristic of the distinctively American faith in the power of the individual conscience. In this confidence in the power of her own views, she presaged not only the early Quakers but also the nineteenth-

century Transcendentalists, Ralph Waldo Emerson, and the "opposi-
tional quality" in such classic literature of the American Renaissance as
Nathaniel Hawthorne's *Scarlet Letter* and *Uncle Tom's Cabin*, by Harriet
Beecher Stowe.

"I spake rashly and unadvisedly" at court, Hutchinson continued. "I
do not allow the slighting of ministers nor of the Scriptures nor anything that is set up by God. If Mr. Shepard doth conceive that I had any
of these things in my mind, then he is deceived. It was never in my
heart to slight any man, but only that man should be kept in his own
place and not set in the room of God." Instead of seeing the ministers
as closer to God than herself, she saw all people as at an equal distance
from God. This view was not shared by the magistrates and ministers,
who saw themselves as her authorities, as in the fifth commandment,
"Honor thy father and thy mother."

Thomas Leverett said, "The assembly [of ministers] may know
what you have delivered" in the paper she turned in, but "somebody
should express what you say to the congregation which heard not."

Cotton presumed to speak on Hutchinson's behalf to the congregation: "The sum of what she said [in writing] is this: that she did not fall
into these gross and fundamental errors till she came to Roxbury. And
she doth utterly disallow herself and condemn herself for her miscarriage and disrespect that she showed to the magistrates when she was
before them. And she confesses the root of all was the height and pride
of her spirit," words that he had urged her to add. "So, for her slighting
the ministers, she is heartily sorry. She is sorry, and desires all that she
hath offended to pray to God for her to give her a heart to be more
truly humbled."

Speaking aloud Cotton's thoughts, Thomas Shepard questioned the
earnestness of her repentance. "I confess I am *wholly* unsatisfied in her
expressions to some of these gross and damnable errors. I fear it doth
not stand with true repentance. Any heretic may bring a sly interpretation upon any of these errors and yet hold them to their death. Therefore, I am unsatisfied, [though] I should be glad to see *any* repentance
in her. That might give me satisfaction."

In the same spirit, John Eliot said, "Mistress Hutchinson did affirm
to me, as she did to Mr. Shepard, that if we had come to her *before* her
restraint or imprisonment, she could and would have told me many

things, but now we had shut and debarred ourselves from that help by proceeding against her. . . . We are not satisfied."

"Two things [need] to be cleared," Cotton ordered her. "What you do now hold, and what you did hold."

"My judgment is not altered though my expression alters," she replied.

"This you say is most dangerous!" the Reverend Wilson cried. "For if your judgment all this while be not altered, but only your expressions—when your expressions are so contrary to the truth!"

"I should be glad to see *any* humiliation in Mistress Hutchinson," the Reverend Symmes said. "I fear these are no new things but she hath anciently held them, and had need to be humbled for her former doctrines and for her abuse of diverse Scriptures."

The Reverend Peter added, in a voice amazed, "We did think she would have humbled herself, for her opinions are dangerous and fundamental and such as takes down the Articles of Religion"—the thirty-nine statements of doctrine of the Church of England—"as denying the resurrection and faith and all sanctification."

Thomas Dudley, the deputy governor, who had listened without comment until now—perhaps because as neither a clergyman nor a member of this church he had no role in this proceeding—decided to insert his canny logic, whether or not it was called for. "Mistress Hutchinson's repentance is only for opinions held *since* her imprisonment, but [she is saying that] before her imprisonment she was in a good condition and held no error, but did a great deal of good to many. Now, I know no harm that Mistress Hutchinson hath done *since* her confinement. Therefore I think her repentance will be worse than her errors, for if by this means she shall get a party [of supporters] to herself—and what can any heretic in the world desire more? And for her form of recantation, her repentance is in a paper, whether it was drawn up by herself or whether she had any help in it, I know not and will not now inquire to. But sure her repentance is not in her countenance. None can see it there, I think."

The Reverend Peter added to the chorus of Hutchinson's defamers, recalling "once speaking with her about the Woman of Ely," a woman in England who was said to preach weekly to men and women and possibly also to baptize. This woman's ministry was in the cathedral town of

Ely, near Cambridge, about sixty miles south of Alford. At the time Ely was home to many Familists, merchants like Will and strong-minded women like Anne who sought more autonomy and power than English village life allowed. According to the Reverend Peter, Hutchinson "did exceedingly magnify her [the Woman of Ely] to be a 'woman of a thousand, hardly any like to her.' And yet we know that the Woman of Ely is a dangerous woman, and holds forth grievous things and fearful errors."

Hutchinson defended herself, "I said of the Woman of Ely but what I heard, for I knew her not nor never saw her."

The Reverend Wilson, whose resentment was fueled by his memories of being so often humiliated by Hutchinson, addressed her directly. "You *say* that the cause or root of these your errors was your slighting and disrespect of the magistrates and your unreverent carriage to them ... but that is not all, for I fear and believe there was another and a greater cause, and that is the slighting of God's faithful ministers and condemning and crying down them as 'Nobodies.'" Flushing at the recollection of that term applied to him, he went on, "Yet I think it was to set up *yourself* in the room of God above others, that you might be extolled and admired and followed after, that you might be a great *prophetess*, and undertake to expound Scriptures and to interpret other men's sayings and sermons after your mind. And therefore, I believe, your iniquity hath found you out! And whereas before, if any dealt with you about anything, you called for witnesses and for your accusers, ... [but] now God hath left you to yourself, and you have here confessed that which before you have called for witnesses to prove. Therefore, it grieves me that you should so mince your dangerous soul and damnable heresies, whereby you have so wickedly departed from God and done so much hurt!"

Before Anne Hutchinson could reply, the Reverend Shepard said, "It is needless for any other now to speak, and useless, for the case is plain."

In desperation, she clung to her one link to orthodoxy. "Our teacher knows my judgment, for I never kept my judgment from him." Cotton remained silent, according to the transcript, but his writings suggest that he did not agree. In his view, while her statement may have been true at one time, it was no longer. He felt she had changed her doctrine and that he had not noticed it until later, when pressed by others to suspect her.

"In the ship," the Reverend Symmes again reminded the assembled, "she was often offended at the expression of 'growing in grace' and 'laying up a stock of grace' and that 'all grace is in Christ Jesus'"—suggesting that her "change" had occurred at least as long ago as 1634, before her ship landed in Boston.

"I know she hath said it and affirmed it dogmatically," Wilson stated, "that the grace of God is *not* in us, and we have *no* grace in us but only the righteousness of Christ imputed to us, and if there be *any* acting in us it is Christ only that acts. 53 Isaiah. Galatians 2."

"Mistress Hutchinson may remember that in her speaking with me," added the Reverend Richard Mather, of Dorchester, who had visited her in Roxbury, "that she denied all grace to be in us, [saying] that there was neither faith, nor knowledge, nor gifts and grace, no, nor life itself, but all is in Christ Jesus. And she brought some Scriptures to prove her opinions. I wonder that Mistress Hutchinson doth so far forget herself as to deny that she did not formerly hold this opinion of denying gifts and grace to be in us." The Reverend Mather was presently writing the *Bay Psalm Book*, which in 1640 would become the first book published in North America.

The Reverend Peter looked at her, his face set in anger. "I fear you are not well principled and grounded in your Catechism. I would commend *this* to your consideration—that you have stepped out of your place" as a woman. "You have rather been a husband than a wife; and a preacher than a hearer; and a magistrate than a subject. And so you have thought to carry [in yourself] all things in church and commonwealth, as you would, and [you] have *not* been humbled for this."

The Reverend Shepard added, "This day she hath showed herself to be a notorious imposter. She *never* had any true grace in her heart." This remark contradicted the Calvinist doctrine of the perseverance of the saints—that if a soul is elect, its election is eternal—and the notion, generally accepted then, that no one can detect for sure the status of another's soul. It is also akin to one of the errors that Anne Hutchinson was accused of holding—the presumption that she could tell who was or was not saved. The magistrates and ministers charged her with, in the words of David Hall, "brushing aside any doubts about [her] ca-

pacity for spiritual discernment" and urging "New England congregations to draw the strictest possible line between the sacred and the profane." This, ironically, is what the men were doing when they cast her
out for her beliefs.

The Reverend Shepard continued, "It is a trick of as notorious subtlety as ever was held in the church to say there is no grace in the
saints, and now to say" there is, "and that she all this while has not
altered her judgment but only her expressions. I would have the
congregation judge whether *ever* there was any grace in her heart or
no, whether ever she was in a good estate, because the ground of her
opinions hath been built upon feigned and fantastical revelations as she
held forth two in the court—one for the certain destruction of old England"—her shipboard prophecy, recounted by Symmes—"and another
for the ruin of this country and the people thereof for their proceeding
against her," which she had related in the Cambridge courtroom.

The Reverend Peter added, "We are not satisfied in her repentance,
in that she lays her imprisonment to be the cause of all her errors, as *if*
she were innocent before."

"I cannot but reverence and adore the wise hand of God in this
thing," intoned the Reverend Wilson. Inferring the wishes and aims of
God, he said, "I look at her as a dangerous instrument of the Devil,
raised up by Satan amongst us to raise up divisions and contentions,
and to take away hearts and affections one from another." Echoing
Dudley's words in November attributing all of the colony's troubles to
her, the minister said, "Whereas there was much love and union and
sweet agreement amongst us before she came, yet since [then] all
union and love hath been broken, and there hath been censurings and
judgings and condemnings one of another. And I do conceive *all* these
woeful opinions do come from *this bottom*, for if the bottom hath been
unsound and corrupt, then must the building be such. And the misgov-
ernment of this woman's tongue hath been a great cause of this disorder, which hath been to set up *herself* and to draw disciples after *her.*
And therefore, she says one thing today and another thing tomorrow,
whereas we should speak the truth plainly. Woe be to that soul that
shall build upon such bottoms! Our souls should *abhor* and loathe to
come so far short in repentance. . . . Therefore, I leave it to the church
to consider how safe it is to suffer so erroneous and so schismatical and

so unsound a member amongst us, the congregation of the Lord. Therefore, consider whether we shall be faithful to Jesus Christ, or whether it can stand with his honor to suffer such a one any longer amongst us. If the blind lead the blind, whither shall we go? Consider whether we may longer suffer her to go on still in *seducing to seduce* and in *deceiving to deceive* and in *lying to lie* and in condemning authority and magistrate. Therefore, we should sin against God if we should not put away from us so evil a woman, guilty of such foul evils!"

In the minds of the men, her "lie" was her recantation, which they judged to be false. As John Winthrop wrote later, some of her remarks were "circumlocutions, and seemed to lay all the faults to her expressions. . . . And this she affirmed with such confidence as bred great astonishment in many, who had known the contrary, and diverse alleged her own sayings and reasonings, both before her confinement and since, *which did manifest to all that were present that she knew that she spake untruth.*"

In the meetinghouse, Thomas Oliver, saddened by the lengthy speeches adumbrating Hutchinson's perceived evils, said, "I did not think the church would have come thus far so soon, especially seeing [that] when I talked with her [this morning] I saw her come so freely in her confession of her sin in condemning magistrates and ministers."

The Reverend Eliot countered, "It is a wonderful wisdom of God to let them fall by that whereby they have upheld their opinions, . . . for she hath carried on all her errors by lies, as that she held nothing but what Mr. Cotton did, and that he and she was all one in judgment."

"The matter is now translated," John Cotton said, meaning it was now settled. Still, he preferred not to be the man who cast out the "notorious liar" Anne Hutchinson. Someone else would have to so cleanse the First Church of Jesus Christ at Boston. Cotton noted that the week before she had been "dealt with [by me] in point of doctrine. Now she is dealt with in point of practice, and so it belongs to the pastor's office."

Before letting his brother Wilson do the deed, Cotton again justified himself. "I know not how to satisfy myself in it but according to that in Revelation 22:15," which reads, "For without [outside the community of God] are dogs, and sorcerers, and whoremongers, and murderers, and idolators, and whosoever loves and makes a lie." Cotton continued, "Though she has confessed that she sees many of the things which she held to be errors, and that it proceeded from the root pride of spirit, yet I see this pride of heart is not healed but is working still. God hath let her fall into a manifest lie—yea, to *make* a lie—and therefore as we received her in amongst us, I think we are bound upon this ground to remove her from us, and not to retain her any longer, seeing she doth prevaricate in her words, as that her judgment is one thing and her expression is another."

In Cotton's view, according to a letter he wrote two years later, the form of excommunication required in such a case as Hutchinson's was among the most severe: "The greatest censure, of anathema *maranatha*, that is, for Mistress Hutchinson," who showed "pertinacity and obstinacy against Christ Jesus." The phrase "anathema *maranatha*" comes from the apostle Paul's first letter to the Corinthians 16:22, "If any man love not the Lord Jesus Christ, let him be anathema, *maranatha*," meaning he should be rejected by God's church and delivered to Satan.

In the meetinghouse, Davenport supported Cotton by saying, "God will not bear with mixtures in this kind." Davenport turned to Hutchinson. "Therefore," he said, "you must freely confess the truth, take shame to yourself that God may have the glory, and I fear that God will not let you see your sin and confess it till the ordinance of God hath taken place against you. It seems to me God hath a purpose to go on in the course of his judgment against you."

One final supporter of hers rose. The shoemaker Richard Scott, husband of her youngest sister, Katherine, had traveled to America with the Hutchinson family in 1634. He said, "I desire to propound this one scruple, which keeps me that I cannot so freely in my spirit give way to excommunication. Whether it were not better to give her a little time to consider of these things because she is not yet convinced of her lie, and so is in distraction, and she cannot recollect her thoughts."

Cotton was not moved. "This now is not for point of doctrine, wherein we must suffer her with patience, but we now deal with her in point of fact or practice, as the making and holding of a lie," by which, he felt, she had deceived him and many others. "Now there may be a present proceeding."

The Reverend Shepard said, "I perceive it is the desire of many of the brethren to stay her excommunication, and to let a second admonition lie upon her." But, he countered, with one who maintains her course of lies before God and the congregation, it would not be "for the honor of God and the honor of this church to bear with patience so *gross* an offender."

The Reverend Mather, who had spoken just once before, invoked the apostle Paul's letter to Titus 3:10. "The Apostle says, an heretic, after once or twice admonition, reject [him] and cut [him] off like a gangrene." The Dorchester minister pointed at Hutchinson. "Now, she hath been once admonished already. Why then should not the church proceed?"

At this point, a man identified as a stranger spoke. "I would desire to know, if the church proceeds against her, whether it be for doctrine or for her lie. If for her lie, then I consent. If it be for her doctrine, she hath renounced that as erroneous."

The Reverend Wilson answered the stranger. "For my part, if the church proceeds, I think it is and it should be for her errors in opinion as well as for point of practice, for though she hath made some show of repentance, yet it doth not *seem* to be cordial and sincere." Looking around the meetinghouse, Wilson announced, "The church consenting to it, we will proceed to excommunication." He paused, considering his words, now that the process of cleansing the church was almost complete.

"Forasmuch as you, Mistress Hutchinson, have highly transgressed and offended, and forasmuch as you have *so* many ways troubled the church with your errors, and have drawn away many a poor soul, and have upheld your revelations, and forasmuch as you have made a lie. Therefore, in the name of our Lord Jesus Christ and in the name of the church, I do not only pronounce you worthy to be cast out, but I do cast you out! And in the name of Christ, I do deliver you up to Satan, that you may learn no more to blaspheme, to seduce, and to lie!"

Thus condemned to Satan, Hutchinson may have heard certain words that her father had recited to her running through her head. "I am to go whither it pleases God," was the Reverend Marbury's final statement to the Court of High Commission. "But remember God's judgments. You do me open wrong. I pray God forgive you."

John Wilson was still shouting, "And I do account you from this time forth to be a heathen and a publican"—a reference to the Gospel of Matthew 18:15–17, "If thy brother shall trespass against thee, . . . tell it unto the church: and if he refuse to hear the church also, let him be unto thee as an heathen man, and a publican"—"and so to be held of all the brethren and sisters of this congregation and of others. Therefore, I command you in the name of Christ Jesus and of this church as a leper to *withdraw yourself out of the congregation!* That as formerly you have despised and condemned the holy ordinances of God and turned your back on them, so you may now have no part in them nor benefit by them!"

Anne Hutchinson had the same reaction as four months earlier, when during his sermon the Reverend Wilson had commanded her to depart the assembly. Holding her head high, she stood, turned, and walked swiftly to the meetinghouse door. Now she took the proffered hand of her friend Mary Dyer, whom she had aided after her difficult birth. A group of Anne's supporters, shrunken by the many banishments, disfranchisements, and voluntary exiles from the colony, clustered around the rude wooden door that led out to the late-winter light.

John Winthrop watched his neighbor and rival stand at the door, a middle-aged woman, six months pregnant, pale and weak. It seemed to him that even now she reveled in her state.

If she seemed proud, and doubtless she did, it may have been because her mind tended toward passages such as 1 Samuel 16:7: "But the Lord said unto Samuel, Look not on his countenance, or on the height of his stature; because I have refused him: for the Lord seeth not as man seeth; for man looketh on the outward appearance, but the Lord looketh on the heart."

Winthrop was unaware, as he watched Mistresses Hutchinson and Dyer in the rear of the meetinghouse, of the events in October that had followed Dyer's stillbirth. Within a week, however, word of the "monster" that Dyer had borne—and that Hutchinson and Hawkins, with Cotton's support, had secretly buried—would reach the governor, horrifying him. He had always admired the charming and attractive young Mary Dyer, but now she seemed "of a very proud spirit," "much addicted to revelations," and "notoriously infected with Mistress Hutchinson's errors." Of the Dyer baby, he would report in his journal:

It was so monstrous and misshapen as the like that scarce been heard of. It had no head but a face, which stood so low upon the breast, as the ears, which were like an ape's, grew upon the shoulders.

The eyes stood far out, so did the mouth. The nose was hooking upward. The breast and back was full of sharp prickles, like a thornback [an ocean dweller with thornlike spines]. The navel and all the belly with the distinction of the sex were where the lower part of the back and hips should have been, and those back parts were on the side the face stood.

The arms and hands, with the thighs and legs, were as other children's, but instead of toes it had upon each foot three claws, with talons like a young fowl. Upon the back above the belly it had two great holes, like mouths, and in each of them stuck out a piece of flesh.

It had no forehead, but in the place thereof, above the eyes, four horns, whereof two were above an inch long, hard, and sharp.

The infant's condition is consistent with a severe birth anomaly, anencephaly, the partial or total absence of the brain, according to modern medical experts. The horns, talons, and prickles are, however, embellishment.

"Many things were observable in the birth and discovery of this monster," the governor would note. The Dyers were "Familists, and very active in maintaining their party. The midwife, one Hawkins' wife, of St. Ives, was notorious for familiarity with the Devil, and is now a prime Familist. This monster was concealed by three persons about five months." Intimating a communal revulsion like that later associated with the witches of Salem Village, Winthrop reported that most women present at the birth "were suddenly taken with such a violent vomiting, as they were forced to go home, others had their children taken with convulsions, and so were sent home, so as none were left at the time of the birth but the midwife and two others, whereof one fell asleep. At such time as the child died, the bed where in the mother lay shook so violently, as all in the room perceived it."

Learning of the birth, Winthrop would order that Mistress Hawkins be questioned and the corpse exhumed. "The child was taken up" from its grave, he reported, "and though it was much corrupted, yet the horns and claws and holes in the back and some scales were found and seen of above a hundred persons."

The governor would continue to be troubled that such a "proper and comely woman" as Mistress Dyer had given birth to something so grotesque. Looking back to the previous fall, he would recall the October day of the birth. It was the Sunday on which his trusted friend, the Reverend John Wilson of the Boston church, had called Anne Hutchinson out of that church for her "monstrous" and "notorious" errors and commanded her to depart the assembly. When Mistress Hutchinson had walked out, who had accompanied her? It was Mary Dyer, who only hours later gave birth. Monstrous errors beget monstrous births.

Now, just as Mistress Hutchinson was again about to depart this meetinghouse, one of her supporters called out to her, "The Lord sanctify this unto you!"

Winthrop stared as she turned back to face him and all the other magistrates, church elders, and even her former teacher. The governor was struck that "her spirits, which seemed before to be somewhat dejected, revived again, and she gloried in her sufferings."

"The Lord judges not as man judges," she said to all her judges. "Better to be cast out of the church than to deny Christ."

Hand in hand with Mary Dyer, Anne Hutchinson exited the church.

14

THE WHORE AND
STRUMPET OF BOSTON

It was a wintry day in spring when Anne Hutchinson set out on her journey to Rhode Island. The snow on the ground was thigh deep, but the robin had begun its hopeful song, and swallows chippered in the barns.

Although the common route from Massachusetts to the settlements south was by water, around the tip of Cape Cod, Anne Hutchinson decided to walk. Her journey started ten miles south of Shawmut, at the house on the six-hundred-acre Hutchinson farm on Mount Wollaston, in modern-day Quincy, extending east from Wollaston Heights to the sands of Wollaston Beach. Anne and her children had come here by sea on March 28 with their portable goods and then spent a few days visiting with the Wheelwrights.

Mary Hutchinson Wheelwright still lived on Mount Wollaston, near Anne and Will's farmhouse and her husband's former meetinghouse, along with her five children—Katherine was now seven and a half—and her and Will's aging mother, whom Mary would care for until Susan Hutchinson's death in 1646. Mary was awaiting spring weather before heading north to join John in Exeter, New Hampshire, where the banished preacher lived with twenty other families just north of Massachusetts Bay Colony, across the Merrimack River. Anne had considered going to New Hampshire with the Wheelwrights until her oldest son, Edward, returned from Rhode Island in March with the news that Will had purchased suitable land on Aquidneck on which he and other men were building houses and preparing a new community.

Unlike her sister-in-law, Anne did not have the luxury of waiting for good weather. A few days after her excommunication, the magistrates had informed her that her sentence of banishment would go into effect by the following month. Until then, she had to stay in her own house. In late March, just before she and her children arrived at their house in Wollaston, more than a foot of snow fell. Winter, it seemed, would not loose its hold.

On the first day of April 1638, accompanied by horses and carts loaded with the family's goods, Anne Hutchinson began her six-day walk. In addition to twenty-four-year-old Edward, who served as a guide, the group included nineteen-year-old Bridget; seventeen-year-old Francis; Anne, who was almost twelve; ten-year-old Mary; eight-year-old Katherine; William, six; four-and-a-half-year-old Susan; and the baby, Zuriel, who had just turned two. Bridget carried her four-month-old son, Eliphal, who had been baptized in Boston during his grandmother's imprisonment. Bridget's husband, John Sanford, who was in his early thirties, held the hands of his two sons by his late first wife, four-year-old John and Samuel, age two (whom he likely also carried). The Dyers—William, who had already been to Rhode Island and back, and Mary and their small children—and several other families accompanied them.

Anne and Will's son Samuel, who was then thirteen, is often assumed to have been present because a "Samuel Hutchinson" appears in the early records of Rhode Island. However, the records of early Exeter, New Hampshire, suggest that Samuel first went north with his uncle John Wheelwright. A "Samuel Hutchinson" was one of eight men, including Wheelwright, who on April 3, 1638, were granted by the Sagamore Indians a large plot of land along the Merrimack River, east to the Piscataqua. This was likely not Will's younger brother Samuel, then forty-seven, who in 1638 remained in Massachusetts and died, after 1644, in England. Anne and Will's son Samuel, at nearly fourteen, may have been close enough to the *de facto* age of a freeman to be included in the Exeter land grant. Within a year or two, this younger Samuel Hutchinson moved from New Hampshire south to Portsmouth, Rhode Island, where he held land and voted in the town meeting.

Several older Hutchinson offspring remained in Massachusetts: twenty-two-year-old Richard; twenty-year-old Faith, who was now five months pregnant with her first child; and Edward's wife, the former Katherine Hamby, a lawyer's daughter from Ipswich, England, and their infant son.

Anne Hutchinson and her companions walked from Wollaston in Quincy, east of the Blue Hills, through Braintree and Brockton, possibly as far east as Taunton, to what is now Pawtucket, Rhode Island. Along the way they passed countless beaver dams. They crossed the many rivers and streams on the ubiquitous canoes that would soon be their main mode of transportation. Each night they slept in wigwams that they found or made in haste. They built fires for warmth and for cooking.

As they walked, the land gradually flattened and became less rocky and there was more spring growth. Where the snow began to melt, the ground was muddy. This journey from town to country was not unlike her 1612 journey, as a newlywed, from London to Alford, although then she knew her destination and did not have to walk.

On the sixth day, as Anne's company approached Providence Plantation, they passed out of the territory of the chartered colony of Massachusetts, as the court had ordered her to do. At that moment, according to Edmund Morgan, "Massachusetts lost a brilliant mind."

The Reverend Roger Williams's Providence was set on a peninsula at the wide mouth of the Seekonk River, which flows south into Narragansett Bay. This sparsely populated settlement had begun two springs before, after Williams's death-defying exodus from Massachusetts. One bitter night in January of 1636, Pastor Williams of Salem had received a letter from Governor Winthrop warning him that the General Court had ordered his removal and that soldiers were coming to Salem to put him on a ship to England. At midnight Williams had fled into the deep woods south of Salem. Ill and unable to survive on his own, the minister was sheltered and fed for several winter months by Wampanoag Indians. In the spring he moved south to modern-day Seekonk, where he built beside the river a hut of saplings covered with boughs. His wife, children, and a few followers joined him there. But the governor of the nearby Plymouth Plantation—where Williams had lived six years before while studying Indian languages—accused him of trespassing. Williams and his followers paddled up the Seekonk River to a place at the base of a hill near a spring that the Narragansetts agreed to sell to him in exchange for tools, wampum, and trinkets. He named this settlement for the providence of God.

Roger Williams, a pioneer of the concepts of freedom of conscience and the separation of church and state, had a theological mind not unlike Hutchinson's. He saw no just cause for an English king to presume to grant Indian territories, a view that alienated the Massachusetts authorities. In his view, civic leaders had no business governing religious worship or doctrine, and church members, not public taxes on all citizens, should pay church expenses. He rejected the then-common idea that God entered into human affairs in making covenants with pious settlers such as John Winthrop. Edmund Morgan, a biographer of both Williams and Winthrop, elucidated this contrast:

> John Winthrop might persuade himself that God had sealed a covenant with Massachusetts simply by bringing a company of people safely across the Atlantic Ocean. Roger Williams could not. John Winthrop might see the hand of God offering him authority whenever the voters of Massachusetts cast their ballots for him. Roger Williams could not. And when Puritans talked of the divine right of kings or of the people's holding the powers of government in trust for the Almighty, Williams wanted to see the deed of gift. Where and when and how, he wanted to know, did God transfer His powers to the people or anyone else? For that matter, when and where and how did God take any people since the Jews into covenant with Him? If he did so momentous a thing, He would scarcely leave the people unaware of it. It would not require a speech by John Winthrop to make the fact known. To read the presence of God into human transaction was blasphemous.

When Winthrop and the orthodox ministers of Massachusetts banished heretics like Hutchinson in order to protect their First Church of Christ, Williams replied, "If the New England churches had been truly Christ's, they would have neither needed nor wanted this kind of protection."

Hutchinson doubtless shared this view. The historian William McLoughlin theorized that to her Winthrop's Bible commonwealth was "a retrograde movement that would lead toward a church of hypocrites—people who professed and displayed outward conformity to local norms but who inwardly were not truly one with God. Like all Calvinists, Hutchinson believed that men have been so depraved since

Adam's fall . . . that self-interest leads them to . . . behave well only out of fear of damnation." In her view, according to McLoughlin, the colony's founders' insistence "that God had made a covenant with the settlers of New England to establish a special community" led to "the same kind of formal, spiritually dead established church that they had fled England to escape. Ultimately," she felt, "this would breed only smugness, complacency, and self-righteousness with outward forms substituted for inward faith." Moreover, like Williams, she did not believe that God makes covenants with chosen nations, defining their enemies as his enemies.

Her colleague in dissidence, Roger Williams, had been born in London around 1603. The son of a tailor and nephew of a mayor of London, Williams had studied theology at Cambridge, where he became Puritan, and had been ordained a minister of the Church of England at twenty-four. Three years later he turned Separatist and decided to sail to Boston, arriving in December 1630. The Boston church offered him the job that Cotton would later accept—serving as the church's teacher who would replace John Wilson when he was away in England. Williams refused, choosing to preach instead at Salem, where more congregants shared his Separatist views. Later, after Cotton arrived in Massachusetts Bay, the two ministers engaged in doctrinal battles that they published as pamphlets. Williams's *The Bloody Tenet of Persecution* argued that it was wrong to punish or remove people for their beliefs. Cotton replied with *The Bloody Tenet Washed and Made White in the Blood of the Lamb*, to which Williams came back with *The Bloody Tenet Made Yet More Bloody by Mr. Cotton's Endeavor to Wash It White in the Blood of the Lamb*.

Williams's Providence Plantation, with fewer than a hundred residents, already had a reputation as a maritime center in the spring of 1638, when Anne Hutchinson arrived. She traveled the sixteen miles south from there to Aquidneck by ship, down the Seekonk River to Narragansett Bay and the windswept marsh, beach, pastureland, and pebbled cove of her new home.

Early in the second week of April, she and Will were reunited. They had been living apart for nearly six months, by far the longest separation in their twenty-six years of marriage. He was delighted to see her but distressed to find her in such a weak state, especially in late pregnancy, a combination he had never observed in her before.

Rhode Island was even more primitive than Boston had first seemed. While it would later join with Providence Plantation under the crown as the chartered Colony of Rhode Island, it was now just the is-land of Aquidneck. The sixty or seventy men, women, and children who had accompanied her and Will were its only European settlers. It had no houses save those few that these men had begun. Until the houses were completed, the families lived in pits dug in the ground, with floors of planks and dirt walls covered with tree bark. Still, Anne was not discouraged, for—as she had reminded the General Court in November—she knew that the bounds of her habitation were deter-mined by God.

The first settlers of Portsmouth, most of whom arrived a few weeks after Anne Hutchinson in late April and early May, divided up the choice land between the Great Cove and Mount Hope Bay so that each man received a house lot of two or three acres, which he could supplement with larger plots of several hundred acres for farming, slightly to the south. The men paid two shillings per acre for the land. The Hutchinson house lot was on the western beach of the cove, be-sides the cove's Little Bay, east of the spring and north of the Great Field and the Calf's Pasture, based on a study of the original Portsmouth land grants. The house lots of William Coddington, John Coggeshall, John Clarke, and John Sanford (the Hutchinsons' son-in-law) were roughly a thousand yards to the north and west, possibly ex-tending northwest to the waters of Mount Hope Bay.

No sign remains of the houses that these men built in the spring of 1638, which appear from contemporary sketches to have been two-story structures with many windows and a large chimney on one end—less comfortable than the settlers' Boston mansions but far airier and more spacious than the houses at Plymouth Plantation. However, around 1950 a local man walking his dog along a beach on the Great Cove uncovered a midden, or seventeenth-century domestic garbage heap, on the Hutchinsons' former land. Archeologists excavated this site in the early 1970s. Their finds, many of which are displayed in the Portsmouth Public Library, include scores of clay pipes made in Bristol,

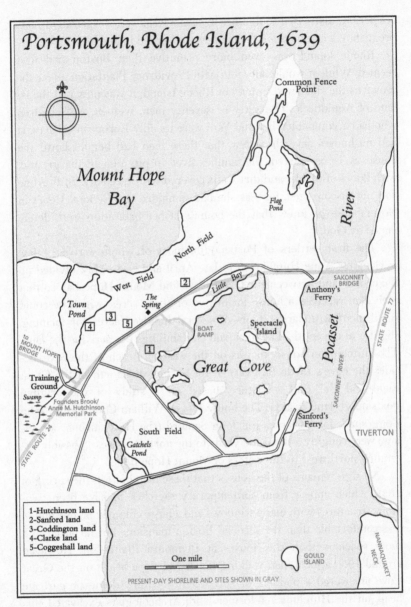

Portsmouth, Rhode Island, 1639

Common Fence Point

Mount Hope Bay

Flag Pond

River

North Field

SAKONNET BRIDGE

West Field

The Spring

Little Bay

Anthony's Ferry

Town Pond

BOAT RAMP

Spectacle Island

to MOUNT HOPE BRIDGE

Great Cove

Pocasset

SAKONNET RIVER

STATE ROUTE 77

Training Ground

Swamp

Founders Brook/ Anne M. Hutchinson Memorial Park

Sanford's Ferry

TIVERTON

South Field

STATE ROUTE 24

Gatchels Pond

1-Hutchinson land
2-Sanford land
3-Coddington land
4-Clarke land
5-Coggeshall land

One mile

GOULD ISLAND

NANNAQUAKET NECK

PRESENT-DAY SHORELINE AND SITES SHOWN IN GRAY

England, in the early seventeenth century, fragments of German and English pottery of the same and even a slightly earlier vintage, Delftware pottery, an English earthenware chamber pot, thimbles, buttons, nails and spikes, hooks, lead shot, a spoon, a Jew's harp, and many animal bones. Based on the bones, the Hutchinsons' diet appears to have been as pleasant in banishment as it was in Boston. Freshly killed pheasant, hare, turkey, venison, beef, mutton, lamb, quahogs, and oysters were likely accompanied by pottages, stews, corn mush, fresh eggs, and fruit pies and compotes.

In this fledgling community the men agreed to graze all their sheep and cattle together on the northernmost tip of the island, which they fenced off and called Common Fence Point, overlooking the waters of Mount Hope Bay. South of the spring, and next to the land granted to William Baulston, the former innkeeper of Boston, they chose a field to be their training ground and meeting place. They gathered here at irregular intervals for town meetings, starting on May 13, 1638, when the thirteen men present voted, among other matters, that "Mr. William Hutchinson is permitted to have six lots for himself and his children, laid out at the Great Cove." A week later the land allotments included, "To Mr. William Hutchinson six acres being ten rod [fifteen and a half yards] in breadth bounded by the Great Cove on the east and fourteen at the west, so it runs eighty pole in length westward," plus six acres each to "Samuel Hutchinson," probably his young son, in absentia; "Edward Hutchinson, Senior," his brother; "Edward Hutchinson, Junior," his oldest son; and his son-in-law John Sanford. The meeting place was also used, on occasional Mondays, for military exercises. It is now the site of the Founders' Brook and Anne M. Hutchinson Memorial Park, established in 1930. The bubbling brook that runs alongside this charming park is the remnant of the founders' spring.

A few weeks after Anne Hutchinson's arrival on Aquidneck, an earthquake shook the island. John Winthrop, who assiduously kept abreast of all her doings even in banishment, saw this tremor—it occurred as "Mistress Hutchinson and some of her adherents happened to be at prayer"—as proof of "God's continued disquietude against the existence of Anne Hutchinson."

Still, he continued, in the privacy of his study on Shawmut Peninsula, to worry about the breadth of her influence. Under his leadership the Church of Boston and the General Court continued to punish Hutchinsonians and others, especially women who seemed likely to make similar trouble. In April 1638 the church cast out Judith Smith, the maidservant of Anne's brother-in-law Edward Hutchinson, for her "obstinate persisting [in] sundry errors." Six months later the court ordered Katherine Finch whipped for "speaking against the magistrates, against the churches, and against the elders." The following summer Finch was called before the court for not behaving "dutifully to her husband," and released upon her promise to reform. In September 1639, after a widow named Phillipa Hammond stated publicly "that Mistress Hutchinson neither deserved the censure which was put upon her in the Church, nor in the commonwealth," the Boston church excommunicated Hammond "as a slanderer and reviler both of the church and the commonwealth." The court ordered a minister of Weymouth, Robert Lenthall, who "was found to have drunk in some of Mistress Hutchinson's opinions, as of justification before faith," to retract these views in writing. (Lenthall left Massachusetts for Rhode Island in 1640.) In late 1638 Hugh Peter's church at Salem obediently followed suit, excommunicating four women who, inspired by Hutchinson and Williams, refused to worship with the congregation and denied the colonial churches were "true." The Boston church later cast out two other prospective Hutchinsonians: Sarah Keayne for "irregular prophesying in mixed assemblies;" and Joan Hogg "for her disorderly singing and her idleness, and for saying she is commanded of Christ so to do."

However, by the end of 1639, eighteen months after Hutchinson departed, Massachusetts was relatively free of her taint, Winthrop felt. "All breaches were made up," he reported, "and the church was saved from ruin beyond all expectation." Antinomianism was discredited, sanctification and justification were linked, and women were again meek. Most local women would have attacked her earlier, he felt, "if their modesty had not restrained them." In the Boston church "there appeared a great change," for "whereas, the year before, they were all (save five or six) so affected to Mr. Wheelwright and Mrs. Hutchinson, and those new opinions, as they slighted the present governor [himself] and the pastor [Wilson], looking at them as men under a covenant of works, and as their greatest enemies; but they [Winthrop and Wilson], bearing all patiently, and not withdrawing themselves (as they were strongly solicited to have done), but carrying themselves lovingly and helpfully upon all occasions, the Lord brought about the hearts of all the people to love and esteem them more than ever before." Governor Winthrop credited himself and Pastor Wilson, "guided by the Lord," with diverting ruin.

Whether or not Winthrop was right about God's "continued disquietude against" Anne Hutchinson, she was indeed suffering physical distress. The unaccustomed weakness she had experienced in the fall and through the winter of her imprisonment continued into spring. She had throbbing headaches and bouts of violent vomiting. Now forty-six years old, she was roughly seven months pregnant. Pregnancy does not always proceed as expected, she was well aware. She had seen many infant and maternal deaths, even with her fine record as a midwife. Most women her age could not conceive, and if they did, the ensuing pregnancy was often difficult.

Still, she must have been distressed to go into labor in May, about six weeks before she expected her sixteenth child, and deliver a strange mass of tissue nothing like an infant. In appearance and size it resembled a handful of transparent gooseberries or grapes. She previously may have seen this birth anomaly, which is now known as a hydatidiform mole. Relatively rare, it occurs most often in women older than forty-five and is the result of one or two sperm fertilizing a blighted ovum. (The Reverend John Cotton's description of it to his congregation—"Several lumps of man's seed, without any alteration, or mixture of any thing from the woman"—was oddly prescient of modern biology.) Most molar pregnancies end in early miscarriages, but some, like Anne's, are carried almost to term.

After the delivery Anne bled profusely, as is typical after late-term miscarriages. Her family feared she would die. They sought the assistance of a local preacher who supported her views, twenty-eight-year-old John Clarke, the 1637 émigré to Boston whose name preceded Will's on the Portsmouth Compact. Clarke had been educated at Cambridge and possibly also the University of Leyden. At the time, ministers had some medical training and were occasionally called on to serve as doctors of medicine, a profession that in its modern sense did not exist. Arriving at the Hutchinson house, the Reverend Clarke found her "feeling her body to be greatly distempered and her spirits failing, and in that regard doubtful of her life." In a letter to his colleague Cotton, Clarke described her condition as "doubtful and dangerous."

In Boston, Cotton related this news to Winthrop, who immediately wrote to Clarke requesting a much fuller account of Hutchinson's "unnatural" pregnancy. Winthrop appears to have taken pleasure in the news. "Mistress Hutchinson being big with child, and growing toward the time of her labor, as others do," he reported later with exuberance,

> she brought forth not one (as Mistress Dyer did) but (which was more strange to amazement) thirty monstrous births or thereabouts, at once; some of them bigger, some lesser, some of one shape, some of another; few of any perfect shape, none at all of them (as far as I could ever learn) of human shape. These things are so strange that I am *almost* loath to be the reporter of them, lest I should seem to feign. . . . But see how the wisdom of God fitted this judgment to her sin every way, for look—as she had vented misshapen opinions, so she must bring forth deformed monsters. And as [there were] about thirty opinions in number, so many monsters. And as those were public, and not in a corner mentioned, so this is now come to be known and famous over all these churches, and a great part of the world.

Hutchinson's late miscarriage was soon the talk of Boston. Cotton "made use of it in public" at the next lecture day, choosing it as his text. Mistress Hutchinson's "unnatural birth," he told his wide-eyed congregation, "might signify her error in denying inherent righteousness" and saying that "all was Christ in us, and nothing of ours in our faith and love." The ministers of Massachusetts neither doubted—nor failed to convey—that God punished the heretic, and anyone who followed her should also be punished.

For these men, the deformed birth, like that of Mary Dyer, demonstrated the obvious link between the intellectual woman and the Devil. Winthrop saw Dyer's stillborn as a Satanic mix of "woman child, a fish, a beast, and a fowl, all woven together in one, and without an head." Women who bore such babies were, like witches, possessed by the Devil.

Winthrop soon noted that Mistress Hutchinson, for "converting" a man on Rhode Island, "gave cause of suspicion of witchcraft."

The Reverend John Wheelwright, hearing from colleagues of these excited exchanges between Winthrop, Clarke, and Cotton, wrote from New Hampshire to correct the Massachusetts governor. The monsters that Winthrop described were, in Wheelwright's view, nothing but "a monstrous conception of his brain, a spurious issue of his intellect."

Nevertheless, wild rumors arose in Boston of Hutchinson's promiscuity. A widely circulated theory was that Henry Vane had fathered both deformed births. Twenty years later, in England, a nobleman recalled that "Sir Henry Vane in 1637 went over [as] governor to New England with two women, Mistress Dyer and Mistress Hutchinson," and "he debauched both, and both were delivered of monsters."

There is a tendency in some accounts of Hutchinson's career to eroticize her relationships with men other than her husband, despite the lack of historical evidence for this conjecture. Hawthorne finds her standing "loftily" in the Cambridge courtroom, surveying the powerful men she awed: "unknown to herself, there is a flash of carnal pride half hidden in her eye." A late-twentieth-century biographer of Henry Vane presumed a sexual attraction between the youthful governor and Anne.

> Vane joined her following soon after he arrived [in Boston], attracted by her eloquence, the intensity of her conviction, and his pleasure at finding her views reinforcing his own. . . . Here was no tedious recital of some past event, but a continual outpouring of spiritual force, unregulated, not really conscious of itself, and therefore unpredictable and exciting.
>
> Soon Anne was also drawn to young Vane. . . . As she lectured she was particularly aware of the sensitive face, the brooding eyes, those soft hands that would never grip a musket or a sword or a dagger, hands made only for the pen and the book. And even more she was aware of his attentive sympathy, the nuances and shifts of mood that matched her own. Vane was the young Seeker, drawn to a woman who was mother and sister and in some remote and subtle way lover, with whom he could share distant mutual ecstasies.

These presumptions make no sense in light of her long and happy marriage to Will, with whom she conceived a child roughly every eighteen
months for well over twenty years. Still, the heroine, unlike the hero, is
sexualized. John Winthrop was also an intimate of the much younger
Henry Vane, and these two men continued a warm correspondence
long after Vane returned to England. John Cotton hosted Vane (and,
over the years, many other young men) in his home for periods of
months. But nowhere is there even a suggestion of a sexual connection
between the men.

As news and gossip sailed back and forth across the water,
Winthrop still worried over the impression his colony made on royal
authorities. In September 1638, after Archbishop Laud again demanded
the return of the colonial charter, the Great and General Court of Massachusetts excused itself from complying. London issued further threats
until 1640, when Charles I recalled Parliament because he needed funds
to fight the Scottish Covenanters. This session of Parliament, which
had not met for twelve years, lasted only three weeks, until the king
dissolved it again. A few months later, however, when the Scots invaded
England, Charles again recalled Parliament. Two years later, civil war
broke out between King Charles and Parliament. The latter eventually
took power, and in 1649 King Charles was beheaded. These political
changes in England effectively ended the first "great migration" to
New England, for the Puritans now held power in England. Following
a decade, the 1630s, in which four thousand English families—roughly
fifteen thousand individuals—left for the New World in three hundred
separate voyages, Puritan emigration largely ceased.

In Boston, Winthrop continued to monitor and, if possible, guide
the activities of "that wandering sheep" Anne Hutchinson. In February
1640 he and the Boston church, still hoping to wring from her a recantation, sent three church members "(men of a lovely and winning spirit,
as most likely to prevail) to see if they could convince and reduce her,
according to 2 Thessalonians 3:13." No doubt Winthrop was aware of
the echoes of the three magi who came to the infant Jesus and of the
three men who visited Abraham and Sarah, bringing news from God.

The three men of Boston took the same overland route to Rhode
Island that Hutchinson had taken nearly two years before. Again, snow
covered the ground. Arriving on Aquidneck, they beached their canoes,

were "entertained at our Brother Coggeshall's house," and inquired as to the location of the Hutchinson house. The men of Boston—Captain Edward Gibbons (who had urged caution before excommunication at her church trial), John Oliver (a son of the surgeon Thomas), and William Hibbins—found Anne outside, in her garden. In an account of this event by Robert Keayne, a brother-in-law of the Reverend Wilson and one of the few merchants of Boston who had opposed Hutchinson, Anne, seeing the men approach, asked them, "From whom do you come, and what is your business?"

"We are come in the name of the Lord Jesus," said one, "from the Church of Christ at Boston, to labor to convince you of the—"

"From the Church of Boston?" she cried, according to Keayne. "I know *no* such church, neither will I own it! You may call it the 'Whore and Strumpet of Boston,' but no church of Christ!"

In the account of John Oliver, who was present, the dialogue lasted longer. In advance, Oliver noted, John Coggeshall had warned the Boston men that the Portsmouth settlers "did not know what power one church had over another church," "conceive one church hath not power over the members of another church," "do not think they are tied to us by our covenant," and "denied our commission and refused to let our letter [from the Boston church] to be read" in public. Oliver reported that after he and his colleagues told Anne Hutchinson they "had a message [for] her from the Lord and from our church," she said, "There are lords many and gods many, but I acknowledge but one Lord. Which Lord do you mean?"

"We came in the name but of one Lord, and that is God."

"Then so far we agree," she replied. "Where we do agree, let it be set down."

"We have a message to you from the church of Christ in Boston."

"I know no church but one."

"In Scripture," they said, "the Holy Ghost calls them churches."

"Christ had but *one* spouse."

"He had in some sort as many spouses as saints," they countered.

"For your church," she replied, "I will not acknowledge it any church of Christ."

According to both Oliver's and Keayne's accounts, the men "of a lovely and winning spirit" left her and went in search of her husband, hoping for a more compliant response. Finding Will, they requested his help in reducing his wife. He answered with the only spoken words actually attributed to him: "I am more nearly tied to my wife than to the church. I do think her to be a dear saint and servant of God."

Oliver, Gibbons, and Hibbins returned to Boston in mid-March. Winthrop noted in his journal that it was "a close, calm day. There fell diverse flakes of snow of this form, very thin, and as exactly pointed as art could have cut in paper."

Early Rhode Island, unlike Massachusetts, did not organize a formal church. In keeping with their belief in greater freedoms than those permitted in Massachusetts, the people of Portsmouth worshiped in a far looser way. As a result, there are few extant records of their religious activities. The Reverend John Clarke, who attended Anne after her miscarriage, preached in Portsmouth, but there was no church founded or meetinghouse built there during this period, and what congregation there was soon split over whether or not to worship on the Lord's Day. They "gathered a church in a very disordered way," Winthrop noted in 1639, and "took some excommunicated persons." Cotton added that "most of them [held] all manner of filthy opinions."

Hutchinson was said to preach even more in Rhode Island than she had in Boston, which suggests she held Scripture meetings for women and perhaps men. "The grand mistress of them all," as the Bostonian Edward Johnson called her, "ordinarily prated every Sabbath day, until others, who thirsted after honor in the same way with herself, drew away her auditors." A local history of Portsmouth notes that the "rapid growth of Pocasset," the town's Indian name, in the late 1630s "was due chiefly to the temporary popularity of Mrs. Hutchinson's religious teachings." At the same time, there is no record of her leading any worship service outside her home in Rhode Island or supporting the idea of a woman preaching in a church. For suggesting that idea, a man was whipped in Portsmouth in 1639. Nevertheless, Portsmouth and Providence were both far more lenient in this regard than Massachusetts.

Even with Rhode Island's loose organs of government, civil troubles arose. The top official, William Coddington, who had quietly suggested to the Massachusetts court that Anne's punishment was disproportionate to her acts, seemed in his magistracy to become imperious and autocratic. He alienated his neighbors by allotting land as he

liked and supporting the establishment of a church like those in
Massachusetts Bay. Early in 1639 Hutchinson befriended a prominent
radical named Samuel Gorton, who attacked the legitimacy of all governing magistrates. A forty-seven-year-old clothier from London who
knew Greek and Latin but had not attended college, Gorton had landed
in Boston in 1637, soon left for parts south, and would in 1643 settle
the town of Warwick, Rhode Island.

On Thursday, April 28, 1639, Samuel Gorton and a dozen other
men of Portsmouth rebelled against William Coddington. They ejected
him from power and formed a new body politic. It is not entirely clear
that Anne Hutchinson supported Gorton's rebellion, for she soon broke
with Gorton, but the rebels chose as their new governor Will Hutchinson, who appears never to have sought political power. The town meeting record of April 30, 1639, reads, "We whose names are underwritten
[William Hutchinson, first, and more than thirty other men] do acknowledge ourselves the loyal subjects of King Charles, and in his
name do hereby bind ourselves into a civil body politic, and do submit
unto his laws according [to] matters of justice. . . . We have freely
made choice of William Hutchinson to be ruler or judge among us." A
month later Winthrop reported, "At Aquidneck the people grew very
tumultuous, and put out Mr. Coddington and the other three magistrates, and chose Mr. William Hutchinson only, a man of a very mild
temper and weak parts, and wholly guided by his wife," who "had been
the beginner of all the former troubles in the country, and still continued to breed disturbance."

Coddington fled to the southern end of Aquidneck Island, where on
May 1 he created the settlement of Newport, which had a far deeper
harbor, and claimed its magistracy by default. Coddington wrote to
Winthrop in late 1639 to say he had separated from the Hutchinsons
and would welcome Winthrop's help in setting up a church. Massachusetts recognized Coddington as Newport's governing authority,
further isolating the Hutchinson group. Late that year William Coddington named himself the governor of the united "Colony of Rhode Island." Perhaps to mollify the residents of Portsmouth, in March 1640
he named Will Hutchinson as one of his three assistant governors. (For
a time, then, Will served as both governor and assistant governor of
the island.) Meanwhile, Massachusetts Bay prepared to annex land on

Narragansett Bay, giving Anne Hutchinson reason to fear that Massachusetts would soon take over her new little colony, either by royal charter or by military force. By the summer of 1640, according to an English visitor named Lechford, Aquidneck was home to "about two hundred families" clustered in Portsmouth, to the north, and Newport, to the south. While neither town had an organized church, Lechford noted, some residents of Portsmouth met to "teach one another, and call it prophecy."

Will Hutchinson's tenure as a governor of Rhode Island lasted hardly a year. In early 1641 he decided to step down. Like many dissident Rhode Islanders, the Hutchinsons no longer believed in human magistracy, or the rule of governors and judges. In their view, a saint—in whom the Holy Spirit dwells—cannot be ruled by a secular authority or by anyone else not ordained by God. This seemingly anarchic and fatalistic reliance on the absolute will of God arose from Hutchinson's strict interpretation of Cotton's doctrine of unconditional election. While it did not please John Winthrop, it was perfectly consistent with the Calvinist view of God's omnipotence and humanity's utterly depraved state.

Various Christian sects emerged during this period in Rhode Island, although there is no evidence that Anne and Will joined them. Many Rhode Island settlers defied the Congregational ministers, much as the Antinomians had in Boston. "Conflict was intrinsic to the congregational system," according to David Hall. "Too much was vague, too much was open to interpretation."

Many of Anne's earliest and strongest supporters, including the Coddingtons and the Dyers, would later join the Society of Friends, founded by George Fox in England in 1647 and imported to Rhode Island in 1655. Becoming Quaker (initially a derogatory term for the bodily shaking of Friends during worship) was for many Hutchinsonians "the natural ending," according to the Bradstreet biographer Helen Campbell, because "the heart of Anne Hutchinson's doctrine [was] a belief in the 'Inward Light.'" Quakers believed that one knows God through this inner light from the Holy Spirit, which is not unlike Anne's notion of the Spirit dwelling in the saint's soul. They supported toleration of other faiths, refused to swear oaths to king or country, and eventually would refuse to take up arms. Rejecting the need for ministers and church services, they believed that women and men are equally capable of leading worship. In David Hall's view, Hutchinson "anticipated certain Quaker themes."

The Quakers, who had little presence in New England until the late 1650s, were but one of many new sects—including Anabaptists, Baptists, Rogerenes, and Gortonists—that flourished (or were imagined to flourish) in early Rhode Island and were disallowed in early Massachusetts. Anabaptists were the spiritual descendants of the sixteenth-century rebels who had taken over the German city of Münster; even the specter of Anabaptism terrified orthodox Puritans, as Dudley had expressed in court in November. Anabaptists and Baptists—followers of John Smyth, who founded the Baptist Church in England in 1604—rejected infant baptism, believing that this sacrament, like the Lord's Supper, should be reserved for aware, regenerate adults. Some Hutchinsonians—although apparently not Anne—shared this view. Winthrop noted in his journal in 1639 some gossip that he had heard: "a sister of Mistress Hutchinson," Katherine Marbury Scott, "being infected with Anabaptistry, went last year to live at Providence," where "Mr. Williams was taken (or rather emboldened) by her to make open profession thereof, and accordingly was rebaptized"—given adult baptism—"by one Holyman, a poor man late of Salem. Then Mr. Williams rebaptized some ten more. They also denied the baptizing of infants, and would have no magistrates."

Williams soon abandoned Anabaptism. In his final effort to purify his church, he denounced all the New England churches. In his view, anyone who had communion with the Church of England—most colonial churches did—was not a true church. Williams refused to worship with anyone but himself. He would not even say a blessing at meals with his wife because she sometimes attended public worship.

To keep Massachusetts pure, the colonial court made laws against all who professed these faiths. In 1644 the General Court ordered that Anabaptists were banished, upon pain of death, and in 1658 it extended this punishment to Quakers.

Whether or not his information was accurate, Winthrop reported in 1641 that Anne Hutchinson "turned Anabaptist." His journal is one of the few sources of information about her life in Portsmouth because he recorded every detail he heard, but its veracity must be questioned on account of his distance and especially his desire to discredit her. According to him, she supported passive resistance to authority, "denied all magistracy among Christians, and maintained that there were not [any] churches since those founded by the apostles and evangelists, nor could any be." Horrified, he recounted how "Mistress Hutchinson and those of Aquidneck Island broached new heresies every year. Diverse of them turned professed Anabaptists, and would not wear any arms, and denied all magistracy among Christians, and maintained that there were not churches since those founded by the apostles and evangelists, nor could any be, nor any pastors ordained, nor seals administered. . . ." In the fall of 1641, he lamented, "She continued on in the wilderness, as yet she was."

Like him, she felt some missionary zeal in trying to correct her opponents' misconceptions. She sent a letter to clarify and justify her views to the General Court of Massachusetts in early 1639. The magistrates refused to "read it publicly because she had been excommunicated." No copy of her letter survives; indeed, we have nothing in her hand.

In the summer of 1641 she sent two of her relatives on a mission to Massachusetts on her behalf. Her twenty-year-old son, Francis, her father's namesake, and her twenty-two-year-old son-in-law, William Collins, traveled from Portsmouth to Boston, where they likely did not stay at the family's old house facing the Winthrop house on Shawmut. (Ownership of the house and its garden, orchard, "courtyards, stables, stalls, outhouses, commons, and appurtenances" had been transferred to Edward Jr. in 1638 and then in June 1639 to Will's brother Richard Hutchinson, a wealthy London ironmonger who appears never to have occupied it. Edward and his family likely remained in the house until Richard Hutchinson divided the property and sold it in two parts in 1658.) William Collins was a nonconformist minister from Barbados, in the West Indies, where, according to Winthrop, "he had preached a time and done some good, but so soon as he came to [Hutchinson in Rhode Island he] was infected with her heresies." He had also married the Hutchinsons' fifteen-year-old daughter, Anne. In 1640 Collins had written several letters to people in Boston charging that the Massachusetts ministers and magistrates were "anti-Christian" and the king of England was like the king of Babylon, who oppressed the people of God.

The General Court, learning that William Collins and Francis Hutchinson were within its jurisdiction, called up the young Hutchinsonians and demanded an explanation for their presence. The two young men refused to appear before the court, so "they were brought [and] led" to the meeting of September 7, 1641. Collins acknowledged to the court that he had written a letter "and maintained what he had written, that there were no gentile churches (as he termed them) since the Apostles' times, and that none now could ordain ministers." Francis Hutchinson disavowed the rumor that he would not sit at table with his mother. Like his mother, he "reviled the church" of Boston as a "strumpet." At this, that church, which the year before had refused Francis's request to be removed as a member, promptly excommunicated him. The court ordered that both men be fined and imprisoned.

> Mr. William Collins, being found to be a [doctrinal] seducer, and his practices proved such, he is fined one hundred pounds, and to be kept close prisoner till his fine be paid, and then he is banished, upon pain of death.
>
> Francis Hutchinson, for calling the church of Boston a whore, a strumpet, and other corrupt tenets he is fined 50 pounds, and to be kept close prisoner till it be paid, and then he is banished, upon pain of death.

To the court, these sums were small in comparison with the amount that the Hutchinsons had cost the state: "That family had put the country to so much charge in the synod and other occasions, to the value of 500 pounds, at least."

The two young men consistently refused to renege on their support of Anne Hutchinson's views, and so they remained in the Boston prison for several months. In early October the court tried to end the standstill by reducing their fines from one hundred to forty pounds, for Collins, and from fifty to twenty pounds, for Francis. "And if they give security to pay the same within six months, it is referred to the Governor to send them away."

Finally, on December 10, the court dismissed and banished the young men, who had paid no part of their fines. Collins and Francis were "enjoined to depart out of our jurisdiction immediately after the

Sabbath, at their peril," and "were not to return again into our jurisdiction at their utmost peril." At the same court meeting, incidentally, a man named "William Hatchet, for bestiality with a cow, is condemned to be hanged, and the cow to be slain and burnt or buried." The court also granted the Reverends John Cotton and Nathaniel Ward each six hundred additional acres of land.

Around this time, on a distant part of the globe, an even more famous heretic than Anne Hutchinson passed away. In a rented villa on a hill just east of Florence, seventy-seven-year-old Galileo Galilei died on January 8, 1642. Like Hutchinson, he had recanted his views before his church. During his 1633 trial for heresy before the Holy Office of the Inquisition, in Rome, he had signed a disavowal of his view that the earth moves and circles the sun. Spared execution, he was held prisoner for five months in the archbishop of Siena's apartment and then allowed to return to his villa, under house arrest.

By the time of Galileo's death, life on Rhode Island for the Hutchinsons was difficult but stable. Their continuing troubles with Coddington were sometimes alarming, especially after Coddington discussed with the General Court of Massachusetts the possibility of subsuming Newport—and perhaps all of Rhode Island—under the Bay Colony's control. To Anne, Portsmouth now felt as familiar as Boston once had. She could speak freely of her beliefs and ideas. She and Will were surrounded by children and grandchildren. Bridget Hutchinson Sanford, now twenty-three, had given birth to two little boys at Portsmouth: Peleg in May 1639 and Endcome in February 1641. Faith and her husband, Thomas Savage, who had accompanied the exiles to Aquidneck but decided to stay in Mount Wollaston, had two sons—Habijah, who was baptized in Boston on August 12, 1638, and Thomas, born in May 1640. Edward and his wife, Katherine, who still lived on Shawmut, had their second child, Elizabeth, in November 1639 and then a boy named Elisha, in November 1641. The family welcomed each baby with joy.

In the midst of this new life, a great loss occurred. Anne's beloved Will died at fifty-five, the same age as Anne's father at his death. Will was buried in Portsmouth, although no marker remains. His exact date and cause of death are unknown because the settlement had no formal church, which would have been the typical repository of records for baptisms, marriages, and burials. For some time after Will's death, Anne retreated from society into mourning, as she had following her daughters' deaths in Alford, although it is hard to imagine much retreat for a widow with six dependent children.

Hoping to exploit her weakness, ministers from Massachusetts came to visit her on Aquidneck. Anne Hutchinson remained bold despite her recent loss. She refused, once again, to recant. The ministers suggested that Massachusetts would soon take over Rhode Island and Exeter, New Hampshire.

Anne Hutchinson resolved to move again as soon as possible. Her wanderings were not over. In hardly eight years, she had left England and then Boston. Now she would have to leave Rhode Island.

She meditated on the best course to take, although there is no record of what Scripture she considered. Her last recorded revelation from Scripture, according to the collections of the Rhode Island Historical Society, was that the Lord had prepared a city of refuge for her outside the English jurisdiction. Her aim was to travel far enough from Massachusetts to escape its meddling visits. This journey, unlike those before, would entail separating from her nation of birth. In that sense, it recalled the Scrooby Pilgrims, from west of Alford, who had sailed for Holland in 1607.

Anne Hutchinson and her older children consulted maps and discussed her options. She considered Ossining, New York, on the Hudson River, but decided instead to head southwest to the Dutch settlement of New Amsterdam on the Atlantic Ocean at a place called Pelham Bay. Hutchinson sent a letter to the Dutch authorities seeking permission to abide among the Dutch. They granted her request to live within the colony of New Amsterdam. She arranged to purchase land and ordered a contract.

In the summer of 1642 the fifty-one-year-old widow packed once more. She sent her furniture and other heavy belongings over land, on carts, along with her horses, cattle, and hogs. She hired boats to convey her party of sixteen to their new home 130 miles away. They would travel from the northern end of Aquidneck southwest into Narragansett Bay, passing east of Prudence Island and Newport, out to what is now Long Island Sound. Several servants and two of her grown children decided to accompany her in her exodus. Francis, who was now

twenty-one, came along to help, as did her sixteen-year-old daughter
Anne and her husband, William Collins.

Moving abroad without Will would be awkward and strenuous, but
she still had several children to raise. Little William was ten, Susan was
eight, and Zuriel but six. These youngest Hutchinsons were as quick-
witted as the rest, with the added sophistication that comes from the
presence of older siblings. The house was lively with their antics, and
she had much to teach them. The best way to accomplish this, she believed, was to make a new start.

15

HER HEART
WAS STILLED

The boats carrying Anne Hutchinson and her party of sixteen from Rhode Island to the Dutch settlement of New Amsterdam passed many islands clustered in a place that its inhabitants would soon call the Bronx, after its first European settler, Jonas Bronck, who had arrived a few years before. The vessels sailed between two small islands and traveled inland along a river heading north. The land on both sides of the waterway now known as the Hutchinson River was an inviting mix of virgin forest and tidal marsh. Other than the splashing of the oars, all that the Hutchinsons could hear were the calls of innumerable birds.

Blue herons and white egrets fed among the tall marsh reeds. The reeds recalled Lincolnshire, where they were used for roofing and insulation. A half mile up the river, a tributary wended east into the marsh in what is now Pelham Park, the largest green space in the city of New York.

From this tributary a hill rose, gradually at first and then steeply. Atop the hill stood a huge, egg-shaped, glacial rock. As the boat approached the shore, the Hutchinsons could see that the rock was split in two, its halves separated by a crevice. Anne asked the sailors to beach the boat and unload here. On land, several of her younger children, delighted with their freedom after two days on the sea, climbed the hill, picking blueberries as they walked. Near the summit they took turns climbing through the eighteen-inch-wide crevice of what is now called the Split Rock.

Anne and her family camped out on this hillside above Long Island Sound, living in an abandoned farmhouse until they could erect their own house. Of the widow's twelve living children, seven were with her—Zuriel, Susan, William, Katherine, Mary, Anne, and Francis. Of the other five, Edward and Richard, now twenty-nine and twenty-six, lived in Boston. Twenty-five-year-old Faith was also in Massachusetts, with her husband, Thomas Savage, and their little boy on Wollaston, now part of Braintree. Bridget and John Sanford had remained on Rhode Island with their sons. Seventeen-year-old Samuel appears also to have stayed on Rhode Island, for he is mentioned in Portsmouth documents during the 1640s and 1650s.

To Anne's great relief, the Hutchinsons were the only English settlers on Pelham Bay. Dutch settlers had arrived here in 1614 and created a permanent trading center, the Dutch West India Company, near modern-day Albany. In 1626 Peter Minuit, New Amsterdam's first director-general, had purchased the island of Manhattan—"island of the hills"—from local Indians for beads and trinkets worth sixty guilders, or twenty-four dollars.

In 1642 when the Hutchinsons arrived, New Amsterdam consisted of fewer than a thousand Dutch settlers spread from the tip of Manhattan north to modern-day Westchester County. The majority of them were clustered in rough wooden houses built along narrow dirt streets far south of Pelham Bay. Unlike the New England settlers, the Dutch lacked for skilled farmers and craftsmen, and many drank to excess. At the same time, they and their Dutch Reformed ministers tended to be far more tolerant than the English in matters of religious belief, which explains their welcome to Anne Hutchinson and other dissident Puritans as well as to Quakers, Lutherans, and Jews. However, the general chaos and instability of this community would lead, eventually, to the surrender of the colony, by director-general Peter Stuyvesant to England in September 1664. At that point New Amsterdam would become New York.

In 1642, however, the bellicose Willem Kieft was still the Dutch colony's director-general. Kieft was a short-sighted, heavy-handed administrator whose cruelty to the natives proved disastrous not only for the Indians but also for the Dutch. When Kieft arrived in 1638, the local Indians—the Mahican, who spoke Algonquian, and the Mohawk, who spoke Iroquois—were already feuding. Kieft entered the fray. In exchange for valuable beaver pelts, he indiscriminately traded muskets and shot to both sides in the natives' conflict. Moreover, he demanded an annual tribute from the Indians of maize and wampum, which the natives refused to provide. Dutch livestock invaded the natives' corn-fields, and the natives retaliated by killing and eating the colonists' pigs and cattle, infuriating the Dutch. Starting in 1640, the Dutch and the Indians had been at war. In intermittent battles over the two years be-fore Anne Hutchinson's arrival, hundreds of Indians were massacred, and scores of Dutch settlers were killed and their homes and farms burned.

The Hutchinsons lived beside, rather than among, the Dutch. Al-though both were Protestant, they shared neither language nor culture. Anne's Dutch neighbors saw her as harmless but odd. For instance, she would not keep firearms in her house. At any moment, the Dutch warned her, the local Siwanoy Indians—Algonquian speakers within the Mahican nation who hunted, fished, and inhabited palisaded vil-lages of wigwams—could go on a rampage. Her neighbors urged her and her sons to keep arms.

Hutchinson replied that she had had no trouble with the natives in Massachusetts or Rhode Island. In Boston she had opposed all English efforts to suppress the natives, including the shameful Pequot War. On Aquidneck the Narragansetts and the English had become friends. Her attitude was later mocked by the same Edward Johnson of Boston who had dismissed her before as "a woman that preaches better Gospel than any of your blackcoats." Johnson wrote that Hutchinson, "being amongst a multitude of Indians, boasted they were become all one Indian." Ac-cording to the scholar Andrew Delbanco, Johnson "found in Anne Hutchinson an even more 'cunning Devil' than were the Pequots, and drenched his *Wonder-Working Providence* in frank delight at her suppres-sion. Johnson exemplified ... that in order to ratify its godliness New England had had to find its local Satans." Among Satan's various forms were the "savage" native, the Antinomian, the Quaker, and the "witch."

This "local Satan" thrived, even in exile. On January 19, 1643, on Rhode Island, Anne's daughter Bridget and her husband had a boy they named Restcome, making their brood six boys. Faith expected her fourth child in the summer. Edward's wife was also pregnant, with a fourth child due in November.

Anne Hutchinson continued to study Scripture, alone and with her children, but she no longer had English-speaking neighbors with whom to meet. She prepared stews of seafood, meat, and fowl and the usual berry pies. In the spring of 1643 she planted an herb garden like those she had tended in Lincolnshire, Massachusetts, and Rhode Island. In "Mrs. Hutchinson," Nathaniel Hawthorne envisions this Bronx scene:

> Her final movement was to lead her family within the limits of the Dutch Jurisdiction, where, having felled the trees of a virgin soil, she became herself the virtual head, civil and ecclesiastical, of a little colony. Perhaps here she found the repose, hitherto so vainly sought. Secluded from all whose faith she could not govern, surrounded by the dependents over whom she held an unlimited influence, agitated by none of the tumultuous billows which were left swelling behind her, we may suppose, that, in the stillness of Nature, her heart was stilled.

In March 1643 the Reverend Roger Williams sailed to England to unite under one charter the towns of Providence, Portsmouth, Newport, and Warwick. His goal was to maintain regional independence from Massachusetts. Not long before, the Massachusetts General Court had sponsored the murder of the Narragansett sachem Miantonomo, an admirer of both Williams and Vane who had negotiated the sale of Aquidneck to the Hutchinsonians. Williams feared further incursions on his and the Narragansetts' territory by the colony of Massachusetts.

The Reverend Williams succeeded in securing from England a charter merging these four towns as "a single colony called Providence Plantations, governed by a President and 4 Assistants," according to John Sanford, Anne's son-in-law. Bridget's husband was at first an assistant of the chartered company, then its head magistrate, and eventually, in 1653, its fifth president.

Meanwhile, Roger Williams and William Coddington continued to feud. Coddington wished to keep the island that contains Newport and Portsmouth independent from the rest of the colony so that he could govern it on his own. Williams refused to give in, and in 1663 the united colony, now generally called Rhode Island, was fully chartered by the crown.

This "Charter of Rhode Island and Providence Plantations," issued to Williams and the Reverend John Clarke, who had assisted Anne following her miscarriage, guaranteed religious freedom—in keeping with the predilections of its founders. "No person within the said colony, at any time hereafter, shall be any wise molested, punished, disquieted, or called in question, for any differences in opinion in matters of religion, and do not actually disturb the civil peace of our said colony; but that all and every person and persons may ... freely and fully have and enjoy his and their own judgments and consciences, in matters of religious concernments, throughout the tract of land hereafter mentioned."

This Rhode Island language leads directly to the Third Amendment to the Constitution of the United States, which was approved by the First Congress in 1789: "Congress shall make no law respecting an establishment of religion, or prohibiting the free exercise thereof." These words and the underlying concept owe as much to the Hutchinsonians on Aquidneck as to Roger Williams in Providence Plantation—as well as to the 1634 charter of the colony of Maryland, the earliest such document in English North America to allow religious toleration.

An early champion of freedom of conscience, Anne Hutchinson supported the notion—now widely accepted in America—that individuals can believe as they wish and question authority. In this respect her contribution is ongoing. In discussing heresies of the ancient world, religious historian Elaine Pagels noted, "Anyone who has seen foolishness, sentimentality, delusion, and murderous rage disguised as God's truth knows that there is no easy answer to the problem that the ancients called discernment of spirits. Orthodoxy tends to distrust our capacity to make such discriminations and insists on making them for us. Given the notorious human capacity for self-deception, we can, to an extent, thank the church for this. Many of us, wishing to be spared hard work, gladly accept what tradition teaches." Yet "we have seen the hazards—even terrible harm—that sometimes result from unquestioning acceptance of religious authority." Anne Hutchinson was one of many determined souls who were not willing to accept religious authority without question.

The Hutchinson family continued to grow. In the summer of 1643 Faith gave birth to her fourth child, Hannah, who was baptized in Wollaston on July 2. In Portsmouth on Rhode Island, Bridget was again pregnant. That baby, who was born the following March, would be named William, after his grandfather. (Bridget's only daughter, Anne, did not arrive until March 1652, following eight sons, and she died at age two.)

On Pelham Bay, Anne Hutchinson was soon to turn fifty-two. By mid-July there would be early carrots and turnips to pull, and sage, lemon balm, and feverfew to hang for drying. Most days, the summer heat did not bother her. Breezes blew in from Long Island Sound. On free afternoons she led her younger children along the Indian trails wending throught the woods around her farmhouse, just as she had taken her older children on walks from Alford up into the Wolds. From the hilltop above the Split Rock, she and her children could see the islands of Long Island Sound and watch cormorants dive into the sea.

The weather was clear on the July day that Anne's Dutch neighbors told her to remove her family from her house. The Siwanoy warriors are coming, the neighbors said. They have sent a warning; we must disappear. The Siwanoy were responding to a surprise attack, ordered by Kieft, on a band of natives camping on Manhattan Island the previous February, in which Dutch soldiers had killed eighty Indian men, women, and children.

Hearing the warning from her neighbors, Anne Hutchinson repeated her long history of good relations with the natives. She would not arm herself, nor would she and her children abandon their home. She had great faith in herself and even more faith in Christ. Should any harm come to her, she would trust in the will of God.

The Siwanoy warriors stampeded into the tiny settlement above Pelham Bay, prepared to burn down every house. The Siwanoy chief, Wampage, who had sent a warning, expected to find no settlers present. But at one house the men in animal skins encountered several children, young men and women, and a woman past middle age.

One Siwanoy indicated that the Hutchinsons should restrain the family's dogs. Without apparent fear, one of the family tied up the dogs. As quickly as possible, the Siwanoy seized and scalped Francis Hutchinson, William Collins, several servants, the two Annes (mother and daughter), and the younger children—William, Katherine, Mary, and Zuriel. As the story was later recounted in Boston, one of Hutchinson's daughters, "seeking to escape," was caught "as she was getting over a hedge, and they drew her back again by the hair of the head to the stump of a tree, and there cut off her head with a hatchet." It is not clear if Anne Hutchinson had a moment—before she gave up the ghost—to begin one of the psalms, to utter the words, "I do verily believe that He will deliver me," or even to say, "Thy will be done."

The Siwanoy warriors dragged the settlers' bodies into the house, followed by their cattle. The men set fire to the dwelling, which burned to the ground. There were, it seemed, no survivors, nor any burial or grave for the dead.

16

THIS
AMERICAN
JEZEBEL

"Was Anne Hutchinson *really* scalped?" I remember asking my great-aunt Charlotte when I was about nine.

"Of course she was," replied Aunt Charlotte, never one to mince words, "and all her little children too."

This was not entirely true. One little Hutchinson child—and the five older ones who were not present—survived the rampage, as my late aunt no doubt knew. Surely she had read Hawthorne's retelling of Hutchinson's "impressive story," with its "awful close":

Her last scene is as difficult to be portrayed as a shipwreck, where the shrieks of the victims die unheard along a desolate sea and a shapeless mass of agony is all that can be brought home to the imagination. The savage foe was on the watch for blood. Sixteen persons assembled at the evening prayer; in the deep midnight, their cry rang through the forest; and daylight dawned upon the lifeless clay of all but one. It was a circumstance not to be unnoticed by our stern ancestors, in considering the fate of her who had so troubled their religion, that an infant daughter, the sole survivor amid the terrible destruction of her mother's household, was bred in a barbarous faith, and never learned the way to the Christian's Heaven. Yet we will hope, that there the mother and the child have met.

Although she was no longer the "infant daughter" that Hawthorne imagines, nine-year-old Susan Hutchinson did indeed survive. While the Siwanoy warriors were killing and incinerating her mother, siblings, and servants, Susan Hutchinson was out of sight of the house. She had gone out by herself that brilliant late-summer day to pick blueberries on the meadow below the Split Rock. She heard the screams of her family and saw the massive plume of smoke rising from the house. She was terrified to think what would happen to her.

The Siwanoy found Susan Hutchinson hiding, according to Bronx legend, in the crevice of the Split Rock. The girl's English coif, worn above a light blouse and petticoat, may have been the first clue they noticed that the family they had massacred was not Dutch. The Siwanoy took Susan captive, and the chief, Wampage, adopted her. Wampage also took on Susan's mother's name, calling himself "Ann-Hoeck" from then on, for it was customary for a Siwanoy warrior to assume the name of his most illustrious victim. The neighboring land was called Ann-Hoeck's Neck. The river was given Anne's surname, and so the modern highway beside it is the Hutchinson River Parkway, known to locals as "The Hutch."

Susan Hutchinson spent eight or nine years with the Siwanoys and is said to have left the tribe reluctantly. Two and a half years after her capture, John Winthrop reported that "A daughter of Mistress Hutchinson was carried away by the Indians near the Dutch," and she "forgot her own language and all her friends." At age eighteen Susan Hutchinson traveled to Boston, where her brother Edward and other relatives still lived. (John Winthrop was now dead.) A few months later, on December 30, 1651, Susan married John Cole, a twenty-six-year-old English settler. Susan and John's first child was born in Boston in 1653. They moved to Rhode Island and had ten more children. Susan Hutchinson Cole died on Rhode Island, at age eighty, in 1713.

Anne Hutchinson was thus survived by six children—nine-year-old Susan; Samuel, eighteen; Bridget, twenty-four; twenty-six-year-old Faith; Richard, twenty-seven; and Edward, who was just thirty—and eventually more than thirty grandchildren.

Little is known of her sons Richard and Samuel as adults.

Bridget stayed on Aquidneck with John Sanford and their many children. After he died she remarried and moved to Maine.

Faith lived on Mount Wollaston with her husband, the loyal Thomas Savage, and their children, who at the time of Anne's death were five-year-old Habijah, three-year-old Thomas, and the newborn, Hannah. Faith gave birth to Ephraim in 1645, Mary in 1647, Dyonisia in 1649, and, on February 17, 1652, a boy named Perez. Three days later Faith Hutchinson Savage died of complications related to the birth. (Thomas Savage later married Mary Symmes, a daughter of the Reverend Zechariah Symmes with whom his mother-in-law had tangled, and had eleven more children.)

Faith and Thomas Savage's oldest son, Habijah Savage, married Hannah Tyng in Boston in 1661, had several children, served as the captain of an artillery company in Boston, and died at age thirty on Barbados. In Cambridge in 1685, Habijah's eighteen-year-old daughter Hannah Savage—Anne's great-granddaughter and my seventh great-grandmother—married the Reverend Nathaniel Gookin (1656–1692), a Harvard graduate and pastor (of the First Church in Cambridge) who was then the president of Harvard College.

The Hutchinsons' oldest son, Edward, stayed in Boston, where he made peace with the church and held public office. He had seven children with his first wife, Katherine Hamby, who died at thirty-five in Boston in 1650, and four more with his second wife, Abigail Vermaies Button, who appears in 1656 court records giving evidence, ironically, against an accused witch, Eunice Cole of New Hampshire. Yet Edward continued to fight for causes associated with his mother. A supporter of religious toleration, he "deserves honor," according to the historian James Savage, "for his firmness in opposing cruelty to the Quakers." Edward's name appears on a 1668 petition calling for the release of imprisoned Baptists.

Edward Hutchinson became a captain in the colonial army in 1657 and eight years later served in King Philip's War. King Philip was the settlers' name for Metacomet, son of Massasoit and chief sachem of the Wampanoags. In this war the English settlers opposed and ultimately defeated the allied Narragansett, Nipmuck, and Wampanoag tribes. On August 2, 1675, according to James Savage, Captain Edward Hutchinson "received a wound from the Indians in a treacherous assault when he was marching to a peaceful meeting with them, of which he died [August] 19th at Marlborough, age 62, as the gravestone says."

Edward Hutchinson's fourth child, Anne Hutchinson, had been born and baptized in Boston in November 1643, two months after the murder of her grandmother. This Anne Hutchinson later became a Quaker and married Samuel Dyer, who in October 1637 had been a two-year-old huddling in a kitchen on Shawmut as his mother, Mary Dyer, delivered her deformed baby. Anne Hutchinson and Samuel Dyer lived on Rhode Island and had eight children. After he died in 1678 she married again, had three more children, and died in 1710. Another daughter of Edward's, Susanna, who was born in June 1649, married a Newport man, Nathaniel Coddington, one of William Coddington's sons.

Many of Edward's progeny became merchants, as Will Hutchinson and his family had been. "The entire clan" in this line, according to historian Bernard Bailyn,

> devoted itself to developing its property and the network of trade. . . . They prospered solidly but not greatly. Their enterprises were careful, not grand. They were accumulators, down-to-earth, unromantic middle-men, whose solid, petty-bourgeois characteristics became steadily more concentrated in the passage of years until in Thomas, in the fifth generation, they reached an apparently absolute and perfect form.

Thomas Hutchinson, Edward's great-grandson, born in 1711, was a wealthy merchant and historian who became chief justice of Massachusetts and then the Loyalist governor of the colony just prior to the Revolutionary War. It was this "celebrated and unhappy governor," James Savage noted, who instigated the Boston Tea Party by attempting to enforce English law by landing the cargo of the tea ship *Dartmouth*. Thrown from office by the revolutionaries in 1774, Thomas Hutchinson returned as an exile to England, where he died in 1780. According to Bailyn, Governor Hutchinson inspired "morbid," "paranoic" distrust and "animosity" in the revolutionary Samuel Adams, who considered him a tyrant and dissembler from whom "the liberties of this country [have] more to fear . . . than from all other men in the world."

Like his great-great-grandmother, Thomas Hutchinson "refused to adjust [his] singular convictions to the will of the community," Bailyn wrote. The Loyalist governor was both "fascinated and chilled" by Anne Hutchinson's career: "Her sincere religious passion, he felt, was in itself no more humane than the destructive fervor of her enemies." Thomas Hutchinson's own description of her, in his *History of the Colony and Province of Massachusetts-Bay*, opens in a manner suggestive of a Jane Austen novel, with which it was roughly contemporaneous:

> There came over with Mr. Cotton, or about the same time, Mr. Hutchinson, and his family, who had lived at Alford in the neighborhood of Boston. Mr. Hutchinson had a good estate and was of good reputation. His wife, as Mr. Cotton says, "was well-beloved, and all the faithful embraced her conference and blessed God for her fruitful discourses."

Governor Hutchinson pointed out the "respect" and "notice" that Anne Hutchinson received from Cotton, Vane, "and other principal persons. Her husband served in the general court, several elections, as representative for Boston, until he was excused at the desire of the church." The "chilling" part follows:

> So much respect seems to have increased her natural vanity. Countenanced and encouraged by Mr. Vane and Mr. Cotton, she advanced doctrines and opinions which involved the colony in disputes and contentions . . . and had like to have produced ruin both to church and state. The vigilance of some, of whom Mr. Winthrop was the chief, prevented, and turned the ruin from the country upon herself and many of her family and particular friends.

According to Governor Thomas Hutchinson, to avoid the ruin of Massachusetts, Massachusetts had to ruin her. Indeed, during Anne Hutchinson's three and a half years in Boston, she was present mostly as an absence. For the most part the men of power hardly knew of her contributions. She was called up by the court only so she could be removed. The power she held—as prophet, preacher, and leader—was by definition private, outside the public sphere. As a *woman of power*, she was an oxymoron. She had to be cast out.

But her absence was never total. Within a few years of her death, her descendants held public power. Her son-in-law John Sanford was governor of the colony of Rhode Island, as was her grandson Peleg Sanford. Thomas Hutchinson governed Massachusetts less than 150 years after her expulsion. In the twentieth century her sixth great-grandson Franklin Delano Roosevelt was president of the United States. President Roosevelt's wife, Eleanor, put Anne Hutchinson at the top of her list of great American women, according to Joseph Lash, the Roosevelts' biographer. President George H. W. Bush was a ninth great-grandson of Anne's. Bush's son, George W., who in 2001 assumed the highest office in the most powerful country in the world, is her tenth great-grandson. Through her powerful male descendants, Anne Hutchinson continues to leave her mark.

Still, an absence remains. In nearly four centuries, not one founder or president has been a woman. Women serve as a minority on the nation's Supreme Court, in its Congress, and on the president's Cabinet yet remain outcasts at America's highest office. Senator Hillary Rodham Clinton, who is said to consider running for president, enjoyed remarkable success with her memoir, *Living History,* according to booksellers, because of her "status as a dual symbol of female victimhood and power." The literary critic Amy Schrager Lang noted that "the gender-specific problem of the public woman prefigures the larger dilemma of maintaining the law in a culture that simultaneously celebrates and fears the authority of the individual," especially "when the individual is female. The fact that Anne Hutchinson, the classic American representative of a radical and socially destructive self-trust, is a woman . . . complicates her heresy." The "problem of Anne Hutchinson," Lang concludes, "is the problem of the public woman." Could John Winthrop still be correct in observing that it is not proper or comely for a woman to hold power? No wonder that as a little girl I associated my ancestor Anne Hutchinson with shame.

In colonial Boston in the autumn of 1643, the leading men rejoiced at the news of Anne Hutchinson's death. Her destruction seemed the act of a just and loving God. "Let her damned heresies, and the just vengeance of God, by which she perished, terrify *all* her seduced followers from having any more to do with her leaven," remarked Peter Bulkeley, the Concord pastor who had led the Cambridge Synod and charged her with Familism during her church trial. The Reverend Thomas Weld—now a colonial emissary in London—wrote, amazed, "I never heard that the Indians in those parts did ever before this commit the like outrage upon any one family, and therefore God's hand is the more apparently seen herein, to pick out this woeful woman, to make her and those belonging to her an unheard-of heavy example of their cruelty above all others. Thus the Lord heard our groans to heaven, and freed us from this great and sore affliction."

John Winthrop said of her demise, "Thus it had pleased the Lord to have compassion of his poor churches here, and to discover this great imposter, an instrument of Satan so fitted and trained to his service for interrupting the passage [of his] kingdom in this part of the world, and poisoning the churches here—as no story records the like of a woman since that mentioned in the Revelation." Winthrop was referring to the passage in the book of Revelation where God tells the angels of the churches, "I have a few things against thee, because thou suffers that woman Jezebel, who calls herself a prophetess, to teach and to seduce my servants to commit fornication, and to eat things sacrificed unto idols. And I gave her space to repent of her fornication; and she repented not. And I will kill her children with death. . . ."

Following Hutchinson's death, as Winthrop prepared his account of the controversy whose center she had been, he spent countless hours analyzing the aptness of this familiar biblical comparison. Jezebel was a witch, a whore, a heathen—a false prophet, an enemy of God—a worshiper of false gods who defied the true prophet Elijah, and an arrogant, amoral woman whose death was so violent that hardly a trace of her remained.

At his desk one afternoon, Winthrop dipped his quill in ink and wrote, "This American Jezebel." He stopped and underlined two words. Then he continued, not stopping again until the end of this breathless, sentence-long paragraph.

This *American Jezebel* kept her strength and reputation, even among the people of God, till the hand of civil justice laid hold on her, and then she began evidently to decline, and the faithful to be freed from her forgeries; and now in this last act, when she might have expected (as most likely she did) by her seeming repentance of her errors, and confessing her undervaluing of the Ordinances of Magistracy and Ministracy, to have redeemed her reputation in point of sincerity, and yet have made good all her former work, and kept open a back door to have returned to her vomit again, by her paraphrastical retractions, and denying any change in her judgment, yet such was the presence and blessing of God in his own Ordinance, that this subtlety of Satan was discovered to her utter shame and confusion, and to the setting at liberty of many godly hearts, that had been captivated by her to that day; and that Church which by her means was brought under much infamy, and near to dissolution, was hereby sweetly repaired, and a hopeful way of establishment, and her dissembled repentance clearly detected, God giving her up since the sentence of excommunication, to that hardness of heart, as she is not affected with any remorse, but glories in it, and fears not the vengeance of God, which she lies under, as if God did work contrary to his own word, and loosed from heaven, while his Church had bound upon earth.

The biblical Jezebel, whom we know from Hebrew accounts in 1 and 2 Kings, lived more than eight centuries before Christ. Born a princess, she was the daughter of Ethball, a high priest who became king of the Sidonians in the Phoenician city of Tyre, in modern-day Lebanon, on the Mediterranean Sea. Like her people, Jezebel worshiped the ancient Canaanite gods such as Baal, the god of rain and fertility, who takes the shape of a bull or calf. To the Hebrews, whose God had no image or face, the Phoenician gods were pagan idols, not worthy of respect.

As a young woman, Jezebel married Ahab, a Jew who became king of Israel in 874 BCE. In this mixed marriage King Ahab worshiped the Hebrew god, Yahweh, while Queen Jezebel worshiped the Phoenician gods. This arrangement worked for some time in their court in the city of Jezreel. But Jezebel wanted more, so Ahab built a temple and an altar to Baal in Samaria, along the Jordan River. To please her he made a wooden image of Baal, an act proscribed by the Hebrew God: "Thou shalt not make a graven image before thee." 1 Kings 16:33 states, "Ahab did more to provoke the Lord God of Israel to anger than all the kings of Israel that were before him." Queen Jezebel, like others in Israel's reign of "pagan monarchs," had to be destroyed, her "whoredoms and witchcrafts" ended.

The recounting of Jezebel's death in 2 Kings 9 begins with Jehu, a commander in the army of Israel, riding toward Jezreel with his troops. When Jezebel learns that Jehu is approaching, she puts paint on her eyes and adorns her head. This is the cause of her millennial reputation as a tart. Jehu charges toward her palace, where she awaits him at her window. (Winthrop must have seen Hutchinson at the window of her bedchamber on Shawmut, gazing out past his house to the sea.) Jezebel taunts Jehu by invoking the name of another army commander who died after a similar mission: "Had Zimri peace, who slew his master?"

Furious, Jehu orders her thrown from the window of her palace. Her blood spatters. Jehu tramples her body with his horses and chariot. When her servants come to bury her, they can find only her skull, her palms, and her feet. Her absence fulfills the prophecy of Elijah of Gilead, in 2 Kings 9:36, that "in the portion of Jezreel shall dogs eat the flesh of Jezebel; and the carcass of Jezebel shall be as dung upon the face of the field in the portion of Jezreel; so that they shall not say, 'This is Jezebel.'" Jehu arranges further to efface the heroine by slaughtering Jezebel and Ahab's seventy sons, fulfilling the prophecy that the Lord would take vengeance on Jezebel's "poisoned seed."

The Hebrew Bible, like Winthrop's account of Anne Hutchinson, is an orthodox history—history as written by the victors. Just as Hutchinson was to Winthrop "the subtlety of Satan," so Queen Jezebel was, in the minds of the authors of the Old Testament, a false prophet. In removing Hutchinson, Winthrop succeeded in restoring what David Hall called "the myth of New England as a land that God had specially favored." We can only wonder what we might learn if the ancient Jezebel, like Anne, had left transcripts of her opinions and beliefs.

Winthrop's account of Hutchinson's career, first published in London in 1644, contained all the relevant documents, including his descriptions of Dyer's and Hutchinson's abnormal births, the catalog of Hutchinson's eighty-two "erroneous opinions," the petition in support of Wheelwright, summaries of the proceedings of court and church against Hutchinson, and additional pages of his recollections and thoughts. The governor had collected and shipped these writings to his colonial emissary in London, the Reverend Thomas Weld—Hutchinson's jailer and inquisitor in Roxbury—who edited and arranged them for publication. The two men hoped this account of the triumph of Congregationalism over Antinomianism in New England would serve as a warning to the English of the dangers of Antinomian sects.

They also wished to diminish Sir Henry Vane, who was now the leader of the English Independent party, working with Cromwell against the monarchists. Parliament was divided between the Independents, led by Cromwell and Vane (still a strong proponent of religious liberty), and the Presbyterians, many willing to share power with the king. Winthrop could not foresee that his account of Hutchinson would not only antagonize Vane's following but also give moderate Scots Presbyterian leaders like the Reverend Robert Baillie ammunition against the "Congregational"—New England—"Way." Baillie used it as evidence of the failure of the immigrants to New England, accusing John Cotton of "wandering into the horrible errors of the Antinomians, and Familists, with his dear friend Mistress Hutchinson."

Many historians consider Winthrop's "Short Story," as his 1644 work is now known, to be uncharacteristically emotional. Edith Curtis called it the "fantastical" product of "a pen dipped in the bitterness of polemic animosity." The colonial historian James Savage termed it "discreditable," "narrow, vindictive, virulent and malignant." Yet the "Short Story" remains a window on Winthrop's final view of "the sorest trial that ever befell us since we left our native soil."

Its expansive title page contains the first published use of the term *Antinomian* in connection with Anne Hutchinson:

A short story of the rise, reign, and ruin of the Antinomians, Familists & Libertines, that infected the churches of New England:

And how they were confuted by the assembly of ministers there, as also of the Magistrates proceedings in Court against them:

Together with God's strange and remarkable judgments from Heaven upon some of the chief fomenters of these opinions and the lamentable death of Mistress Hutchinson.

Very fit for these times, here being the same errors amongst us, and acted by the same spirit.

> Published at the instant request of sundry, by one
> [Winthrop] that was an eye and ear-witness of the carriage
> of matters there.

The Reverend Thomas Weld appended to the text a brief preface, in which he set the scene: "After we had escaped the cruel hands of persecuting prelates [in England], and the dangers at sea, and had prettily well outgrown our wilderness troubles in our first plantings in New England; and when our commonwealth began to be founded, and our churches sweetly settled in peace (God abounding to us in more happy enjoyments than we could have expected), lest we should, now, grow secure, our wise God (who seldom suffers his own, in this their wearisome pilgrimage to be long without trouble) sent a new storm after us"—the presence and power of Anne Hutchinson.

A year after the publication of the "Short Story," the Reverend John Wheelwright, who was now the pastor at Wells, Maine, published a book refuting it and justifying himself, titled *Mercurius Americanus,*

> or, Massachusetts' great Apologies examined,
> Being Observations upon a Paper Styled,
> A short story of the Rise, Reign, and Ruin of the Familists,
>   Libertines, &c.
> which infected the Churches of New England, &c.
> Wherein some parties therein concerned are vindicated,
> and the truth generally cleared.
>   By John Wheelwright

> London: Printed, and are to be sold at the Bull near the Castle-Tavern in
> Cornhill. 1645.

Wheelwright had left New Hampshire for Maine in 1643, when Massachusetts subsumed Exeter, and then wrote to Winthrop and the court to apologize for his "vehement, censorious speeches" in 1636 and 1637. He requested permission to visit and "give satisfaction" to the Massachusetts court, which was granted—for two weeks in the late summer of 1643. In person, he asked the court to overturn his sentence of banishment. As he awaited the court's answer, he learned that his sister-in-law and six of her children had been killed.

The General Court of Massachusetts, under Governor Winthrop, lifted Wheelwright's banishment the following May. This rapid shift appears to have resulted from Wheelwright's potential usefulness to the colony in gaining public support in Cromwellian England and from Wheelwright's earlier decision to go into exile apart from the Hutchinsonians on Rhode Island. Three years later, in 1647, Massachusetts called back the fifty-five-year-old Wheelwright to become assistant pastor in Hampton, New Hampshire, then part of the colony, where he served without incident. In 1650 he received the deed to a two-hundred-acre farm, and his annual salary increased from forty to fifty pounds. The same year his twenty-year-old daughter Katherine, who had been born during the year of the plague in Alford, returned to Boston and married Robert Nanny, a wealthy merchant in his late forties, who died a few years later. Katherine remained in their house on Cross Street, beside Mill Pond near the landing place for the Shawmut-Charlestown ferry, where the remains of her privy would be uncovered more than three centuries later. She married again, unhappily. She filed for a divorce from her second husband, a Boston merchant named Edward Naylor, and the divorce was granted in 1671. Katherine Wheelwright Nanny Naylor died years later at age eighty-four in Charlestown.

In 1656, when England was under the rule of her father's old school buddy, Oliver Cromwell, the Reverend Wheelwright had returned to the land of his birth. The Parliamentarians had beheaded Archbishop Laud at the Tower of London in 1645, and the king four years later. From 1649 until 1653, England had been a Puritan republic, or commonwealth, with parliamentary rule. In 1653 Cromwell had dismissed the so-called Long Parliament, ending the commonwealth and making Britain and Ireland a protectorate, with himself as Lord Protector, or chief, although he refused the title of king. Oliver Cromwell died in 1658 and was succeeded as Lord Protector by his son, Richard, who lacked his political skill. In 1660 King Charles II took back the throne and executed a few of the Puritans who had opposed his father. Two years after the restoration of the monarchy, the Reverend Wheelwright returned to

Massachusetts as minister of Salisbury, where he served until his death, at eighty-seven, in November 1679.

At the time of Anne Hutchinson's death, her mother, who had married for a second time in 1620, was still alive, in her late seventies. Bridget Dryden Marbury Newman died in April 1645 in Berkhamsted, Hertfordshire. All the Marbury offspring save Anne and Katherine remained in England. Anne's brothers Erasmus, Jeremuth, and Anthony received degrees from Oxford, and one Marbury brother was a London doctor.

John Winthrop died six years after Anne Hutchinson, in Boston, on March 26, 1649. He had been at the center of colonial government and religion since 1630, having been chosen every year as either governor, deputy governor, or assistant to the General Court. Late in life, it was said, he regretted his actions toward the Hutchinsonians. On his deathbed, when asked by Thomas Dudley to sign yet another banishment order, Winthrop said he had "done too much of that work already." A plaque near his grave in Boston reads, "Winthrop dedicated his life to the creation of a model Christian community [and he] died at age 61 years in 1649, no doubt a disappointed man."

By this time, several figures in the Hutchinsonian controversy were back in England, where Cromwell was establishing his Puritan commonwealth and presiding over the trial and execution of King Charles I. The Reverend Hugh Peter had returned in August 1641 on a mission to make excise and trade law more favorable to the colony. Peter joined the Parliamentary party and became Cromwell's chaplain in the army. Later, after the restoration of the monarchy, Peter was committed to the Tower and indicted for high treason for his alleged role in the death of Charles I. Some said he had stood on the scaffold while the king was beheaded; others said he was the hooded executioner. Hugh Peter's head was cut off, stuck on a pole, and placed on London Bridge. Thomas Weld, who had accompanied him back to England in 1641, died there twenty years later, at sixty-five. Even the old Hutchinsonian William Aspinwall, who had gone to Portsmouth, Rhode Island, in 1638, returned to England, where he died in 1662.

John Cotton died three years after John Winthrop, at age sixty-eight, in his house in Boston, two days before Christmas 1652. "His lat-

ter days were like the clear shining of the sun after rain," a younger
contemporary observed. Even the Reverend John Wilson, who remained pastor of the First Church of Boston until his death in 1667,
when he was seventy-eight, remarked after Cotton's death that Cotton
had been, of all things, "a most skillful compounder of all differences in
doctrine or practice according to God." A late poem by Cotton captures
his enduring sense of contentment, which seems to have eluded many
of his peers.

A Thankful Acknowledgment of God's Providence

In mother's womb Thy fingers did me make,
And from the womb Thou didst me safely take:
From breast Thou hast nurs'd me life throughout,
That I may say I never wanted ought . . .

In both my callings Thou hast heard my voice,
In both my matches Thou hast made my choice:
Thou gav'st me sons and daughters, them to peer,
And giv'st me hope thou'lt learn them Thee to fear.

Oft have I seen Thee look with mercy's face,
And through Thy Christ have felt Thy saving grace,
This is the Heav'n on earth, if any be:
For this, and all, my soul doth worship Thee.

Cotton and Winthrop each had a son and namesake who followed
in his stead. John Winthrop Jr. was a governor of the Connecticut
colony, and John Cotton Jr. was a Boston minister. Cotton and
Winthrop were both buried in the old graveyard next to King's Chapel,
near Cotton's friend John Davenport, who died in 1670.

This burying ground, Boston's first, was taken over by the crown
in 1686 to give the Church of England a foothold in Boston. Beside the
burying ground the Church of England built the King's Chapel, which
is partly a monument to the decline of Winthrop and Cotton's Congregational Church. Some Hutchinson descendants—several Savages and

Governor Hutchinson—are also buried here, a block west of where Winthrop and Hutchinson lived and half a block south of the site of the Cotton house. Cotton's and Hutchinson's lines were joined in 1710, when his great-granddaughter Dorothy Cotton (1693–1748) married Anne Hutchinson's great-great-grandson the Reverend Nathaniel Gookin (1687–1734), the son of the Harvard president and Hannah Savage Gookin.

Simon Bradstreet, an assistant during Anne's trials, was later elected governor of Massachusetts. He died in 1697, a quarter century after his wife Anne Bradstreet. Her first volume of poems was published in London in 1650 by her brother-in-law, apparently without her knowledge, under the title *The Tenth Muse Lately Sprung Up in America.* Most of her other work appeared posthumously. The Bradstreets' daughter Dorothy, who was born in Boston in 1633, married Seaborn Cotton, the minister's first son. Anne Bradstreet's father, Thomas Dudley, one of Anne Hutchinson's most brutal foes, lived to the ripe old age of seventy-five. When he died, in his house in Roxbury on the last day of July 1653, this poem, in his own hand, was found in his pocket.

> *Let men of God in courts and churches watch*
> *O'er such as do a* toleration *hatch,*
> *Lest that ill egg bring forth a cockatrice,*
> *To poison all with heresy and vice.*
> *If men be left, and otherwise combine,*
> *My* Epitaph's *I DIED NO LIBERTINE*

Another court assistant in Anne's day—and one of her least tolerant judges—was John Endicott, of Salem, who was elected governor an impressive fifteen times, in 1644, 1649, from 1651 to 1653, and from 1655 to 1664. An efficient administrator, Governor Endicott was known for his harshness to Quakers, witches, and other latter-day Antinomians, with whom he battled until his death in 1665.

One Quaker encountered by Governor Endicott was Anne's youngest sister, Katherine Marbury Scott, who returned to Boston in 1660 as a "grave, sober, ancient woman" to protest the amputation of the ear of another Quaker, Christopher Holder. The General Court under Endicott had ordered that all followers of Anabaptism, the Society of Friends, and other such sects be banished from Massachusetts upon pain of death. In some cases blasphemy was punished with the amputation of an ear, presumably on the theory that the voices the person heard were not God's. Soon after Anne's death Katherine Scott had said the Massachusetts court was "drunk with the blood of the saints," but since then she had lived quietly on Rhode Island. Now, because of her objection to the court's treatment of Holder, the court had her jailed and thrashed with a threefold, corded, knotted whip. The magistrates sent her away and threatened her with death if she returned. Echoing her older sister Anne, Katherine Marbury Scott said to the Massachusetts court, "If God calls us, woe be to us if we come not, [because God] will make us not to count our lives dear unto ourselves— for the sake of His name."

"And we," Governor Endicott promised, "shall be as ready to take away your lives as ye shall be to lay them down." Scott died twenty-seven years later, in Newport, Rhode Island.

Mary Dyer also returned to Massachusetts in protest while Endicott was governor. The Dyers, having followed the Hutchinsons to Rhode Island, returned in 1650 to England, where they became Quakers. Six years later they came back to Rhode Island as Quaker missionaries. Their ship landed in Boston. Learning that Mary Dyer, now in her forties, was in Boston, the General Court ordered her out of its jurisdiction. When Dyer refused to leave the colony, Massachusetts authorities arrested her, stripped her to the waist, and whipped her in public. Tried by the court along with two Quaker men, in 1659 she was convicted of blasphemy and led to the gallows on Boston Common, in front of today's State House. The executioner hanged the two men and put Mistress Dyer on a horse and ordered her away to Rhode Island. Again she returned and was told by the court that she would die if she did not leave. She refused. The court condemned her to death for "rebellious sedition, and presumptuous obtruding herself after banishment upon pain of death." Her son William Dyer petitioned for a reprieve on the condition that she depart within forty-eight hours. Despite his efforts to save her life, she returned to Boston a third time.

On June 1, 1660, Mary Dyer stood motionless on the scaffold on Boston Common as a rope was placed around her neck. At the executioner's command, she climbed the ladder. Before a great crowd, among whom stood the magistrates and ministers of the colony, she said, "My life not availeth me in comparison to the liberty of the truth—" As the executioner yanked away the ladder, her neck snapped. She was sur- vived by her husband, who died at Newport in 1677. A year after her death, at the behest of the freemen of Boston and the order of King Charles II, the court reduced the penalties for religious crimes. There were no more executions of Quakers, although whippings of Quakers continued.

Anne Hutchinson's governor, Sir Henry Vane, also lost his life for his support of religious liberty. Having returned to England in August 1637, a few months before her Cambridge trial, he had married Francis Wray and become a member of Parliament, where he and Oliver Cromwell led the Independent Party against the Presbyterians. He was named treasurer of the navy and knighted in 1640, and he was known during the English civil war as a moderate, arguing for religious toler- ation and a constitutional monarchy. As in Boston, Vane impressed many with his idealism and honor. In 1652 the poet John Milton wrote this admiring sonnet "To Sir Henry Vane the Younger."

> *VANE, young in years, but in sage counsel old,*
> *Than whom a better senator ne'er held*
> *The helm of Rome, when gowns, not arms, repelled*
> *The fierce Epirot and the African bold,*
> *Whether to settle peace, or to unfold*
> *The drift of hollow states hard to be spelled;*
> *Then to advise how war may best, upheld,*
> *Move by her two main nerves, iron and gold,*
> *In all her equipage; besides, to know*
> *Both spiritual power and civil, what each means,*
> *What severs each, thou hast learned, which few have done.*
> *The bounds of either sword to thee we owe:*
> *Therefore on thy firm hand Religion leans*
> *In peace, and reckons thee her eldest son.*

Despite such accolades, Vane also continued to disappoint, even ir- ritate, those with whom he allied. In 1649, after Oliver Cromwell tried and executed King Charles I, Vane became an influential member of the

Commonwealth government. His influence ended in 1653 when he clashed with Cromwell over the latter's decision to dissolve the Long Parliament and establish his own rule. "Oh, Sir Henry Vane," Oliver Cromwell said at the time. "Thou with thy subtle casuistries and abstruse hair splittings, thou art other than a good one! The Lord deliver me from thee, Henry Vane!" Three years later Cromwell had Vane imprisoned briefly for writing a pamphlet, *A Healing Question*, against arbitrary government. After Cromwell's death in 1658, Vane sat in Parliament under Cromwell's son. At the fall of Richard Cromwell's government, Vane argued for the restoration of the Long Parliament. In 1660 Charles II, son of Charles I, retook the throne.

In 1662 Henry Vane was convicted of high treason and sentenced to death, despite his 1649 refusal to participate in the execution of King Charles I. (The corpse of Oliver Cromwell, who had led the trial and execution of the king, was exhumed, and his head was displayed at Westminster Hall.) On June 14, 1662, at the execution stand before the Tower of London, forty-nine-year-old Henry Vane approached the scaffold. He lay his head on the block. The ax severed his neck. The executioner raised Vane's head and cried, "Behold, the head of a traitor!"

"There must have been grim, knowing looks in Massachusetts when news of Vane's death arrived," the historian Michael Winship surmised. "His execution fulfilled a bloody prophecy a minister made slightly before his departure." The minister was Thomas Shepard, of Cambridge, who himself collapsed and died in August 1649 at only forty-five. In a 1638 sermon at the Cambridge meetinghouse, Shepard had prophesied for Vane a ghastly end. According to Winship, the colonial establishment "seemingly had the last word in revelations; Massachusetts still existed; Vane and Hutchinson were dead.

"But Massachusetts had only twenty-two more years of autonomy left in which to chase the theocratic dream of Elizabethan Puritans . . . of a religiously and morally cleansed Reformed Christian polity—one state, one church, one godly path to heaven." The colony's charter was voided for good in 1684 by King Charles II. This Stuart king, whose father the Puritans had beheaded, would do anything to prevent the return to England of "the disorder of two decades of failed Puritan rule." The final governor of the Massachusetts Bay Colony, Simon Bradstreet, was replaced by a series of royal governors selected and sent from abroad. Particularly offensive to the Puritans of Boston, the king who chose the first royal governor of New England (which extended from Nova Scotia to Delaware), Charles II's successor, James II, was a Roman Catholic. In the summer of 1686, two years after the charter was voided, English ships sailed into Boston harbor carrying the order to create the King's Chapel, transplanting the "popish" Church of England to the still-impure New World.

"Thus," Michael Winship noted, Anne "Hutchinson had been right in 1637 when she predicted destruction on the Massachusetts magistrates for trying to export their problems" by banishing her and her followers. She was "right in ways both broader and more symbolic than she had intended, but right nevertheless—their inability to work out a way to live with their hotter brethren and sisters prophesied Puritanism's doom."

Three hundred and fifty years after her prophecy, this "hotter" sister, John Winthrop's "American Jezebel," was welcomed back into the fold. In 1987 Michael Dukakis, Winthrop's political descendant as governor of Massachusetts, formally pardoned Anne Hutchinson. No longer "banished from our jurisdiction as a woman not fit for our society," Anne Hutchinson is again present.

EXPLORING ANNE HUTCHINSON'S
ENGLAND AND AMERICA

Finding the sites of Anne Hutchinson's life requires the imagination of a skilled realtor showing potential buyers a derelict mansion. Under the dismal carpet lies a gorgeous, original wood floor. Can I peel up the edge here to show you? Beneath these layers of grime and paint are beautifully carved moldings. With vision and patience, a potential buyer may envision the mansion as it once was and could still be. It is the same with the seventeenth-century world of Anne Hutchinson: with patience and vision, one can both find and imagine it alive.

The obvious starting place is her Boston house, whose footprint still exists in the modern city—remarkably, given that most of seventeenth-century Boston is gone. The brick, gambrel-roofed Old Corner Bookstore building in downtown Boston, one of the city's oldest standing structures, was built in 1718 on the exact site of her 1634 house. Her son Edward Hutchinson Jr. had sold that house in 1639 to his uncle Richard Hutchinson, who divided the lot in two and sold it outside the family in 1658. An apothecary named Thomas Crease purchased the house and corner lot (at the corner of Washington and School Streets today) in the early 1700s and used the house as both home and office.

In October 1711, in the Great Fire of Boston, the former Hutchinson house burned to the ground. Seven years later Thomas Crease erected a brick structure in the same alignment and orientation on the footprint of the house that Will Hutchinson had built. This brick house still stands, along with much of its original exterior brickwork. Its front door, at 271 Washington Street, opens into the Boston Globe Bookstore, the Old Corner Bookstore's successor, which is devoted to New England memorabilia. Entering the building from the School Street side, one can climb to the second and third floors and view some of its original 1718 timbers, preserved in a hallway. The upper floors of the building, which has been owned by the corporation Historic Boston since 1960, contain the offices of that preservation group, the Freedom Trail, and the Boston Globe Bookstore.

A wonderful little book published in 1939, *The Thomas Creese* [sic] *House: being the Description of a typical townhouse of the early Eighteenth century and containing a History of the site thereof from the time of Anne Hutchinson to the Present day*, describes the original early-eighteenth-century house, its wooden predecessor, and its various changes in the centuries since. In the mid-nineteenth century it housed Tichnor & Fields, the publisher of Nathaniel Hawthorne, Henry David Thoreau, and Louisa May Alcott. The modern-day view from the upper windows of the Old Corner Bookstore building is of street and skyscraper, nothing like the view the Hutchinsons enjoyed from the windows of their house here. That view is best approximated by visiting the second or third floors of any downtown, harbor-front hotel or high-rise.

For a wider perspective on Anne Hutchinson's Boston, a useful aid is the WalkBoston map of the "Shawmut Peninsula Walk: Tracing Boston's Original Shoreline," which offers a "guided tour imagining the past by experiencing early Boston on foot." It superimposes the outline of colonial Boston on the map of the modern city. The original town dock was inland and slightly to the north of today's Long Wharf, home of the Aquarium, the Boston Harbor Hotel, and Rowes Wharf. The town spring was just above the Old State House at the top of Washington Street, a block northeast of the Old Corner Bookstore. Adjacent to the spring was the marketplace and the First Church of Boston, where Anne's excommunication trial was held. On this site a skyscraper now stands.

The church, now known as the First and Second Church of Boston, has moved several times over the centuries. It is presently Unitarian Universalist and located at 66 Marlboro Street, at the intersection with Berkeley Street, in the Back Bay. Until a 1968 fire, it contained a wooden plaque honoring Hutchinson that read "Anne the Pioneer, Anne the Trouble-Maker, Anne the Martyr." The First and Second Church now displays calligraphic memorabilia relating to Hutchinson and other early congregants.

One block north of the Old Corner Bookstore on School Street, past the Old City Hall, is the King's Chapel Burying Ground, where lie the remains of the Reverends Cotton and Davenport, John Winthrop, Governor Thomas Hutchinson, and several Savages descended from Hutchinson. Inside the King's Chapel is the Governor's Box, where Thomas Hutchinson worshiped before fleeing the colony.

The site of John Winthrop's Boston mansion house—diagonally across from the Old Corner Bookstore—is now occupied by the Winthrop Building (278–286 Washington Street), a handsome Victorian skyscraper made of orange brick, which takes up the small block between Spring and Water Streets. The actual stone foundation of Winthrop's first house, in Charlestown, is still visible, near the Bunker Hill Monument, as a result of archeological work done during Boston's Big Dig. Mary and William Dyer lived at the corner of Washington and Summer Streets, just southwest of the Hutchinsons. The Reverend John Cotton's house was across Tremont Street from the modern Boston City Hall, on the eastern edge of Pemberton Hill, which was sometimes called Cotton's Hill.

To the west of Charlestown, in Cambridge's Harvard Square, is the site of Hutchinson's first, or civil, trial. The first meetinghouse of Cambridge was located at the southwest corner of modern-day Mount Auburn and Dunster Streets, where a brick building housing a Nantucket Nectars office and a J. Press haberdashery now stands. The street sign on Dunster says in small letters, "Water Street, 1631." A short block west on Mount Auburn, at Winthrop Square, a Cambridge Historical Commission billboard depicts the history of Newtown and Cambridge.

For those in search of three-dimensional depictions of Hutchinson's life in America, there are several excellent museums of living history. Two in Massachusetts—Plymouth Plantation, south of Boston, and Pioneer Village, north of Boston—are set in the 1620s. Although it is farther afield, St. Mary's City, in southern Maryland, founded in 1634, gives an even better idea of what the Hutchinsons' life was like. St. Mary's City is an actual archeological site, probably the oldest such site of a European settlement in North America. Because Maryland's climate is milder than that of Massachusetts, its colonial houses are closer to the spacious, relatively comfortable abodes enjoyed by the Hutchinsons and their wealthy Boston neighbors than the small, dark interiors of Plymouth Plantation.

These created or re-created depictions of seventeenth-century America are refreshing in light of the tendency to see colonial America as starting around 1770, well over a century after Anne's time. The Smithsonian Museum's exhibit on colonial America, for instance, goes back only to 1775, as does the Women's Military Memorial at the Arlington National Cemetery. Colonial Boston, as depicted in three dimensions in the fine model inside Boston's Old South Meeting House, just across Washington Street from the Old Corner Bookstore, is dated 1773, when Anne's great-great-grandson, the governor of Massachusetts, lived in the city's North End. The model also includes the "Thomas Crease house," as the building was then known.

Monuments to Hutchinson and her contemporaries do exist in modern Boston. Bronze statues of Anne Hutchinson and Mary Dyer grace the front lawn of the Massachusetts State House. The Hutchinson statue, by Cyrus Dallin, was a 1923 gift of the Anne Hutchinson Memorial Association and the Massachusetts State Federation of Women's Clubs. Oil portraits of the Reverend John Wheelwright, Governor John Winthrop, Governor Thomas Dudley, and Governor Simon Bradstreet hang inside the state house, and the Fogg Art Museum, at Harvard University, holds another portrait of Winthrop. A statue of the young Henry Vane in a wide-brimmed cavalier hat stands in the lobby of the Boston Public Library, in Copley Square. "An ardent defender of civil liberty and advocate of free thought in religion, he maintained that God, Law, and parliament are superior to the King," the plaque reads.

Most of these early Boston settlers lived in the area that is now Government Center. To travel from her house on Shawmut to her Cambridge trial in early November 1637, in modern terms, Anne Hutchinson walked from the Old Corner Bookstore site up Washington Street to the top of State Street, passing the meetinghouse and market square, and crossed what is now Government Center and the North End en route to the landing for the Shawmut-Charlestown ferry. The ferry landing was beside Mill Pond, a basin of water between modern-day Haymarket Square, North Washington Street, and Merrimac Street, which was filled in with soil from the top of Beacon Hill during the nineteenth century. A historical marker on the Keany Square Building at 251 Causeway Street—once the northeast corner of the marshy pond—indicates the raised footpath that native Americans used to cross the pond; hence the name of Causeway Street in Boston's North End. The route of the ferry that the Hutchinsons took to and from Charlestown in November 1638 was roughly the span of today's Charlestown Bridge, at the mouth of the Charles River.

Joseph Weld's house, where Anne Hutchinson was held prisoner for nearly six months during the winter of 1637–38, was in the Dudley Square neighborhood of Roxbury, at the intersection of Washington and Dudley Streets. For a modern tour of historic Roxbury, drive or take a bus from downtown Boston west to Dudley Square and walk north two short blocks up Dudley Street to the First Church in Roxbury, at John Eliot Square. (The honors go to Hutchinson's contemporaries Thomas Dudley and the Reverend John Eliot.) The present church, erected in 1804 on the site of the first (1632) meetinghouse of Roxbury, is now Unitarian and offers one weekly service, Sundays at eleven. This is the spot from which William Dawes set off on April 18, 1775, for Lexington and Concord, as Paul Revere began his parallel ride from Charlestown. This site, halfway up a hill, affords a fine view of the skyscrapers of the Back Bay, a neighborhood that in the days of Hutchinson, Dudley, and Eliot was under water. The widow's walks on extant eighteenth-century houses in this Roxbury neighborhood attest to the former proximity of the sea. Continuing north up the hill past the First Church and turning left on Fort Avenue, one reaches the summit and Fort Hill Park, also known as Highland Park. This charming green space, designed in the late nineteenth century by Frederick Law Olmsted, boasts weeping willows, benches, and a historic water standpipe at the former site of the Roxbury high fort.

On the current waterfront, in Dorchester, adjacent to the John F. Kennedy Library, is another treasure trove for students of Hutchinson's life and times: the Massachusetts Archives and Commonwealth Museum, often known as the Big Dig Museum. The archives contain many documents of early colonial Boston, including some written by Hutchinson's male relatives. The museum's ongoing exhibition, Highway to the Past: The Archaeology of the Central Artery Project, contains seventeenth-, eighteenth-, and nineteenth-century artifacts collected and analyzed by archeologists during the fifteen-year excavation of the Big Dig in downtown Boston in the late twentieth century. These include many household objects owned by Anne Hutchinson's niece, Katherine Wheelwright Nanny Naylor (1630–1715), whose privy was unearthed. Naylor was the first child of Anne's brother-in-law John Wheelwright and his second wife, Mary Hutchinson, Will's youngest sister, who immigrated to Boston in 1636. Katherine would have known her aunt Anne well as a toddler in Lincolnshire (which the Hutchinsons left when Katherine was four) and then in Boston and Mount Wollaston as a five-, six-, and seven-year-old.

The original transcripts of Hutchinson's two trials, the most important documentation of her life and thought, are lost to history. The surviving copy of her church trial is an eighteenth-century transcription of the original done by Ezra Stiles, the Newport, Rhode Island, minister who later became president of Yale. It is in the Ezra Stiles Papers at Yale University. The transcript of Hutchinson's civil trial appears in an appendix to volume 2 of Governor Thomas Hutchinson's 1776 *History of the Colony and Province of Massachusetts Bay.* The governor had inherited an "ancient manuscript" containing the original trial transcript, which is believed to have burned in a fire in his house during the Stamp Act riots in 1765.

The Hutchinsons' six-hundred-acre farm south of Boston stretched from Wollaston Heights, a neighborhood in modern-day Quincy, down to Wollaston Beach. The island granted to Will Hutchinson in 1634, which was named Taylor's Island in the court record, is not marked on extant maps, but it was likely located in this southerly part of Boston harbor. In nearby Quincy Center, the National Parks Service runs a visitor center for the Quincy and Adams homesteads. Directly next door to this visitor center is the First Church of Quincy, the successor to the 1636 church in which Anne's brother-in-law John Wheelwright preached. The church's crypt contains the remains of Presidents John Adams and John Quincy Adams. This church, like the First and Second Church of Boston, considers Anne Hutchinson a former member of the congregation, for she occasionally worshiped in Wollaston during her years in Massachusetts. There was once an Anne Hutchinson Square near Quincy's Wollaston depot, as evidenced by historic markers beside the Wollaston fire station on Beale Street west of Newport Avenue.

The Anne M. Hutchinson Memorial Park, also known as Founders Brook Park, in Portsmouth, Rhode Island, is a lovely wooded site just below the Boyd Lane exit off Route 24 south, beside the Mello Garden Store and farm stand. A sign on the highway reads, "Welcome to Portsmouth, Birthplace of American Democracy, established 1638." Among the many memorial rocks placed to honor the Portsmouth Compact and the earliest settlers here is one from April 1996 with a brass plaque that reads, "To the memory of Anne Marbury Hutchinson 1591–1643. Wife, mother, midwife, visionary, spiritual leader and original settler." The brook bubbling in the background is the remnant of the original spring around which the families who followed Anne Hutchinson into banishment created their settlement in 1638. Their meetinghouse and training ground (for military exercises) were located on this spot.

The Hutchinson house lot was on the western shore of the Great Cove and is today accessible on foot or by boat. It is roughly a half-mile walk north of Flo's Clam Shop on Park Street, in Island Park, Portsmouth, or a thirty-minute kayak ride from the nearest kayak rental shop, in Tiverton, Rhode Island, beneath the Sakonnet River Bridge. The kayak trip entails paddling west across the Sakonnet River (avoiding the ferries and large pleasure boats in the channel) and under a small bridge into the Great Cove, passing north of Spectacle Island, aiming for the Mount Hope Bridge on the horizon, cutting through the narrow pass beside the boat ramp frequented by pickup trucks and people fishing, heading for the cement plant beside Route 24, passing through the opening in the stone bridge in the water (which was erected in 1971 by the archeologists who directed the local excavation), and turning in to the isolated beach that was owned in 1638 by Will Hutchinson.

Along the dune above the strand are two bare places where shrubs and beach grasses do not grow. In this spot in the early 1970s, a team of archeologists led by Marley Brown of Brown University and James Deetz of Plymouth Plantation uncovered the remains of a midden, or garbage heap, which they dated to the period of earliest settlement: animal bones, clay pottery from early-seventeenth-century England and Germany, nails, thimbles, spoons, and many clay pipes made in Bristol, England, before 1640. Because this beach is on the site of Will Hutchinson's 1638 house plot, it is reasonable to assume that these objects—now on display at the Portsmouth Public Library, a few miles to the south— were disposed of by the Hutchinsons themselves, thrown into a trash pile not far from their house. The Portsmouth Historical Society (open from 2 to 4 P.M. on summer Sundays) has little from the seventeenth century, but the nearby Tiverton Historical Society (open Thursday through Sunday afternoons in summer) has on display a 1690 house, an early privy, and a kitchen garden like those that Hutchinson planted.

Southwest of Rhode Island, in the coastal Connecticut town of Mystic, the Pequot Museum's impressive collection of artifacts and information about the native culture brings to life the world that existed before the early English settlers arrived. A memorable film of the final battle of the Pequot War depicts many of Anne's male contemporaries, including most notably the fierce Captain John Endicott.

Anne Hutchinson and six of her children died in the northern reaches of modern-day New York City. No remains of her farmhouse there have been uncovered, but the character of the area in which she lived is well preserved because it is amid the 550-acre Pelham Bay Park, the largest public park in New York City. Miles of trails meander through the protected saltwater marsh and forest of the former Dutch settlement in which she lived. The adjacent Pelham Bay Split Rock Golf Course backs onto what must have been her land. Another modern access point to the sites of her brief stay here is the Hutchinson River, the tributary of Long Island Sound beside which she lived, which later gave the adjacent parkway its name.

The massive Split Rock, in which her daughter Susan Hutchinson hid from the Siwanoy during their July 1643 raid, still stands at the juncture of the Hutchinson River Parkway and the New England Throughway, on the right side of the northbound Hutch at the eastbound exit ramp to the throughway. The rock was scheduled for demolition in the late twentieth century when the throughway was built, but at a local historian's objection the proposed road was moved ten feet north to save the historic rock. Each week many thousands of drivers pass the Split Rock at roughly sixty-five miles an hour as they head north on the Hutch or take the exit from the Hutch to New England. But these vantage points offer no more than a split-second view, and there is no way on the high-speed road or exit ramp to stop a car, get out, and explore.

Perturbed that the Split Rock was not otherwise accessible, I asked at the Pelham Bay Split Rock Golf Course how to get a closer look at the rock. No one was able to help me. Outside the clubhouse, a bronze historical plaque elaborated on the story, placing Anne's daughter Susan inside the rock after the massacre but giving no instructions on how to reach the rock. Someone suggested driving south on Shore Drive to the local stable, which might have a map.

At the stable, a young blond woman was standing out front. I introduced myself—her name was Lesli—and said I was looking for the Split Rock, where Anne Hutchinson died. Did the stable have a map, or did Lesli know how to walk to the rock? She didn't, she said, but an old blacksmith who had ridden here for decades might know. She asked Nick, the blacksmith, who said, "Sure I know the Split Rock. It's up the bridle path." She asked him where, he explained it, and she turned to me. "Why don't I just saddle you up a horse and take you there?"

Lesli, riding bareback, led me, on Strawberry, about a mile along the bridle path that initially skirts Shore Road. To our left, we could hear the distant noise of the cars and trucks on the Hutchinson River Parkway. To our right was the vast protected expanse of the woods and marsh of the Pelham Bay Park and eventually the golf course. The smack of an errant golf ball alarmed Strawberry, who began to buck. I had to dismount.

"Run ahead," Lesli instructed me, taking the reins of my horse. "From what Nick said, the Split Rock should be right at the top of this hill." I ran up the bridle path, aware that my family would soon be waiting back at the stable. The road noise indicated that the intersection of the two major highways was close. Then, off to the left, about seventy yards away over brambles and scrub, the Split Rock came into view. Bigger than a minivan, the rock is split through the middle, leaving a gap of about eighteen inches—more than enough space for a nine-year-old to slip inside. If not for the exit ramp, the road noise, and the artificial turf of the golf course, this wooded part of the northern Bronx seems little changed from Anne Hutchinson's time.

As our horses retraced their steps to the stable, Lesli explained that the bridle path makes a loop past the Split Rock. While the loop trip takes several hours, our round-trip had lasted only an hour.

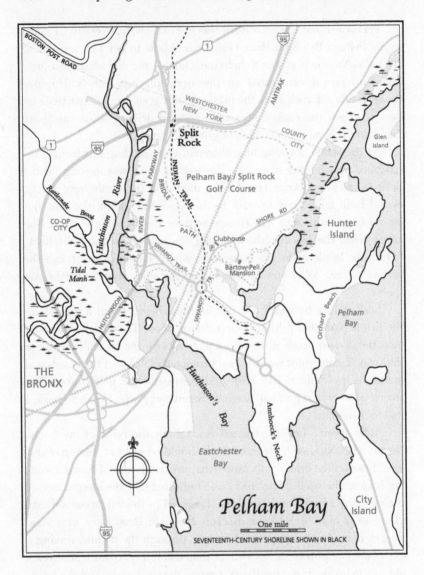

BOSTON POST ROAD

WESTCHESTER
NEW YORK

**Split
Rock**

INDIAN TRAIL

Pelham Bay / Split Rock
Golf Course

Rattlesnake

Broad

Hutchinson River

CO-OP
CITY

Tidal
Marsh

RIVER

SIWANOY TRAIL

HUTCHINSON

THE
BRONX

AMTRAK

COUNTY
CITY

Glen
Island

SHORE RD

Clubhouse

P

Bartow-Pell
Mansion

SIWANOY TR.

Hunter
Island

Orchard Beach

Pelham
Bay

Hutchinson's Bay

*Eastchester
Bay*

Annhock's Neck

City
Island

Pelham Bay

One mile

SEVENTEENTH-CENTURY SHORELINE SHOWN IN BLACK

Across the road from the golf course clubhouse is the beginning of the twelve-mile-long Siwanoy Trail, a rural trail maintained jointly by the Appalachian Mountain Club and the New York City Parks Department. The yellow-blazed trail was designed to view a lagoon, salt marshes, a freshwater pond, large meadows and groves of trees opening into glades, and Long Island Sound. Patches of daylilies mark former doorsteps. Derelict stone walls designate old property lines. The path passes the 1842 Federal-style Bartow-Pell Mansion Museum, which is open early afternoons on Wednesdays and weekends.

Moving back in time, one can travel to England, where Anne Hutchinson spent her first forty-three years. Much of the London she knew in the early seventeenth century is gone, either to the Great Fire of 1666 (which destroyed her father's parish church, Saint Martin in the Vintry, and many other city churches) or to the bombing of World War II. The modern location of the church and vestry in which the Marburys lived from 1605 to 1611 is the northeast corner of Upper Thames and Queen Streets. There is now a park here, and across the street a bronze marker embedded in the sidewalk indicates that this was the Vintry. Among the extant London churches that share the look and feel of medieval churches such as Francis Marbury's are All Hallows-by-the-Tower, St. Katherine Cree, St. Andrews Undershaft, St. Giles Cripplegate, St. Margaret (Westminster), St. Olave (Hart Street), and St. Helen's Bishopsgate.

To get a sense of the early-seventeenth-century London neighborhood in which Anne Marbury Hutchinson lived, one can walk from the Guildhall Library (which holds the parish record of her 1612 marriage) south to the Southwark Bridge (a twentieth-century addition) over the Thames, passing the site of her father's parish church one block shy of the river. The Three Barrel Walk follows the northern side of the Thames, but the river's south side boasts an even wider, more pleasant walkway from which to imagine the city in its Jacobean incarnation. On this southern side, at the re-creation of Shakespeare's Globe Theatre, staffers are well informed about London life in the Marburys' period. Tours of the Globe provide an excellent sense not only of the architecture but also of the activities of that time.

Slightly west along the river, at the Tate Gallery of modern art, take the elevator to the seventh-floor café for a fine view of the modern city. If you imagine the square-mile of the city of London surrounded largely by fields, and turn every crane into a steeple, you have some sense of the London of Hutchinson's day. The most prominent building on the London skyline today, as then, is Saint Paul's Cathedral. The present cathedral is the late-seventeenth-century successor of the medieval church that Francis Marbury and his family knew. While quite unlike the earlier church, Christopher Wren's Saint Paul's still has the consistory hall in its southwest corner, roughly on the spot where the Consistory Court tried Francis Marbury. And Paul's Cross, at which sixteenth- and seventeenth-century Puritans preached, is still outside the cathedral's south wall.

To explore the place where Francis Marbury was imprisoned in the late 1570s, visit the Borough neighborhood south of the Thames, near Southwark Cathedral and Guy's Hospital. Head south on the Borough High Street and turn left into an alley called Mermaid Court to find the original site of the notorious Marshalsea Prison. The jail was moved a bit south in the nineteenth century, when it held for a time the father of Charles Dickens, who later described its inhabitants in *Little Dorrit*.

Among the relatively few London structures that have stood since Anne Marbury Hutchinson's time are Westminster Abbey, the Henry VII Chapel, Prince Henry's Room, the Guildhall, Gray's Inn (whose garden was laid out by Sir Francis Bacon), Staple Inn, Lincoln's Inn and Lincoln's Inn Fields, Middle Temple Hall, the Queen's House at Greenwich, the Tower of London, the Banqueting House on Whitehall, St. James's Gatehouse and Palace, and the churches mentioned above. To learn more about sixteenth- and seventeenth-century London, visit the Museum of London, which has artifacts and three-dimensional models of the city through the centuries.

Finally, one can drive north from London to Lincolnshire, the county in which Anne Hutchinson spent more than half of her life. Lincolnshire "is a bit of a secret," according to a local historian, Jean Howard. "Most people in England don't even know where Lincolnshire is." It is north-northeast of London, on the country's east coast, above Cambridgeshire and East Anglia. Anne Hutchinson's birthplace of Alford, Lincolnshire, is 140 miles—at least a four-hour drive—from London.

En route, about an hour shy of Alford, one passes through the town of Boston, where John Cotton preached for two decades before emigrating. The church of Saint Botolph, still England's largest parish church, is still entered through the seven-hundred-year-old oak South Door that the Hutchinsons, Dudleys, and Bradstreets used. For a modest fee, a visitor can climb a narrow staircase from the nave up 290 steps to a lookout inside the famous stump, or tower. The elegant, gilded pulpit given to John Cotton in 1612 remains, and a newer chapel honors Cotton at the rear of the church. Glass-covered cases display books from Cotton's era, including a leather-bound Holy Bible published in 1609, a 1629 Book of Holy Psalms, and a Brevarium Romanum from 1632.

Continuing on to Alford, a town below the eastern edge of the Wolds, one has no trouble finding the Market Square, which is much as it was when Will Hutchinson sold textiles here, and the adjacent green-limestone church, in which the Reverend Francis Marbury preached. A sign on the church lawn says, "A House of Worship and a Place of Prayer for 650 Years: Welcome to St. Wilfrid's Church." The second-story room in which Marbury taught is directly above the church's front door and South Porch, accessed with permission from the vicar or the warden. The schoolroom now has a fireplace, although it did not then, and its large mullioned windows mimic those in the nave.

Inside the church, to the right of the altar, is the impressive marble tomb of Sir Robert Christopher, who died in 1669, probably the son of the man who built the manor house. In effigy, the knight holds a sword and wears armor and a curled periwig, and his wife, Dame Elizabeth Christopher, lies beside him in an elegant dress, coif, and high-heeled boots. The church's rood screen remains, as does the Jacobean pulpit that was added near the end of the Reverend Marbury's tenure in the church. The silver chalice that he sipped from during communion is kept in a bank vault in the nearby town of Louth, I was told by the vicar of Alford. Because Alford is the largest town in this part of Lincolnshire, its parish includes many churches besides Saint Wilfrid's— Holy Trinity at Bilsby, St. James's at Rigsby, St. Margaret's at Saleby, St. Andrew's at Beesby, St. Margaret's at Well, St. Andrew's at Hannah, St. Peter's at Markby, and St. Andrew's at Farlesthorpe—all of which are pictured on tea towels on sale inside Saint Wilfrid's.

The early-seventeenth-century manor house that was built during Anne and Will's early married life is just up the road from the church. Now a folk museum, it underwent a major restoration project in the early twenty-first century, during which its main timbers were exposed and dated to 1611. The manor house museum contains exhibits on Hutchinson and other prominent citizens, Captain John Smith and Thomas Paine. Behind the manor house, at the forefront of its charming rear garden, is a medicinal garden in honor of Hutchinson. Each April 26 the town observes Anne Hutchinson Day, inspired by the citizens of Portsmouth, Rhode Island, who began honoring her annually in April 1996. While the sites of the Marbury and Hutchinson houses are not marked—although a local antiques shop claims, without evidence, to be where Anne Hutchinson lived—there are still nearly two hundred thatched, mud-and-stud cottages around the town, some available for holiday rentals. The plague stone, one of the most vivid reminders of Anne Hutchinson's time, stands in the garden of Tothby Manor, a private house on a residential street just west of the center of town.

From here in Alford, one can walk west on a path across the fields and up into the Wolds. Rabbits and pheasants dart across the trail. A mile or so along, not far from the Norman ruin of Saint James's at Rigsby, with its small belfry, one reaches Rigsby Wood, where Anne Hutchinson often took her children. When I was there it was almost May, and the bluebells were beginning to bloom. In this place, at least, time stands still.

CHRONOLOGY

1591   Anne Marbury is born in Alford, Lincolnshire, England, on July 17.

1605   The Marbury family moves to London, where the Reverend Francis Marbury becomes vicar of the parish of Saint Martin in the Vintry.

1611   The Reverend Marbury dies in London.

1612   Anne marries Will Hutchinson, of Alford, and returns to her native town.

1630   Her daughters Susan, sixteen, and Elizabeth, eight, die of the bubonic plague.

1634   Anne, Will, and eleven of their children sail to America.

1635–36   Anne's religious discussion groups with other women in Boston are so well attended that she offers a second meeting each week, open also to men.

1636   Henry Vane, who attends her meetings, is elected governor of Massachusetts.

1637   Troubled by growing conflict in the colony, Vane returns to England. John Winthrop is reelected governor.

1637   In November the General Court tries Anne Hutchinson, convicts her of heresy, and banishes her.

1638   In March the Church of Boston examines Anne and excommunicates her. Thirty other families voluntarily accompany her in banishment. The men, including her husband and older sons, sign the Portsmouth Compact, creating the new settlement of Rhode Island.

1638   In June, after bearing fifteen healthy infants over twenty-five years, forty-six-year-old Anne delivers a hydatidiform mole.

1642   Her beloved husband, Will, who was named Rhode Island's first governor, dies.

1642   Removing herself from English control, Anne travels west with her younger children to the Dutch colony that would become New York. She builds a farmstead on a meadow in Pelham Bay, near the Split Rock.

1643   In a rampage on this Dutch settlement, Siwanoy Indians scalp Anne and six of her children and burn down their house. The natives capture and adopt her nine-year-old daughter, Susan. Anne is survived by three older sons, two older daughters, and Susan, who later returns to Boston to marry. The Siwanoy chief, Wampage, renames himself Ann-Hoeck after his most famous victim.

1911   A bronze tablet is placed on the Split Rock as a memorial to the most noted woman of her time. The river near her resting place now bears her name, as does the adjacent Hutchinson River Parkway.

1923   A bronze statue of Anne is erected outside the Massachusetts State House.

1932   A wooded site in Portsmouth, Rhode Island, now the Founders Brook/Anne M. Hutchinson Memorial Park, is dedicated to the founders of Rhode Island.

1987   Michael Dukakis, governor of Massachusetts, formally pardons Anne Hutchinson, 350 years after his predecessor John Winthrop ordered her "banished from our jurisdiction as a woman not fit for our society."

GENEALOGY

Anne Marbury ─┬─ William Hutchinson
(1591–1643)   │   (1586–1642)

    Faith Hutchinson ─┬─ Major Thomas Savage
      (1617–1652)   │   (1607–1682)

        Habijah Savage ─┬─ Hannah Tyng
         (1638–1669)   │   (1640–1688)

           Hannah Savage ─┬─ Rev. Nathaniel Gookin[1]
            (1667–1702) │   (1656–1692)

              Rev. Nathaniel Gookin ─┬─ Dorothy Cotton[2]
                (1687–1743)   │   (1693–1748)

                  Dorothy Gookin ─┬─ Rev. Peter Coffin
                   (1722–1749)   │   (1713–1777)

                      Major Peter Coffin ─────────
                        (1741–1802)

---

[1] A. B. Harvard, 1675, minister of First Church in Cambridge, and acting president of Harvard College, 1682–1692

[2] Great-granddaughter of the Reverend John Cotton

Lucretia Flagg
(b. 1741)

Peter Coffin ─┬─ Anne Martin
(1768–1840) │   (1773–1819)

Lucretia Flagg Coffin ─┬─ Rev. Samuel Joseph May[3]
(c.1805–1865)   │   (1797–1871)

Charlotte Coffin May ─┬─ Alfred Wilkinson
(1833–1909)   │   (1831–1886)

Louisa Forman Wilkinson ─┬─ Philip Johnson Wilson
(1864–1930)   │   (1854–1926)

Philip Johnson Wilson ─┬─ Virginia Eaglesfield
(1896–1984)   │   (1896–1971)

Virginia Wilson ─┬─ Joseph LaPlante
(b. 1930)   │   (1923–1990)

Eve LaPlante

---

[3]Unitarian minister and abolitionist

ACKNOWLEDGMENTS

Many people have helped in the research and writing of this book. My wonderful editor, Renée Sedliar, offered more enthusiasm and support than I could have imagined. Laureen Rowland and Gary Morris of the David Black Agency generously shared their knowledge and talents. My thoughtful first readers were Alison McGandy, Leslie Brunetta, Edward Furgol, Bradford Wright, Glenn Gibbs, and of course my constant first reader, my husband, David. Allison Christiansen, my research assistant, skillfully addressed queries about life in sixteenth- and seventeenth-century England and America.

Bradford Wright, my former American History teacher, started me on this book in more ways than one. Learning last year of the project, he appeared at my doorstep bearing shopping bags full of books about colonial New England, noted American women, religion in early America, and Anne Hutchinson's trials. Since then Brad has dropped by on occasion to leave a relevant historical article, like an Easter surprise, at my front door. Other former teachers to whom I am indebted are Donald W. Thomas, Jonathan Arac, A. Walton Litz, Thomas Kinsella, and Sacvan Bercovitch.

My friend Edward Furgol, a historian and curator, had the patience and knowledge to answer countless questions about English and American history and theology. Ed accompanied me to the seventeenth-century archeological site at Saint Mary's City, Maryland, and provided sage advice about what to see in England. As an early reader of the manuscript, he uncovered several anachronisms that only a historian could. I am also grateful to Ed's family for their hospitality.

Martha Karasek, another longtime friend, invited me into her weekly Scripture study group just as I began this book. I enjoyed not only participating in the group but also experiencing firsthand the sort of meetings that Anne Hutchinson conducted in her Boston parlor in the 1630s. I am grateful to Marti, Lois Showalter, Christine Fusaro, Troy Catterson, Dale Karasek, Harriet Sutfin, and others in the group, which is sponsored by the Ruggles Baptist Church of Boston. In the longer run, my understanding of faith and grace has been deepened by the Reverend Jack Ahern, Andrew Kelly, the Reverend Charles Weiser, Olivia C. LaPlante, the Reverend James Nero, Joseph A. LaPlante, Emer bean Í Chuív, the Reverend Shan O Cuív, and Mary B. Page.

David D. Hall, the living expert on the political and religious controversy that swirled around Anne Hutchinson, generously met with me in his office at Harvard Divinity School, where he is the John Bartlett Professor of New England Church History, and answered further questions by e-mail. He referred me to Michael Winship's remarkable book, *Making Heretics: Militant Protestantism and Free Grace in Massachusetts, 1636–1641* (2002). Besides Winship's and Hall's books (especially the essential source book, edited by Hall, *The Antinomian Controversy*), the books I found most helpful were Selma Williams's 1980 biography, *Divine Rebel: The Life of Anne Marbury Hutchinson;* Mary Beth Norton's *Founding Mothers and Fathers: Gendered Power and the Forming of American Society* (1996); and Norman Pettit's 1989 study, *The Heart Prepared: Grace and Conversion in Puritan Spiritual Life.*

Many archivists, librarians, historians, curators, and others have assisted in my search for new information about Anne Hutchinson and all the sites of her life. In Lincolnshire, Dr. Mike Rogers, curator of the Lincolnshire Archives, generously assisted in unearthing and actually reading historic documents pertaining to the Hutchinson and Marbury families. The local historian and Blue Badge guide Jean Howard drove me all over Alford and environs, showing me the locked schoolroom in which Anne's father taught, the inside of the manor house that was erected in Anne's day, the plague stone now in a private garden, and the clearing where the bluebells bloom in Rigsby Wood each May. Over the next few months Jean answered numerous questions by e-mail and fact-checked portions of the manuscript. The historian and geologist David Robinson, in Louth; the church historian Rosemary Watts, in Lincoln; and the tour guide Barbara Walker, in Lincoln, also helped answer questions about life in Lincolnshire at the turn of the seventeenth century.

In London, I was grateful for the assistance of Hazel Forsyth of the Museum of London, Valerie Austin of the Tourist Board, the warden of

Saint Olave's church, Concetto Marletta, Ally Flanigan, Ariel Palmieri, and several people at the Guildhall Library, including Lynne MacNab, Matthew Payne, and Lloyd Child.

In Massachusetts, I am grateful to Betsy Lowenstein, chief of special collections at the Massachusetts State Library; Elizabeth Bouvier and Martha Clark, curators of the Massachusetts State Archives; Nicholas Graham, librarian of the Massachusetts Historical Society; Stephen Nonack, of the Boston Athenaeum; and Kristen Weiss, of the Peabody Essex Museum. I wish also to thank the librarian Mary Bergman, at a local public library, who secured various rare books that I requested, sometimes repeatedly. Other scholars who assisted in my search were Lad Tobin and Lynn Johnson, of Boston College; Kevin McLaughlin and James Egan, of Brown University; and Barbara Rimkunas, curator of the Exeter (New Hampshire) Historical Society. At the site of the Hutchinsons' Boston home, I was assisted by two preservationists: Stanley Smith, Executive Director, and Jeffrey T. Gonyeau, Project Manager, both of Historic Boston Inc., which owns the site.

In Portsmouth, Rhode Island, I am grateful to retired police chief John C. Pierce Sr., who in the 1950s began unearthing the archeological remains of the Hutchinsons' homestead there. He walked me around the neighborhood and told me how to kayak to the location of the midden. James Garman, a local historian, generously shared with me his early records and maps of the settlement. Robert Pimentel (of the Portsmouth Public Library), Isabella Casselman (of the Portsmouth Historical Society), Laura Mello, Gail Gardiner, Maureen Cain, and Robert Hamilton (of Hamilton Printing Company) also offered assistance, as did Valerie Debrule, of Newport, Rhode Island, head of the Anne Hutchinson Memorial Committee. At the Sakonnet Boathouse in Tiverton, Rhode Island, which rents kayaks, Karla Moran gave me excellent advice about finding the former Hutchinson land. I wish also to thank Robert Driscoll, Portsmouth's Town Manager, for his guidance.

In the Bronx, New York, I am indebted to Lesli Rosier, who had the spunk to say to a stranger who was looking for the Split Rock, "Why don't I saddle you up a horse and take you there?" I also wish to thank the staff of the Pelham Bit Stable/Bronx Equestrian Center, on Shore Road. Kenneth West and Kate Whitney Bukofzer, volunteers for the

Appalachian Mountain Club of New York, provided maps and information about the walking trails in the parkland around the Split Rock.

At Harper San Francisco, I am grateful to Laura Beers, who designed the handsome cover; book designer Joseph Rutt; copy editor Priscilla Stuckey; production editor Lisa Zuniga; proofreader Kimberly McCutcheon; and Jennifer Johns and Roger Freet, who handled publicity and marketing. I wish to thank Jonathan Wyss and Kelly Sandefer, of Topaz Maps in Watertown, Massachusetts, for their skill and care in making the maps, several of which I would have liked to have had on hand while researching the book.

Friends and relatives provided invaluable help. Jane Larsen offered, as always, emotional support and editorial advice. Virginia LaPlante helped with editing and childcare. Phoebe Hoss lent my family her New York City apartment, from which we explored Anne Hutchinson's Bronx home. Angel Garcia, Wendy Brennan, Luzmari Garcia Sanchez, Elaine Soffer, Lily and Johanna Kass, and Katharine Emerson Hoss entertained us in New York. The Reverend Brian Clary solved puzzles concerning ecclesiastical vestments. Carl Dreyfus provided an insider's tour of Roxbury, Massachusetts. Tony Dreyfus made a translation from the Latin. I wish to thank Sarah Wernick for introducing me to Laureen Rowland, and C. Michael Curtis for his longtime encouragement. Among the many people who have comforted and supported my family as I wrote, I am particularly grateful to Andrea and Danielle Mazandi, Liza Hirsch, Nelly Langlais, David Weinstein, Ginny Carroll, and Mary Sheldon.

As for the five people to whom the book is dedicated, I am grateful to David for his generous encouragement, thoughtful advice, and unending support, and to Rose, Clara, Charlotte, and Philip for their excitement and, especially, their patience. I could not have written it without them.

BIBLIOGRAPHY

ARCHIVAL COLLECTIONS

Bostonian Society, Boston, Massachusetts

Deed given by Edward Hutchinson (Jr.) to William Trenton of land formerly the property of John Winthrop. Boston, MA. March 1, 1657.

Commonwealth of Massachusetts Archives, Boston, Massachusetts

Charter of the Governor and Company of the Massachusetts Bay, 1629 [SC1–23x].
Correspondence of Governor Thomas Hutchinson, Vols. 26, 27.
Court records of Massachusetts Bay Colony, Vols. 1–5 [CTO–1700x].
Massachusetts Archives Collection, 1629–1799 [SC1–45x]. Listings under Hutchinson, Anne; Hutchinson, Edward; Hutchinson, Francis; Hutchinson, Richard; Hutchinson, Samuel; Hutchinson, William; and Savage, Thomas.
Records of the Governor and Company of the Massachusetts Bay in New England, 1629–86.

General Records Office, Guildhall, London, England

Early maps of London, circa 1553–1667.
Parish records for the City of London, 1605–12.

Greater London Record Office, County Hall, London, England

Marbury, Francis. Last will and testament. January 30, 1610 (1611).

Historic Boston, Inc., Boston, Massachusetts

Historic Structures Report for the Old Corner Bookstore Buildings, Boston, Massachusetts. Turk Tracy & Larry Architects, LLC. May 2000.

Lincolnshire Archives, Lincoln, England

Alford faculties, 1606–1868 [TER BUNDLE/ALFORD].

Associated Architectural Societies' Reports and Papers, Vol. 34, part 1, pp. 28–29, describing contents of Alford church, 1548 [FUR 1/26].

Diocesan property, seventeenth-century listing [FAC 9/95].

Glebe terrier for Alford, 1601 [TER/3/321].

Hutchinson, Edward (Sr.). Inventory, February 18, 1632.

The Parish Registers of Alford & Rigsby in the County of Lincoln. Vol. I, *1583–1653.*

Quitclaim of interest involving Edward Hutchinson (Sr.) and his wife, Sarah, sealed at Boston, MA. 1635 [MON/1/IV/7/7].

Ringe, Sharon H. "Anne Hutchinson's Challenge to Liberal Theology." N.d. [Anne Hutchinson file, MCD 1486].

Winter, Sister Miriam Therese. "Anne Hutchinson and Spirituality." N.d. [Anne Hutchinson file, MCD 1486].

Massachusetts Historical Society, Boston, Massachusetts

Gay, F. L. "Notes and Documents on Francis Marbury," Massachusetts Historical Society Proceedings, Vol. 48, 1915: 280–91.

Winthrop, John. "A Short Story of the rise, reign, and ruin of the Antinomians, Familists & Libertines, that infected the churches of New England." London, 1644.

The Winthrop Papers, Massachusetts Historical Society Proceedings, Vol. 3, 1631–7; Vol. 4, 1638–44.

Portsmouth Public Library, Portsmouth, Rhode Island

West, Edward H. "The Lands of Portsmouth, Rhode Island, and a Glimpse of Its People." *Rhode Island Historical Society Collections.* Vol. 25, no. 2. July 1932.

———. Original Land Grants of Portsmouth, Rhode Island. Compiled in 1932.

———. "Portsmouth, Rhode Island Before 1800." *The Records of Rhode Island.* Providence, RI, 1932.

———. "The Records of Rhode Island." Speech to the National Genealogical Society, Washington, DC. March 19, 1938.

———. "The Signing of the Compact and the Purchase of Aquidneck." *Rhode Island Historical Society Collections.* Vol. 32, no. 3. July 1939.

Westchester County Historical Society, White Plains, New York

Hufeland, Otto. "Anne Hutchinson's Refuge in the Wilderness." Anne Hutchinson and Other Papers. *Publications of the Westchester County Historical Society.* Vol. 7. 1929.

Articles and Chapters

Bremer, Francis J. "The Heritage of John Winthrop: Religion Along the Stour Valley, 1548–1630." *New England Quarterly* 70 (December 1997): 515–47.

Brown, Anne, and David D. Hall. "Family Strategies and Religious Practice: Baptism and the Lord's Supper in Early New England." In *Lived Religion in America: Toward a History of Practice.* Princeton, NJ: Princeton University Press, 1997.

Brown, David C. "The Keys of the Kingdom: Excommunication in Colonial Massachusetts." *New England Quarterly* 67 (December 1984): 531–66.

Bush, Sargent, Jr. "John Wheelwright's Forgotten *Apology:* The Last Word on the Antinomian Controversy. *New England Quarterly* 64 (March 1991): 22–45.

Caldwell, Patricia. "The Antinomian Language Controversy." *Harvard Theological Review* 69 (1976): 345–67.

Cooper, James F. "Anne Hutchinson and the 'Lay Rebellion' Against the Clergy." *New England Quarterly* 61 (September 1988): 381–97.

————. "Higher Law, Free Consent, Limited Authority: Church Government and Political Culture in Seventeenth Century Massachusetts." *New England Quarterly* 69 (June 1996): 201–22.

Coover, Susan. "Town Man Seeks Recognition for Historic Site." *Newport Daily News* (RI), January 9–10, 1999: A3.

Crum, Christopher. "The female genital tract." In *Robbins Pathologic Basis of Disease,* 6th ed. Ramzi S. Cotran, Vinay Kumar, Tucker Collins, eds. Philadelphia: W. B. Saunders, 1999.

Dexter, F. B. "A Report of the Trial of Anne Hutchinson, Church 1638." Massachusetts Historical Society Proceedings, 2nd ser., 4 (1889): 159–91.

Eells, James. "An address in recognition of six tablets erected to do honor to Governor Henry Vane, Mistress Anne Hutchinson, Governor John Leverett, Governor Simon Bradstreet, Mistress Anne Bradstreet, and Governor John Endicott." Speech given in the First Church in Boston. December 21, 1904.

Garman, James E. "Anne Hutchinson and the Founding of Aquidneck Island." Unpublished article. 1996.

Ginger, Dawn. "Anne Hutchinson." *Lincolnshire Life.* August 1984.

Gomes, Rev. Peter J. "Vita." *Harvard Magazine.* November–December 2002:32.

Hoppin, Nicholas. "The Rev. John Cotton A.M." *Church Monthly* 4 (1862): 40–54; 5 (1863): 161–67.

James, Henry. "Hawthorne." 1879. In *The Shock of Recognition: The Development of Literature in the United States Recorded by the Men Who Made It.* Edited by Edmund Wilson. New York: Doubleday, 1943.

Katz, Celeste. "Monument planned for colonial leader Anne Hutchinson."
    Providence Journal. December 18, 1995.

Kibbey, Ann. "1637: The Pequot War and the Antinomian Controversy." In
    *The Interpretation of Material Shapes in Puritanism: A Study of Rhetoric,
    Prejudice, and Violence.* Cambridge: Cambridge University Press, 1986.

Koehler, Lyle. "The Case of the American Jezebels: Anne Hutchinson and
    the Female Agitation During the Years of Antinomian Turmoil,
    1636–1640." *William and Mary Quarterly,* 3rd ser., 31 (1974): 55–78.

Maclear, J. F. "Anne Hutchinson and the Mortalist Heresy." *New England
    Quarterly* 54 (1981): 74–103.

Rau, Elizabeth. "Anne Hutchinson: Courage Ahead of Her Time." *Providence
    Journal.* February 29, 1996.

Tobin, Lad. "A Radically Different Voice: Gender and Language in the Tri-
    als of Anne Hutchinson." *Early American Literature* 25 (1990): 253–70.

BOOKS

Adams, Charles Francis. *Three Episodes of Massachusetts History.* Vols. 1, 2.
    New York: Russell & Russell, 1965.

———, ed. *Antinomianism in the Colony of Massachusetts Bay, 1636–1638.*
    1894. New York: Burt Franklin, 1967.

Adams, James Truslow. *Dictionary of American History.* New York: Scribner,
    1940.

Adamson, Jack H., and Harold F. Folland. *Sir Harry Vane: His Life and
    Times, 1613–1662.* Boston: Gambit, 1973.

Ahlstrom, Sydney E. *A Religious History of the American People.* New Haven,
    CT: Yale University Press, 1972.

Anderson, Marianne O. *Native Americans: Van Cortlandt & Pelham Bay Parks.*
    New York: Parks & Recreation Dept., 1996.

Andrews, Charles M. *The Colonial Period of American History: The
    Settlements.* Vol. 1. New Haven, CT: Yale University Press, 1934.

Andrews, William, ed. *Bygone Lincolnshire.* Vol. 1. Hull, England: A. Brown,
    1891.

Bailyn, Bernard. *Faces of Revolution: Personalities and Themes in the Struggle
    for American Independence.* New York: Vintage Books, 1990.

———. *The Ordeal of Thomas Hutchinson.* Cambridge, MA: Harvard Uni-
    versity Press, 1974.

Battis, Emery. *Saints and Sectaries: Anne Hutchinson and the Antinomian Con-
    troversy in the Massachusetts Bay Colony.* Chapel Hill: University of North
    Carolina Press, 1962.

Bell, Charles. *A History of Exeter, New Hampshire.* Boston: J. E. Farwell, 1888.

Bercovitch, Sacvan. *The Puritan Origins of the American Self.* New Haven, CT: Yale University Press, 1975.

Berkin, Carol. *First Generations: Women in Colonial America.* New York: Hill & Wang, 1996.

Bobbitt, Philip. *The Shield of Achilles: War, Peace, and the Course of History.* New York: Knopf, 2002.

Bradstreet, Anne. *Anne Bradstreet: To My Husband and Other Poems.* Edited by Robert Hutchinson. New York: Dover, 2000.

Bremer, Francis J. *John Winthrop: America's Forgotten Founding Father.* Oxford: Oxford University Press, 2003.

———, ed. *Anne Hutchinson: Troubler of the Puritan Zion.* New York: Krieger Publishing, 1981.

Bridenbaugh, Carl. *Fat Mutton and Liberty of Conscience: Society in Rhode Island, 1636–1690.* Providence, RI: Brown University Press, 1974.

Brown, John Perkins, and Eleanor Ransom. *The Thomas Creese House: Being the Description of a typical townhouse of the early Eighteenth century and containing a History of the site thereof from the time of Anne Hutchinson to the Present day.* Boston: Little, Brown, 1939.

Burrows, Edwin G., and Mike Wallace. *Gotham: A History of New York City to 1898.* New York: Oxford University Press, 1998.

Caldwell, Patricia. *The Puritan Conversion Narrative: The Beginnings of American Expression.* Cambridge: Cambridge University Press, 1985.

Cameron, Jean. *Anne Hutchinson, Guilty or Not? A Closer Look at Her Trials.* New York: Peter Lang, 1994.

Campbell, Helen. *Anne Bradstreet and Her Time.* Boston: Lothrop, 1891.

Carter, Stephen L. *The Culture of Disbelief: How American Law and Politics Trivialize Religious Devotion.* New York: Basic Books, 1993.

Chapin, Howard M. *Documentary History of Rhode Island.* Vol. 2, *Being the History of the Towns of Portsmouth and Newport to 1647 and the Court Records of Aquidneck.* Providence, RI: Preston and Rounds, 1919.

Clift, Eleanor, and Tom Brazaitis. *Madam President: Shattering the Last Glass Ceiling.* New York: Scribner, 2000.

Cohen, Charles L. *God's Caress: The Psychology of Puritan Religious Experience.* Oxford: Oxford University Press, 1986.

A Collection of Early Maps of London 1553–1667. Introduced by John Fisher. Kent, England: Harry Margary, 1981.

Collins, Gail. *America's Women: 400 Years of Dolls, Drudges, Helpmates, and Heroines.* New York: HarperCollins, 2003.

Collinson, Patrick. *The Elizabethan Puritan Movement.* Oxford: Oxford University Press, 1967.

———. *Godly People: Essays in English Protestantism and Puritanism.* London: Hambledon Press, 1983.

———, ed. *The Sixteenth Century, 1485–1603.* Oxford: Oxford University Press, 2002.

Collinson, Patrick, and John Craig, eds. *The Reformation in English Towns, 1500–1640.* London: Macmillan, 1998.

Cott, Nancy F., ed. *Roots of Bitterness: Documents of the Social History of American Women.* Boston: Northeastern University Press, 1972.

Cotton, John. *The Correspondence of John Cotton.* Edited by Sargent Bush Jr. Chapel Hill: University of North Carolina Press, 2001.

Crawford, Deborah. *Four Women in a Violent Time.* New York: Crown, 1970.

Crawford, Patricia, and Laura Gowing. *Women's Worlds in Seventeenth-century England.* London: Routledge, 2000.

Cressy, David. *Coming Over: Migration and Communication Between England and New England in the Seventeenth Century.* Cambridge: Cambridge University Press, 1987.

———. *Education in Tudor and Stuart England.* London: Edward Arnold, 1975.

Curtis, Edith. *Anne Hutchinson: A Biography.* Cambridge, MA: Washburn & Thomas, 1930.

Daniels, Bruce. *Puritans at Play: Leisure and Recreation in Colonial New England.* New York: St. Martin's Press, 1995.

Deen, Edith. *Great Women of the Christian Faith.* New York: Harper & Row, 1959.

Delbanco, Andrew. *The Puritan Ordeal.* Cambridge, MA: Harvard University Press, 1989.

Demos, John. *Entertaining Satan: Witchcraft and the Culture of Early New England.* New York: Oxford University Press, 1982.

———. *A Little Commonwealth: Family Life in Plymouth Colony.* New York: Oxford University Press, 1999.

———, ed. *Remarkable Providences 1600–1760.* New York: George Braziller, 1972.

Dow, Elaine. *Simples and Worts: Herbs of the American Puritans.* Topsfield, MA: Historical Presentations, 1982. Based on the seventeenth-century herbal guides that were likely used by Anne Hutchinson, *Culpeper's Complete Herbal,* by Nicholas Culpeper, and John Gerard's *Herbal.*

Dudding, Reginald C. *History of the Parish and Manors of Alford with Rigsby and Ailby with Some Account of Well in the County of Lincoln.* Horncastle, England: W. K. Morton, 1930.

Dunlea, William. *Anne Hutchinson and the Puritans: An Early American Tragedy*. Pittsburgh: Dorrance, 1993.

Earle, Alice Morse. *Home Life in Colonial Days*. New York: Berkshire House, 1993.

Emerson, Everett. *John Cotton*. Boston: G .K. Hall, 1990.

Erikson, Kai T. *Wayward Puritans: A Study in the Sociology of Deviance*. New York: Wiley, 1966.

Fischer, David Hackett. *Albion's Seed: Four British Folkways in America*. New York: Oxford University Press, 1991.

Foxe, John. *Foxe's Christian Martyrs*. Book found in most Puritan gentry homes in England in the late sixteenth century. http://www.ccel.org/f/foxe_j/martyrs/home.html.

Fraser, Antonia. *Cromwell: The Lord Protector*. New York: Knopf, 1973.

———. *Faith and Treason: The Story of the Gunpowder Plot*. New York: Doubleday, 1996.

———. *The Weaker Vessel*. New York: Random House, 1994.

Garland, Sarah. *The Herb Garden*. New York: Penguin, 1984.

Garman, James E. *A History of Portsmouth, Rhode Island, 1638–1978*. Newport, RI: Franklin Printing, 1978.

Gaustad, Edwin S. *Liberty of Conscience: Roger Williams in America*. Grand Rapids, MI: Eerdmans, 1991.

———. *A Religious History of America*. New York: Harper & Row, 1966.

———, ed. *Baptist Piety: The Last Will and Testimony of Obadiah Holmes*. Valley Forge, PA: Judson Press, 1994.

———, ed. *A Documentary History of Religion in America to the Civil War*. Grand Rapids, MI: Eerdmans, 1982.

Gordon, Charlotte Conover. "Incarnate Geography: Toward an American Poetics. Anne Bradstreet's Discovery of a New World of Words in Seventeenth Century New England." PhD diss., Boston University, 2002.

Gowing, Laura. *Common Bodies*. New Haven, CT: Yale University Press, 2002.

Hakim, Joy. *A History of US: The First Americans, Prehistory–1600*. New York: Oxford University Press, 1993.

———. *A History of US: Making Thirteen Colonies, 1600–1740*. New York: Oxford University Press, 1993.

Hall, David D. *The Faithful Shepherd: A History of the New England Ministry in the Seventeenth Century*. Chapel Hill: University of North Carolina Press, 1972.

———. *Worlds of Wonder, Days of Judgment: Popular Religious Belief in Early New England*. New York: Knopf, 1989.

————, ed. *The Antinomian Controversy, 1636–1638: A Documentary History.* Middletown, CT: Wesleyan University Press, 1968. The primary text of the documents pertaining to Anne Hutchinson's trials.

————, ed. *Witch-Hunting in Seventeenth-Century New England: A Documentary History, 1638–1692.* Boston: Northeastern University Press, 1991.

Hall, David D., John M. Murrin, and Thad W. Tate. *Saints & Revolutionaries: Essays on Early American History.* New York: Norton, 1984.

Hambrick-Stowe, Charles. *The Practice of Piety: Puritan Devotional Disciplines in Seventeenth-Century New England.* Chapel Hill: University of North Carolina Press, 1982.

Hawke, David F. *The Colonial Experience.* Indianapolis: Bobbs-Merrill, 1966.

————. *Everyday Life in Early America.* New York: Harper & Row, 1988.

Hawthorne, Nathaniel. *The Scarlet Letter.* 1850. Boston: Houghton Mifflin, 1960.

————. *Selected Tales and Sketches.* New York: Penguin, 1987.

Heimert, Alan, and Andrew Delbanco, eds. *The Puritans in America: A Narrative Anthology.* Cambridge, MA: Harvard University Press, 1985.

Hill, Christopher. *God's Englishman: Oliver Cromwell and the English Revolution.* New York: Dial Press, 1970.

————. *The World Turned Upside Down: Radical Ideas During the English Revolution.* London: Penguin, 1972.

Hillerbrand, Hans J., ed. *The Protestant Reformation.* New York: Harper & Row, 1968.

Holifield, E. Brooks. *The Covenant Sealed: The Development of Puritan Sacramental Theology in Old and New England, 1570–1720.* New Haven, CT: Yale University Press, 1974.

Holmes, Clive. *Seventeenth-Century Lincolnshire.* History of Lincolnshire 7. Leeds, England: W. S. Maney, 1980.

Howe, Susan. *The Birth-Mark: Unsettling the Wilderness in American Literary History.* Hanover, NH: University Press of New England, 1993.

Huggett, Jane. *The Book of Children: Children and Childrearing, 1480–1680: Age 7–14.* Bristol, England: Stuart Press, 1998.

————. *The Book of Children: Children and Childrearing, 1480–1680: Birth to Age Seven.* Bristol, England: Stuart Press, 1996.

Hutchinson, Thomas. *The History of the Colony and Province of Massachusetts-Bay.* 1776. Cambridge, MA: Harvard University Press, 1936.

Ireland, William W. *The Life of Sir Henry Vane the Younger.* New York: Dutton, 1906.

Jefferys, C. P. B. *Newport: A Short History.* Newport, RI: Newport Historical Society, 1992.

Johnson, Edward. *Wonder-Working Providence of Zion's Saviour in New-England.* 1654. Edited by J. Franklin Jameson. New York: Barnes & Noble, 1959.

Kenyon, Theda. *Scarlet Anne.* New York: Doubleday, 1939.

Knappman, Kathryn F., ed. *Women's Rights on Trial.* New York: Gale Group, 1996.

Knight, Janice. *Orthodoxies in Massachusetts: Rereading American Puritanism.* Cambridge, MA: Harvard University Press, 1994.

Krieger, Alex, and David Cobb, eds. *Mapping Boston.* Cambridge, MA: MIT Press, 2001.

Krovatin, Dan. *A Matter of Conscience: The Trial of Anne Hutchinson.* New York: Steck-Vaughn, 1993.

Lang, Anne S. *Prophetic Woman: Anne Hutchinson and the Problem of Dissent in the Literature of New England.* Berkeley and Los Angeles: University of California Press, 1987.

Lewis, Ann-Eliza H., ed. *Highway to the Past: The Archaeology of Boston's Big Dig.* Boston: William Francis Galvin, Secretary of the Commonwealth of Massachusetts, 2001.

Liu, Tai. *Puritan London: A Study of Religion and Society in the City Parishes.* Newark, NJ: University of Delaware Press, 1986.

Livingstone, E. A., and F. L. Cross, eds. *The Oxford Dictionary of the Christian Church.* Oxford: Oxford University Press, 1997.

Lockridge, Kenneth A. *A New England Town the First Hundred Years, Dedham, Massachusetts, 1636–1736.* New York: Norton, 1970.

Macfarlane, Alan. *Witchcraft in Tudor and Stuart England: A Regional and Comparative Study.* New York, Harper & Row, 1970.

Marsh, Christopher. *Popular Religion in Sixteenth-Century England: Holding Their Peace.* Hampshire, England: Palgrave Macmillan, 1998.

McLoughlin, William G. *Rhode Island: A Bicentennial History.* New York: Norton, 1978.

Michaels, W. B., and Donald E. Pease, eds. *The American Renaissance Reconsidered.* Baltimore: Johns Hopkins University Press, 1984.

Miller, Perry. *Nature's Nation.* Cambridge, MA: Harvard University Press, 1967.

———. *The New England Mind in the Seventeenth Century.* New York: Macmillan, 1939.

———, ed. *The America Puritans: Their Prose and Poetry.* New York: Anchor Books, 1956.

Moore, Keith L., and T. V. N. Persaud. *The Developing Human: Clinically Oriented Embryology,* 6th ed. Philadelphia: W. B. Saunders, 2003.

Morgan, Edmund S. *The Puritan Dilemma: The Story of John Winthrop.* Glenview, IL: Scott, Foresman, 1958.

———. *The Puritan Family.* New York: Harper & Row, 1966.

———. *Roger Williams: The Church and the State.* New York: Harcourt, Brace, 1967.

———. *Visible Saints: The History of a Puritan Idea.* New York: New York University Press, 1963.

Morison, Samuel Eliot. *The Founding of Harvard College.* 1935. Cambridge, MA: Harvard University Press, 1995.

Morris, Robert. *Clothes of the Common Man and Woman, 1580–1660.* Bristol, England: Stuart Press, 2000.

———. *Headwear, Footwear and Trimmings of the Common Man and Woman, 1580–1660.* Bristol, England: Stuart Press, 2001.

Murphy, Cullen. *The Word According to Eve: Women and the Bible in Ancient Times and Our Own.* Boston: Houghton Mifflin, 1998.

Norton, Mary Beth. *Founding Mothers and Fathers: Gendered Power and the Forming of American Society.* New York: Knopf, 1996.

———. *In the Devil's Snare: The Salem Witchcraft Crisis of 1692.* New York: Knopf, 2002.

Ousby, Ian. *Blue Guide England.* London: A & C Black, 1995.

Pagels, Elaine. *Beyond Belief: The Secret Gospel of Thomas.* New York: Random House, 2003.

Parry, R. H., ed. *The English Civil War and After, 1642–1658.* Berkeley and Los Angeles: University of California Press, 1970.

Pettit, Norman. *The Heart Prepared: Grace and Conversion in Puritan Spiritual Life.* Middletown, CT: Wesleyan University Press, 1989.

Phillips, Roger, and Nicky Foy. *The Random House Book of Herbs.* New York: Random House, 1990.

Pierce, John T., Sr. *Historical Tracts of the Town of Portsmouth, Rhode Island.* Portsmouth, RI: Hamilton Printing Company, 1991.

Plimpton, Ruth. *Mary Dyer: Biography of a Rebel Quaker.* Boston: Branden, 1994.

Porter, Darwin, and Danforth Prince. *Frommer's England 2002.* London: Hungry Minds, 2002.

Porterfield, Amanda. *Female Piety in Puritan New England: The Emergence of Religious Humanism.* New York: Oxford University Press, 1992.

Reynolds, David S. *Beneath the American Renaissance: The Subversive Imagination in the Age of Emerson and Melville.* Cambridge, MA: Harvard University Press, 1988.

Rhode Island Historical Society Librarian. *The Early Records of the Town of Portsmouth.* Providence, RI: E. L. Freeman, 1901.

Richter, Daniel K. *Facing East from Indian Country: A Native History of Early America.* Cambridge, MA: Harvard University Press, 2002.

Roberts, Gary Boyd. *Ancestors of American Presidents.* Santa Clara, CA: Carl Boyer, 1989.

Rugg, Winnifred K. *Unafraid: A Life of Anne Hutchinson.* Boston and New York: Houghton Mifflin, 1930.

Rushing, Jane Gilmore. *Covenant of Grace.* New York: Doubleday, 1982.

Rutman, Darrett B. *Winthrop's Boston: A Portrait of a Puritan Town.* Chapel Hill: University of North Carolina Press, 1965.

Sarti, Raffaella. *Europe at Home: Family and Material Culture 1500–1800.* New Haven, CT: Yale University Press, 2002.

Savage, James. *A Genealogical Dictionary of the First Settlers of New England, Showing Three Generations of those who came before May, 1692.* 4 vols. Boston: Little, Brown, 1862.

Scott, Anne Firor. *Making the Invisible Woman Visible.* Urbana: University of Illinois Press, 1984.

Seasholes, Nancy S. *Gaining Ground: A History of Landmaking in Boston.* Cambridge, MA: MIT Press, 2003.

Sheppard, Gerald T., ed. *The Geneva Bible.* 1602. New York: Pilgrim Press, 1989.

Shonnard, Frederic, and W. W. Spooner. *History of Westchester County, New York.* Harrison, NY: Harbor Hill Books, 1974.

Shriver, George H., ed. *Dictionary of Heresy Trials in American Christianity.* Westport, CT: Greenwood Press, 1997.

Shurtleff, Nathaniel B. *A History of the Old Building on the Corner of School and Washington Streets, Boston.* Boston: Damrell and Upham, 1887.

———, ed. *Records of the Governor and Company of the Massachusetts Bay in New England.* Vol. 1, *1628–1641.* Boston: William White Press, 1853.

Sobel, Dava. *Galileo's Daughter: A Historical Memoir of Science, Faith, and Love.* New York: Penguin Putnam, 2000.

Spence, Jonathan D. *The Memory Palace of Matteo Ricci.* New York: Penguin, 1983.

Steele, Ian, and Nancy Rhoden, eds. *The Human Tradition in Colonial America.* Wilmington, DE: Scholarly Resources, 1999.

Stout, Harry S. *The New England Soul: Preaching and Religious Culture in Colonial New England.* New York: Oxford University Press, 1986.

Taylor, Alan. *American Colonies.* Edited by Eric Foner. Penguin History of the U.S. Vol. 1. New York: Viking, 2001.

Thwing, Annie H. *The Crooked and Narrow Streets of Boston.* Boston: Marshall Jones, 1920.

Tomalin, Claire. *Samuel Pepys: The Unequalled Self.* New York: Knopf, 2002.

Trigger, Bruce, ed. *Handbook of North American Indians.* Vol. 15, *Northeast.* Washington, DC: Smithsonian, 1978.

Tyler, Moses C. *History of American Literature 1607–1765.* 1890. Ithaca, New York: Cornell University Press, 1949.

Ulrich, Laurel Thatcher. *The Age of Homespun: Objects and Stories in the Creation of an American Myth.* New York: Knopf, 2001.

———. *Good Wives: Image and Reality in the Lives of Women in Northern New England, 1650–1750.* New York: Random House, 1991.

———. *A Midwife's Tale: The Life of Martha Ballard, Based on Her Diary, 1785–1812.* New York: Random House, 1990.

Waller, George M., ed. *Puritanism in Early America.* Boston: D. C. Heath, 1950.

Wedgwood, C. V. *A Coffin for King Charles: The Trial and Execution of Charles I.* New York: Macmillan, 1964.

Weis, Frederick L. *Colonial Clergy of New England.* Lancaster, MA: Descendants of the Colonial Clergy, 1936.

Wheeler, William B., and Susan D. Becker. *Discovering the American Past: A Look at the Evidence.* Vol. I, *To 1877.* Boston: Houghton Mifflin, 1986.

Whitehill, Walter Muir, and Lawrence W. Kennedy. *Boston: A Topographical History.* Cambridge and London: Harvard University Press, 2000.

Williams, Selma R. *Divine Rebel: The Life of Anne Marbury Hutchinson.* New York: Holt, Rinehart, and Winston, 1981.

Winship, Michael P. *Making Heretics: Militant Protestantism and Free Grace in Massachusetts, 1636–1641.* Princeton, NJ: Princeton University Press, 2002.

Winthrop, John. *The Journal of John Winthrop, 1630–1649.* Edited by Richard S. Dunn, James Savage, and Laetitia Yeandle. Cambridge, MA: Harvard University Press, 1996.

Wood, William. *New England's Prospect.* 1634. Edited by Alden T. Vaughn. Amherst, MA: University of Massachusetts Press, 1989.

Woodley, Roger. *Blue Guide London.* London: A & C Black, 2002.

Wrightson, Keith. *English Society 1580–1680.* New Brunswick, NJ: Rutgers University Press, 1992.

Ziff, Larzer. *The Career of John Cotton: Puritanism and the American Experience.* Princeton, NJ: Princeton University Press, 1962.

———, ed. *John Cotton on the Churches of New England.* Cambridge, MA: Harvard University Press, 1968.

Zinn, Howard. *A People's History of the United States.* New York: Harper & Row, 1980.

INDEX

Page numbers of illustrations appear in italics.